Puppy's Tales
Puppy Papers 2

puppy Sharon and Steven Toushin

Published by
Wells Street Publishing
1363 North Wells Street
Chicago, Illinois 60610
Printed in the United States

Copyright © 2007 Wells Street Publishing
First Printing 2007

All rights reserved. Except for brief passages quoted in newspapers, magazines, radio or television reviews, no part of this book may be reproduced in any form or by any means, electronic or mechanical, including photocopying or recording, or introduced into an information storage or retrieval system, or transmitted in any form, or by any means scanned, uploaded and/or distributed via the Internet or via any other means, with-out written permission in advance from the Publisher is illegal and punishable by law.

ISBN 978-1-884760-06-6

Cover design by Steven Toushin
Photographs of puppy by Rob Perisho

Substance Over Image

Table of Contents

Introducing Steven..6
Introducing Puppy...12
Steven's Beginnings...15
Steven Meets puppy..20
Danger and Fear...23

Chapter 1: Spring 2004...33

Tina's Place: Puppy's First Public Play...35
Playing at the Bijou..43
Dying With Dignity..53
IML 2004..59

Chapter 2: Summer 2004...71

Learning to Deep Throat...77
GLLA: Puppy's First Event..104
First Review of *The Puppy Papers*...112

Chapter 3: Fall 2004..117

Life's Detours, Distractions, Interruptions and Changes............................124
Natasha..129
The Three of Us..134
Help! Arthur Found *The Puppy Papers*!...142

Chapter 4: Winter 2005..197

Boston Fetish Flea Market..202
The Art Of Cocksucking...216
Our Collaboration: *Destruction of the Moral Fabric of America*....................248
Playing at the Leather Rose..250

Chapter 5: Spring 2005... **277**
The Butler and Maid..287
Collaring Ceremony..316
(Slave Offering and Contract)
IML 2005..326
Piercings...329
Mark of Ownership..332

In Memory of BB Gun and Desperado..342

Reviews of *The Puppy Papers* 349

Introducing Steven

As a dominant man in the BDSM lifestyle, I take pride in knowing the dynamics of my personality, my dominance, and the fabulous feelings it gives me in a relationship. When I make a connection with a submissive woman and we're in sync, the feeling of erotic power embraces me. This feeling of erotic power becomes more encompassing and more empowering when total control is given to me out of trust and respect; and it is this total trust and respect that defines my relationship with puppy. The pleasure I strive for is the power of control. I absolutely need this power; it enraptures me. It is within this power exchange that the world does not exist outside of ourselves. This erotic power exchange intensifies and climaxes in our kinky sexual play, which is my piece of erotic heaven.

I had my first taste of an S/M relationship back in 1963 when I was 17 and still in high school. It lasted about a year. Since then, all of my relationships have been based on domination and submission, bondage and discipline, sadism and masochism, top and bottom. This is what I want, what I need, and what I look for. I play easy; I play rough; I play with fear; I play with consent. I know the difference between right and wrong; safe and sane are subjective. I am not middle-class BDSM. I am a Sadist, Top, Dominant, and Master who wants control over a consenting masochist, bottom, submissive, slave.

Because I know myself, I know the basic make-up of the woman I am looking for, a woman who has a need to please, who derives pleasure from giving pleasure, who puts her lover's needs before her own, a woman who will embrace with me the mindset, play, lifestyle, and philosophy of this kind of relationship in more than just casual play. I want a woman who shares the same philosophy of life as I do and a woman who freely gives herself to me in mind, body, and soul, allowing me to mold, direct, cherish, and be responsible for her. I have to add that the control part of the relationship does not extend to her work and responsibilities outside of our personal life together.

All of my relationships start from the BDSM play and sexual side. Open and honest communication from that side can then easily cross over to the social side. I look for sexual chemistry, compatibility, intellect, and the knowledge that she is comfortable with herself and with me. If we get past the play, we are compatible and comfortable with each other, and the Top/bottom structure is understood, then other factors come to light. Does she offer me intellectual stimulation, continuing sexual excitement, trust, friendship, and respect? If the answer is yes, and if our personalities complement each other, then like any other budding relationship, we play it out and see where it takes us.

I am not monogamous and I tell women this fact up front. Over the past forty years, I've played with hundreds of women. Some of them lasted one play date, while many others for three or more play dates. I've had play relationships that lasted a few years, one off-and-on-again relationship for 27 years, and I've been married twice.

How did I meet so many women? God only knows the answer to that. Well that's not quite true. My businesses are sexual in nature and have been frequently busted, resulting in numerous trials. Because of this, my name and businesses have appeared in newspapers and on the news for over 35 years. Consequently, many people knew of me, and many women found my notoriety exciting.

Also, back in the 1970s, I rode a motorcycle and would advertise my kink by wearing leather arm and wristbands and sometimes a leather collar. The collar was worn to symbolize being rough and unconventional, not to indicate Top or bottom. In the 1960s and 1970s very few people outside of the leather lifestyle knew that a collar indicated that the person wearing it was a slave or bottom.

Since my businesses and lifestyle were never hidden, women were drawn to me because I represented what they wanted: to be bad, to rebel. Life has been good to me. I've had the opportunity to play with all types of women, from housewives, lawyers and doctors, to the rich and spoiled. For whatever reason, these women just wanted to break away from their daily lives and do something crazy for a moment. It is the *Belle de Jour* fantasy (Louis Bunuel's classic film starring Catherine Deneuve). I met these women at my children's school, the neighborhood where my businesses are located, the health club, restaurants, and places where I often frequented.

I've sat and listened to women who have hidden kinky fantasies and women who wanted to be submissive and give up control, but who felt they had to be the strong one in their relationships. These women wanted to be made to do kinky things, but were afraid to ask their partner or husband because they felt that giving up control in the bedroom also meant giving up control outside of the bedroom. Some women had played and secretly tasted the dark forbidden fruits of their fantasies outside of their relationships. But all of these women were afraid that if they revealed their fantasies, they would lose the respect of their partner and that their fantasies would be used to hurt or shame them in the future.

It didn't matter whether the women I played with were newbies, novices, or experienced players. Some of them were impossible to be with and, at times, it was like walking on eggshells. Many others were wonderful, exciting, and we enjoyed each other's company. Some wanted to start changing the rules after we had been together for a while. Others wanted to get more serious and have a more "acceptable" and conventional relationship. Almost all of them asked if I would ever consider changing my profession. The answer is no.

Now, as a man, I view and express things differently than a woman. In my opinion, men and women see the world and relationships in different ways. How many authors and poets have written about this? So I want to give you my opinion on this very important subject. The major difference between men and women is rooted in how they view time. A woman's reality of life is grounded in the basics of her biological clock where the outcome is predictable. For example, women know they will have their period every 28 days; they know when pregnant, it will be nine months until delivery; and they know they have a childbearing window that will close at menopause. A woman's clock never stops ticking.

Men do not have this internal biological clock. Men rely on an external clock that is derived from their imagination, needs, wants and desires, thus creating the illusion of exact time. For example, a man knows there are two minutes left to the football game. However, during these "two minutes," the clock will stop and start many times, until eventually some thirty minutes have gone by before the game has ended. The illusion of these "two minutes" is a metaphor for a man's outlook on life and relationships. Man has no timetable or schedule for the way things ought to be. He is the dreamer who wonders about what is on "the other side of the mountain," where time is put on hold. In other words, women are defined by the reality of time, while men are defined by the illusion of time. This difference in the meaning of time is the difference in how men and women approach life, love, and relationships. These differences will appear, at one time or another, in any relationship whether it is conventional, Dominant/submissive, or Master/slave. No one is immune.

[Note from puppy: From a woman's perspective, the above two paragraphs have nothing whatsoever to do with this introduction. However, they do serve to illustrate that men (yes, even Masters) tend to forget the point of something and end up getting lost in their own world of illusion. It further demonstrates that since He is the Master and He wants it here, this is where it will stay!]

So why do I continue wanting relationships and what do I bring into the conventional part of a BDSM relationship? I like being in a relationship; I need it and I want it. I love the excitement of being with another person, the closeness, the companionship, the comfortable trust, being responsible to that person, taking responsibility for that person's well-being, and being responsible to the relationship. I've always known that the things I need and want in a woman are specialized, which narrows the playing field. Many women are uncomfortable with my sexual, legal, and business history. However, I also bring honesty, integrity, kindness, understanding, and my need for a sexual, rough sex, Top/bottom, Dominant/submissive relationship. My only concerns have been in finding or being found by women who want to be in a relationship with someone like me.

When I first met puppy, it was all about simple Dominant/submissive play. I wasn't necessarily looking for a relationship. I had been in and out of several over the last few years besides playing with others a few times a week. In fact, I was already playing with a few other women when I met puppy. Although I am not monogamous, those other relationships ended about four or five months after I started playing with puppy. As far as a long-term or committed relationship, I didn't reject the idea, but I wasn't going to jump into anything foolishly.

Puppy had been with a Top who taught her about obeying, serving, and her affinity for pain and pleasure, but that was all. After a few times together, puppy and I seemed comfortable and compatible with each other in play, so as far as I was concerned, I wanted to find out where this could go. I soon learned that she derived pleasure from pleasing, was easy to play with, and responded well. A few more months went by and I was still enjoying myself. I played with her any way I desired and she went along and gave herself to me with great enthusiasm. As far as our Dominant/submissive relationship outside of the bedroom, she was learning and following my structure and protocols.

Puppy and I had been together for a while, and wouldn't you know it? The realities of life entered into our Dom/sub world, but things didn't change. I was still comfortable with puppy; she did not have an erratic personality or try to change the relationship. She gained strength in the relationship and in her submissive identity. As I have gotten to know her, I have learned to appreciate her kind, truthful, honest, and respectful nature, as well as her loyalty and her love. I trust her judgment, and I value her comments. I also discovered her ability to write and to create, which brought more depth to our relationship. She kept the play and sex exciting, erotic, satisfying, and interesting, which is very important to me. As the relationship grew and expanded, she has always remained true to the Dom/sub structure, which is now a Master/slave relationship. Puppy has learned well.

Steven Toushin, early 2000

Introducing puppy

At the time I met Sir, I had been in an intermittent Dominant/submissive relationship for a couple of years. One part of me didn't want this relationship to end and another part of me knew it had run its course, that the relationship wasn't going to grow. I had just moved to a new home in a new state and started a new job. It was a time of exciting growth, change, and exploration for me. I was moving forward and didn't want anyone holding me back. I had gotten a taste of Domination/submission and I needed more.

For me, it was never about a need to be bad or to rebel. It was more like I had outgrown the confines of my life. There was something missing and I didn't know what it was. I needed to move into a different dimension of living, to expand my horizons. I had spent my life consumed by family, church, education, and career, always looking for something to fill an undefined need.

I had never even heard of Domination/submission or BDSM when an advertisement for a dating site popped up on my computer screen. I tried to close the pop-up, clicked on the wrong spot, and found myself at the dating site. I was simply curious about what was inside the site, so I put together a profile in order to gain access to it, never intending to go any farther than that. After receiving hundreds of boring and sometimes scary replies, I got a letter from someone who said he was a "Master of Domination and submission." The letter made my heart pound; I couldn't get it out of my mind, so a few days later I sent a response.

After a few weeks of corresponding, I met the man who would become my first Master. In retrospect, I realize he wasn't really a Master at all, but simply a Top, and only interested in a one-dimensional, scening or playing relationship. However, he opened the door to a whole new world for me. After the first time we were together, I knew, without a doubt, that I was on the right path to filling that undefined need in my life.

I discovered, much to my surprise, that being submissive to a Dominant man created a satisfying and fulfilling peace within me. It made me feel completely relaxed and alive. It took me out of my busy, demanding world and allowed me to be present in the moment, to really focus on the person I was with. When I was told to kneel or crawl or stand naked in the middle of the room for inspection, it was as if an unseen levitating force took me to another dimension, far above the life I had previously known. It was a place without boundaries, a place of mind expansion, of transcendence; and strange as it may seem, it was a place of safety. It made me feel very giving and generous in spirit. Looking back, I can see that it created a need to communicate, to connect with someone on a much deeper or higher level. I was immediately hooked and wanted to go farther; I wanted more.

However, the man who introduced me to all of this lived in a world with concrete boundaries. He wasn't interested in anything but inflicting pain, not interested in what I was experiencing, and not about to share his experiences with me. I never knew whether or not I was making him happy. He kept me at arm's distance, never allowing himself to make a connection, never allowing himself to feel anything, never communicating. In my naivety, I thought he must surely be the only person on earth who knew of this secret world, but after the first couple times, he seemed determined to withhold it from me. I think he was more interested in the chase than anything else. Once he had me, he turned his attention elsewhere. It was all very frustrating, but I stayed with him because I kept hoping for more of what I had experienced in those first couple months.

In the meantime, I started reading and exploring on my own. As I started learning more about BDSM, I tried playing with a few other men who called themselves "Master." Sometimes it was good, sometimes not, but nothing ever went beyond a superficial level. Dominance seemed to be just a fantasy to all of them, a game. They all seemed incapable of making a connection, incapable of fully appreciating the Dominant/submissive dynamics. For them, it was all about sex or about doing specific "forbidden" activities and fetishes. I didn't really mind that; I was having fun just exploring different things and different people. I wasn't looking for a serious relationship. After all, I was married and had no intention of ending my marriage.

So that's where I was when I met Sir. I thought He would be just another person to have some fun times with before moving on. I knew the first time I met Him that He was someone special, a gentleman in the truest sense of the word. I was swept away by His kindness, politeness, and consideration. He was different than all the others; this wasn't just a fantasy for Him. I felt like He could take me to places I had never been before, perhaps places I had never allowed myself to go. I was fascinated when He talked about edge play and pushing limits. When we first met, we sat in a restaurant and talked. He communicated more to me in that one conversation than all the other "Dominant" men plus my husband put together. Before that conversation was over, He had me completely under His control, simply by being Himself. It seems like such a long time ago. I got a tiny glimpse of His world that day; I had no idea what I was getting myself into.

As time went on, He allowed me to enter into more and more of His world until His world also became mine. His character and integrity have remained consistent over time, and my love and respect for Him have continued to grow. His honesty and willingness to communicate are matchless, and He is always faithful to His word. Besides all that, the sex is always wonderful, always exciting and, in case you miss it throughout the rest of this book, it always makes my pussy very, very wet. I can't imagine ever going back to a life without this man who has become my one and only true Master. He is the center of my world.

Steven's Beginnings

sharon wrote:

Dear Master,

　　Now that i've told You (in *The Puppy Papers*) how i discovered BDSM, i think it must be Your turn to tell me how You got started in the lifestyle. What and when was Your first S/M experience? When did You know and understand that this lifestyle is right for You? Were You always dominant? How did You discover Your dominance? Inquiring minds want to know!

Love,
Your slave puppy

Steven wrote:

Dear puppy,

　　I have always been strong with my hands; and I have always played and made love roughly, but not harshly. I have the need to feel the other person. I don't like the feel of hands moving lightly over my body. I want to feel my lover; and I want her to feel me.

　　Back in high school in 1963, I had a girlfriend. We had been going together for about three months, and had already made love about a dozen times when our desires and fantasies led us into S/M (BDSM). Combined with laughter, nervousness, excitement and intensity, we naïvely explored this strange new world.

　　One afternoon when her parents weren't home, we were in her bedroom lying half-naked on her bed when she asked me if I would do something to her. She said I had to promise that I wouldn't tell anyone, not a soul. I was very curious, so I said I wouldn't tell anyone. She then asked me to swear on my mother's life, on my father's grave, and on the rest of my family, and if I did tell anyone, may God strike me dead on the spot. I swore. She then asked me to never make fun of her or throw whatever she was going to ask of me back in her face, not to call her sick or weird, and I could not use it to hurt her if we should fight. She also asked me not to laugh or make fun of her when she told me. I had no idea what she was going to say.

　　She began by describing the things I did that excited her, things like pulling her hair tightly when we kissed or when we fucked. She liked that I gently or roughly spanked her ass when we made love, hurt her nipples, alternated between being rough and tender when we kissed, and the way I created intensity before and during our lovemaking Then, she finally told me what she wanted.

When she was alone, she would pluck her pubic hairs out with a tweezers. It would hurt, so she would stop. She loved how the pain felt afterwards, but couldn't get into it as deeply as she wished because she was doing it to herself and couldn't relax. Still, the feelings excited her and the thoughts of it stayed with her for days. She wanted to know if I would do this to her. With nervous excitement, I said yes, and then said, "I have no idea what I'm doing." So I told her that she had to tell me what she wanted me to do, and she also had to let me know whether I was doing what she wanted while I was doing it. She said, "I'll show you what I want," and, "Whatever you ask me, I'll tell you." I also asked her to tell me if I was hurting her in an uncomfortable way. She said, "Don't worry, I love how rough you get."

This was the first time she had ever expressed that appreciation to me. We had never really talked about what I did. I just did it, and since she didn't object, I kept on doing it. I had been rough with my hands since my spin-the-bottle days and none of the girls had ever said they didn't like it. I wasn't brutally rough, but I did have a gentle intensity in the act of kissing, so I had gotten a reputation among the girls of being an intense kisser.

When I started to pluck her pubic hairs, I pulled quickly while watching her body's reaction and her facial expressions. When she winced, I asked if she was okay and, according to my memory, it seemed like it took forever for her to answer me. In reality, it was only a few moments before she said, "I'm fine; DON'T stop."

I found that when I slowly pulled the hair without plucking I could lift her body right off the bed while she yelled and breathed heavily. If I plucked slowly, she had a pained reaction on her face and body, and she cried out. If I plucked fast, her whole being gave a warm erotic sigh with deep and intense breathing. I got one reaction when I plucked the hair from her soft belly at the top of the pubic line, another reaction when I plucked near her clit, and yet another reaction when I plucked in the soft spot at the top of her inner thigh near her lips. Within five minutes, I had perfected my routine and my girlfriend was lost in her own world.

For the next five or six months we experimented with hair pulling; bondage with belts, ties, and ropes; spankings with hair brushes, my hands, and anything else we could find in the kitchen, garage, basement, or her parents' closet, as well as other kinky fantasies. We always talked and laughed about what we were doing, and as we got crazier with our experimenting, we started calling ourselves perverted.

During those first weeks, we went to several bookstores in the east and west Village (Greenwich Village in N.Y.C.) and nervously asked about books on sexual perversions. We learned that we were doing S&M and we wanted to learn more. We gave ourselves names: I was "S" for sadist and she was "M" for masochist. A few years later, I learned that we were a Top and bottom in an S&M relationship. We were together for about eight months before we broke up because she wanted more out of our relationship than I did. We remained good friends.

A few months after we broke up, she was seeing another young man, but one night I got a call from her. She asked if we could talk; I said yes. She told me that she had, jokingly and in a round-about way, asked her boyfriend if he ever thought about tying someone up or about spanking a girl. He told her those were sick thoughts and anyone who had those thoughts needed a lot of mental help. She said she laughed and told him he was right, realizing that he would shame and belittle her to everyone if he knew her real needs.

She asked if I still wanted to play, and if I did, it had to be secretly. I said yes. I asked her if she would have any feelings of guilt because she would be cheating on her boyfriend. I needed to know if she was sure about us playing. She said she was sure, that this was what she wanted. I ended our conversation by telling her that if she changed her mind, she should call me the day before. She said she would. We planned a time when her parents would not be home; she didn't call.

When I went to her home, I knocked on the door and waited about a minute. When the door opened, she stood there, and then she backed up. She did not speak or look at me; her eyes were cast down. I walked in and closed the door behind me. She dropped to her knees in front of me with her arms draped at her sides. She had never done this before. I was nervous and just stood there staring for a moment, trying to understand what she was doing.

Then it happened; the feeling was overwhelming. She was freely giving herself to me, giving me her sweet submissiveness, her strength. That was the first time I felt total control over another person, total power was being given to me by another person. The feeling that came over me was majestic; I was the omnipotent OZ; I was Master, Lord, and King of my universe. She was giving me this awesome gift, the gift of herself. I lost all inhibitions as I looked down on her and told her to bark for me, to bark loudly.

Over the next year, our communication had no boundaries. Also during this period, I spent a great deal of time thinking about her and talking to myself about our time together. I never had any doubts or conflict; I knew exactly who I was and what I was supposed to do.

My girlfriend/ex-girlfriend/play partner had gone through the metamorphosis from a young girl to a woman. She learned, understood, accepted, and became comfortable with the sexual place within herself.

Our rough play had brought out her desires; her desires brought out her kinkiness; and her kinkiness brought out my kinkiness and strengthened my dominance. My dominance brought out her submissive sexual identity. Although my sexually dominant nature was already established, it wouldn't have developed as quickly without her strength of character, her desire, and her openness. On two occasions, she initiated the moment that further defined our personalities and set in motion the dynamics that defined our relationship, first as a Top and bottom, and then as a Dominant and submissive.

The night that she knelt before me was a defining moment in my life. She gave me her mind, her body, and her soul, and I became intoxicated from her submissiveness. I understood within myself the true meaning and feeling of dominance. As time went on, I learned to understand and embrace the responsibilities of my dominance in a Dominant/submissive relationship. But from that night on, I knew without a doubt how all of my relationships were going to be.

Sir

Steven Toushin, 1963 – 17 years old

Steven Meets puppy
Thu, 22 Apr 2004
sharon wrote:

Dear Master,

    i've been daydreaming back to the day we first met, 1 ½ years ago. The minute i first saw You at Starbucks, i knew You were someone special. You looked so handsome and distinguished in Your black jacket. You walked right up to me and greeted me, unlike anyone else i had met under similar circumstances. The others would often leave me standing there for a half-hour while they watched from around a corner.

    You seemed very relaxed...and You smiled. You weren't annoyed that the place was too crowded; and You weren't ashamed to be seen walking down the street with me. You seemed very comfortable, natural, polite, flexible, and yet in control of things. When i sat across from You in the restaurant, i kept watching the sparkle in Your blue eyes and thinking how deliciously sexy You looked.

    When You talked, Your New York accent was captivating. It made You seem very distinguished. In case You haven't noticed, i still thoroughly enjoy watching You and listening to You talk.

    It was hard to focus on what You were saying, although i do remember being a little nervous when You mentioned knives and hoods. But You seemed so charming and confident (not pushy or rude) and trustworthy that You probably could have talked me into anything right there in the restaurant. You didn't though. You didn't seem obsessed, and You didn't act like You owned me just because we met for lunch. It was just a casual lunch, talking about whips, watersports, knives, and puppy-play, like most people would talk about the weather. You didn't seem to expect anything from me...no orders or rules or demands.

    We walked to Your home and You gave me a tour. i don't recall seeing the dogs there that day. i do remember standing in Your dungeon when You gave the slightest hint that You might be interested in playing (i think it was the sparkle in Your eyes) and then You walked me back to my car.

    i thought You would turn around at the entrance to the parking garage and i was afraid i would never see You again. Instead, You walked me all the way to my car and got in! i had no idea what was on Your mind. i was so nervous it's a miracle i managed to maneuver the car all the way back to Your house. i still had no idea what You had in mind... and then You kissed me.

    No one had ever kissed me like that before. Powerful and gentle at the same time. i didn't know how to respond. You breathed into me...i had never felt anything like that before ...exotic, like i was floating. You gently squeezed my throat and then very slowly let go. You had complete control over me.

    You were very intriguing and mysterious. i wanted so much to go back up to Your dungeon loft to explore Your world, but You wanted me to think about it... You made me wait.

Love,
Your slave puppy

Steven writes:

    I watched the future puppy of this book enter Starbucks. She is a tall, slim, quietly attractive woman. When we sat to talk, she paid attention and responded without the typical "I have played a little so I know it all" attitude. She had played with people who gave themselves titles. She smokes, not good. Still, I had a warm feeling about her; she was very open in her answers and body language. I asked her questions and I talked about myself; I wanted her to feel comfortable.

    When we parted, I told her to think about what we had discussed and her feelings about the day. I wanted time and space between us; I wanted her to be sure that she wanted to meet again.

    She left me feeling curious, perhaps excited. I cannot play with someone unless I feel physically attracted to her. I need responses and reactions; they are important to me both in play and in sex. I need to know that my partner is able to feel and to let go of her inhibitions. I romanticized about the play and what her responses might be if we got together.

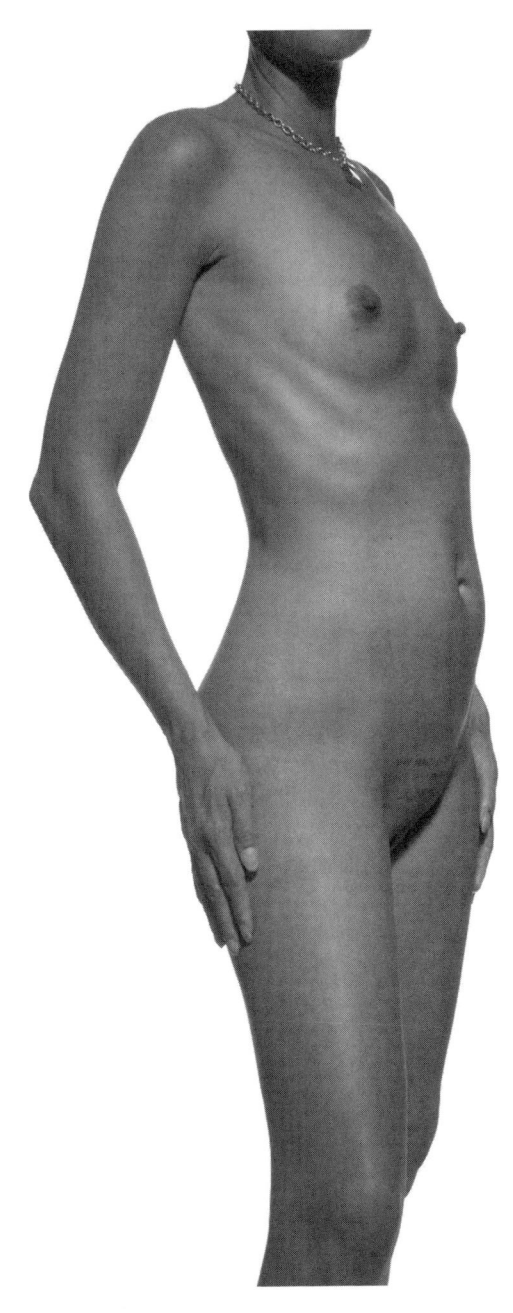

puppy

Danger and Fear

Steven writes:

Puppy and I have listened to people at events and in on-line discussion groups talk about finding a BDSM partner. These discussions have always centered on the slogan "Safe, Sane and Consensual," and for many people, this is the only correct BDSM philosophy. In my opinion, the safe, sane, and consensual doctrine was born out of fear and it has diluted BDSM with political correctness, leaving a tamed and civilized version of what once was S/M.

The general consensus in these discussions has been that a person should not go out and scene with someone they hardly know. It is often stated that there should be at least three to four weeks or even a few months of communication before agreeing to scene together. Other warnings include that you should do a full background check on the person; you should meet in public 3 to 5 times; and whenever you go with them, you should always leave a letter with a friend stating the name of the person you're with, along with their phone number, email address, and the location of where you will be. The bottom should also make arrangements to call a friend when he/she arrives at the destination and at some point during the meeting. This phone call is to let the friend know that he/she is safe.

In addition, these discussions always include advice on a mandatory negotiation process, meaning that in any discussion with a new prospective Top, the bottom must negotiate and set limits to the scene. Thus, it is the bottom's scene and if the Top drifts too far away from what has been planned and negotiated, the scene stops. As I see it, these rules have reversed the roles of Top and bottom by taking control away from the Top and giving it to the bottom. This type of safe, sane, and consensual mindset is not the circumstances under which puppy and I met and first scened. For one thing, puppy and I did not negotiate.

I believe that there are other acceptable philosophies in the world of BDSM. I believe that if you meet someone on-line, you need to talk on-line and on the phone, and then you need to have a face-to-face meeting with them. However, I believe that a week or two of emailing and a couple phone conversations are all that is needed before having a face-to-face meeting. By this point, you should have been able to size up the person and know whether or not you want to scene with them.

Puppy is not controlled by fear. Compared to the safe, sane, and consensual philosophy, she takes chances and risks. For her, there is an element of excitement in taking a chance. We have talked numerous times about being safe, about the idea of negotiation, and about taking risks. In the next few letters, I asked puppy to write about why she enjoys playing in danger with little or no negotiation.

Steven wrote:

Dear puppy,

Explain your views on playing in the element of danger. Do you like the element of fear? The unknown?

Sir

sharon wrote:

Dear Master,

I don't think I'm attracted to the elements of fear or danger. The adrenalin rush of doing or repeatedly doing something dangerous, like skydiving or racecar driving, just isn't something that I seek out or particularly enjoy. However, I do get very stimulated by the unknown and the unexpected, without ever giving thought to whether the unknown is dangerous or not. That's why giving total control to someone else for even a brief period of time is very exciting and appealing to me...I don't know what is going to happen. It is the unpredictable that is most erotic to me. If everything was negotiated, discussed, and planned out, it wouldn't make any difference how dangerous the activity itself was, it would just be ho-hum...so what.

Fear is an unpleasant emotion created in the mind....the *anticipation* of danger. If I don't think about something ahead of time, if I don't anticipate what will happen, it seems to me that I'm preventing fear from taking root and paralyzing my life. So in answer to Your question about playing in the element of fear, I do not play in fear. I play in the element of trust. I am not afraid. I have not perceived danger in any of my explorations into BDSM. I rely on my instincts to know whether I can trust someone and while my instincts are not infallible, they have kept me safe thus far.

I won't try to convince anyone else that I'm right about this, or anything else for that matter, but in my opinion, meeting someone from the Internet is less risky than picking up someone in a bar or at a party and then going home with them. Things are much more likely to get carried away and result in miscommunication, harm, injury or rape when people have had a couple drinks. Neither drugs nor alcohol have ever been involved in any of the BDSM scenes I've been involved in. The purpose is not to make yourself numb in order to endure the "torture," or to become uninhibited enough in order to summon up enough courage to be that "other" sexual person. The purpose of domination and submission is to fully experience both the interaction and the sensations. The purpose is to accept who you are – not to pretend to be someone else.

I'm sure there are plenty of people who, if they had the same experiences I've had, they would claim the scenes were devastating, traumatic, scary, or disappointing. I think, at least to some extent, those feelings are the result of fantasizing and anticipating what would happen – but reality is never quite the same as fantasy. If I knew what was going to happen or what I wanted to happen, I wouldn't be present in the moment. My mind would be somewhere else; there would be no need to pay close attention. Then if things didn't go exactly as expected, I would probably be angry because the other person spoiled my fantasy.

Of course, if a person doesn't enjoy giving up control and she is apprehensive about the unexpected and unknown, she is not going to enjoy the same things as I do. If a person just wants to be "bad" or "rebellious" and tries to hang on to some (or all) of the control, she will miss out on what I consider to be the erotic excitement of the unexpected and unknown. If I set the rules and limits and know exactly what will and will not happen, I may as well just stick with mental fantasies that I can control, and have sex with myself so there is no risk involved….except the risk of eternal boredom.

Love,
Your slave puppy

Steven wrote:

Dear puppy,

Did you negotiate, set rules, or discuss what you wanted with Rob or with anyone else before you scened with them for the first time? Did you have any idea what would happen in the first scene?

Sir

sharon wrote:

Dear Master,

    Rob often asked me what my "limits" were and I would tell him I didn't know. How was I supposed to know whether or not I liked something if I never tried it? There was no discussion or negotiation beforehand about what would happen during any of the scenes, although he did tell me exactly what to wear the first time. The first time we were together, he blindfolded me, tied me spread-eagle on the bed and started flogging me hard, to the point that my backside was a deep purple from my knees to my waist and it lasted for a couple weeks. It never occurred to me to say, "stop."

    I don't need to know everything about a person before going out with him. I find out what I need to know and just let the rest evolve. When I first met Rob, he told me he was a doctor and that he was married and had three daughters. Of course, he could have been lying….and as it turned out, he was actually a psychologist, not a doctor…but in any case, I felt he would not risk doing anything that would threaten either his professional or personal life. I guess that was just a personal judgment, a gut feeling, on my part.

    When I first got involved in bdsm, I only played with married, professional men who had something to lose if they harmed me in any way. My only fear was not that I would be hurt or harmed, but rather the fear that my husband would find out what I was doing.

    As time went on and I started to better understand the mindset of people involved in bdsm, I ventured on to unmarried men, like the cop, who still had something to lose if he harmed me in any way.

    When I met You, You advertised Your businesses and where You lived on the Internet and then I met You in person right in Your own neighborhood. If anything ever happened to me, it wouldn't be hard to track You down. I also felt You wouldn't risk Your business by causing harm to some foolish woman from the suburbs. It did enter my mind that because You were so open and straightforward about Your lifestyle and activities, that there was a much bigger risk of my husband finding out.

Love,
Your slave puppy

Steven wrote:

Dear puppy,

What do "consent" and "consensual" mean to you? Which mindset do you ascribe to?

Sir

sharon wrote:

Dear Master,

When I got started in BDSM, I didn't know any of the terms that were used by people in this lifestyle. It wasn't until after I had been with Rob a few times that I even heard of the terms "Top" and "bottom," and even then he never explained what they meant. He said he appreciated that I didn't try "topping from the bottom." I had no idea what he was talking about and he just laughed when I told him that.

Whether it was consent or consensual, it seemed logical to assume that by showing up at a hotel room to meet a virtual stranger, I was consenting to whatever he wanted to do. After all, I was there to have sex, so it's not like I had to worry about being raped.

As I understand the terms now, "consensual" means there is discussion and negotiation before a scene and the bottom lays down specific rules or guidelines about what she will and will not allow. I understand "consent" to mean that once an agreement is reached that a Top and bottom will scene or play together, there is no negotiation or discussion of limits. Although I wasn't aware that there were options in this regard when I was initiated into BDSM, I was definitely of the "consent" mindset. I think it had a lot to do with the fact that I didn't know what it was all about and I was depending on him to show me. In fact, I was quite relieved when he started telling me exactly what to do as soon as I walked through the door.

I can understand the "consensual" mindset if the bottom has tried something and had a bad experience (like ending up in the emergency room) that she doesn't want to repeat, or if she can't do something due to health reasons. I don't understand how (or why) a person would want to enter the lifestyle and then put limits on things like blindfolds, handcuffs, marks, or having someone watch them in the bathroom. If I'm going to refuse to do things that make me feel uncomfortable, nervous, afraid, or embarrassed, then why would I get involved in BDSM in the first place? It's the tension of doing something that I've never done before or that I'm embarrassed to do, pushing the limits, that I find exciting. If I am not able to trust my partner(s) enough to let them do as they please, then perhaps another lifestyle would be more suitable for me, or else I should be a Top.

Love,
Your slave puppy

Steven wrote:

Dear puppy,

How long were you talking with Rob and the others before you met and scened with them? Did you meet any of them face-to-face before you decided to scene with them?

Sir

sharon wrote:

Dear Master,

I always met the men in a public place before we scened together. The first time I met Rob, I expected he would want to talk for a few minutes and then get a hotel room...I was ready, but he was not. He told me to go home and think about it and let him know. Then we corresponded by e-mail for at least another month before he decided it was time to play. This lengthy correspondence had me very frustrated. It seemed like I had to beg him to see me again. In reality, it was only once every few months that he was able to take a morning off from work in order to play. When playing with married men, it was always a daytime thing, whenever they could play hookey from work for a couple hours. Their wives kept close track of them....which just goes to show that they were anything but dominant at home. Most guys wanted to meet after we had corresponded for about a week. We never talked on the phone ahead of time and I never met anyone more than once before we played.

Love,
Your slave puppy

Steven wrote:

Dear puppy,

Were you scared or nervous before you walked into a hotel room the first time? Were you scared or nervous the first time Rob tied you down and whipped you and then fisted you?

Sir

sharon wrote:

Dear Master,

    I was very nervous when I first got to the hotel room, mostly because I was afraid Rob wouldn't like the way I looked or that I wouldn't be what he expected. He asked me if I needed to make a phone call to let someone know I was safe. I told him that no one had any idea where I was, who I was with, or what I was about to do, and I was certainly not going to tell anyone now. Until he asked that question, it never occurred to me that I had something to be afraid of. In fact, it wasn't until I answered the question that I thought, "That was a dumb thing to say!" Then it was at that point when I decided I would be better off to just kept my mouth shut.

Love,
Your slave puppy

Steven wrote:

Dear puppy,

    Did you panic at any time during the first or second scene?

Sir

sharon wrote:

Dear Master,

    I don't recall ever panicking during a scene. Freeze like a deer caught in the headlights, yes. Panic, no. I think the closest thing to panic was when we went to the Leather Rose for New Year's and You told me to get undressed and then walk through the crowd of (dressed) people to get us some food from the buffet. That was the closest I ever came to refusing to do something asked of me. There have been quite a few times that You've asked me to do something and my heart stopped for a moment or two or three…mostly when we've been in a public place…because, You see, I am actually quite shy and conservative. The only way I can go through with any of that is to let go of myself and focus completely on You…my lifeline. I think it's been the same with anyone else I've played with. I would be far too embarrassed to do any of it spontaneously. In certain situations, like whenever You put the hood or gas mask on me, I have to focus on one second at a time in order to keep from panicking. I really do NOT like anything that interferes with breathing. There have been times when I didn't think I could take any more flogging, whipping, electricity, or whatever, and wanted it to stop, but I know that just past that point of desperately wanting it to stop, just past the point where my mind and senses are in chaos, just past the feeling that I can't take any more, is the best part.

Love,
Your slave puppy

Steven wrote:

Dear puppy,

    How did you feel when the first scene with Rob was over? How did you feel weeks later? What were your conversations with Rob about in the weeks following the first scene? Where were your thoughts, emotions, needs, and desires?

Sir

sharon wrote:

Dear Master,

    After that first scene with Rob, I was preoccupied fantasizing about it, reliving it in my mind, and trying to figure myself out, trying to figure out what I liked about it and why. People started asking what I was so happy about. There was no doubt in my mind that I wanted to explore this world further. I remember thinking how amazing it was that this whole other world existed and I had never known anything about it. Because my words always seemed so inadequate, I wrote to Rob on a daily basis trying to better articulate all the wonderful thoughts and feelings I was having.

Love,
Your slave puppy

Steven wrote:

Dear puppy,

    How long was it until you met Rob again for another scene? Were you scared, nervous, fearful, or excited the second time? Was the element of danger apparent the second time?

Sir

sharon wrote:

Dear Master,

The second time we played was about a month after the first scene. I was told to show up at a certain address. I had no idea that anyone else would be there and was quite surprised when a woman answered the door. I was immediately taken upstairs, told to get undressed, and then i was blindfolded. It wasn't until the scene was over that I actually met the man whose cock was between my legs. The whole thing was very exciting, perfect…beyond my wildest fantasies. That one day is what kept me going back to Rob for three years, hoping for more of the same type of imaginative scene…but it was never quite that good again.

Love,
Your slave puppy

Spring 2004

Sat, 1 May 2004
sharon wrote:

Tina's Place: Part 1

Dear Master,

On the way home last night (this morning), i was thinking about what You said about everything being a dance. That seems to be so true when i am with You. It's like a symbiotic flowing dance. i have never felt that way with anyone else before. my father-in-law is an excellent dancer. i remember once when i was about 8 ½ months pregnant (and the size of a whale), we were at a wedding and i was feeling completely miserable. Then he asked me to dance. He weaved us all over the dance floor and i felt as light as a butterfly, thanks to his skill in leading. That was at a time when Arthur and i were separated and i was an emotional eggshell. i was so grateful to him (my father-in-law) for making me feel human again. Anyway, that's how i always feel on my way home from Your house... light as a butterfly, like we've been dancing all night. And it is Your skill in "leading" that makes me feel that way. Thank You.

i had a wonderful time last night. Three of my curiosities answered all in one night! The sushi, sake, and green tea ice cream were a delectable adventure, with the sushi being much better than i expected. i love trying new things. Where i come from, the cuisine is strictly American, Dutch, or Mexican (as in Taco Bell), so all of the restaurants You've taken me to have been a novel, delicious and fun experience. Thank You again!

Due to the way people have talked, i guess i've built up places like Tina's in my mind too much. i expected it to be a glamorous place crowded with glamorous people playing to the extreme all over the place. i expected to feel intimidated, but actually felt quite comfortable being there, thanks to You. You led the dance perfectly and kept me more relaxed and focused than i thought possible.

It does add a different flavor to things knowing that we're being watched, even though i didn't know that for sure until near the end. (laughing) The lack of vision must have heightened my hearing because the sound of your knife opening scared me every time. i don't recall even hearing it at all in the past. Also, the snap of Your deerskin flogger made me jump before it even touched me. That must have been amusing for You to watch. It took me a second to realize it didn't hurt as much as i first thought. i was disappointed that they have that silly rule about no penetration... and do appreciate that You don't necessarily follow the

35

rules... although fisting without fucking is like cake without frosting. But that's okay because Your bed is much better suited for fucking anyway.

The Bijou was also a surprise. i guess i expected it to be more like a gay bar, although i've never been to one of those either. i thought there would be lots of talking, laughing and socializing, etc., while people casually did their own thing out in the open. i must sound incredibly naive to You. Have i told You that i just arrived here from another planet a few months ago? (laughing) i expected the place to be elaborately decorated, to have strobe lights and loud music, but i guess that's not a guy thing.

The thing that intrigued me about the Bijou was that all of the guys had the same look on their face... almost a haunted, pained, vacant expression. i didn't see a smile anywhere. They all seemed tense. i'm not sure if they are always like that or if it was just because a woman was invading their territory. i wanted to give them all a shoulder massage, tell them to relax a little and have some fun. i guess i just don't understand the culture. i'm afraid if You were to ever put me in that sling at the Bijou, i would have to start giggling at all the somber faces lining the walls... or would using the sling put a smile on someone's face... other than Yours, that is. Thank You for the tour...fascinating.

i started my period today, so perhaps Tues & Thurs would work better next week?

i love You.
Your slave puppy

Steven wrote:
Puppy will write more about the evening at Tina's later on. It was our first time playing together in public. I wanted to see how puppy would handle it, how well she would be able to focus on me in a different environment, and whether she would be distracted by other people or things. I wanted to see if she enjoyed public play, if she was an exhibitionist, and if playing in public excited her. I wanted to know how much of herself she would turn over to me, how completely I could control her depth of focus, how deeply I could take her into her erotic self. I wanted to see if I would enjoy playing intimately with her in public. As I planned the evening, I was very much enjoying my thoughts.

The play area was empty when we arrived at Tina's, so I told puppy to undress and had her sit down in front of a large wooden cross. Then I blindfolded her and hand-cuffed her to the cross. I left her sitting there and then returned ten minutes later, placing my switchblade right up to her ear and pressing the button. The blade flew out and puppy jumped. I repeated this two more times over the next twenty minutes. She was now ready to play.

(Tina's was one of the three public BDSM Dungeons in Chicago at that time. It has since closed.)

Sat, 1 May 2004
sharon wrote:

Tina's Place: Part 2

Dear Master,

    Friday night…(smile) i parked exactly where You <u>said</u> to park even though i knew You <u>meant</u> the other lot. my mother always said you're supposed to take a woman for what she means and not what she says. i guess that goes for men too?

    The only thing i knew about the evening was that we would be going to a public dungeon to play. i was a bit nervous about that, but not too much because i feel very safe with You. We went up to Your bedroom and i sat on Your bed while You chose from among three black jackets. i liked the cashmere one and that's what You wore, along with black wool pants, a black silk shirt, and a very sexy-looking black undershirt. You looked delicious. i wanted to snuggle inside the jacket with You.

    i believe that was when You got out a leather bag and started filling it with floggers, a blindfold, handcuffs, lubricant, the cloth hood...and two white towels. (laughing) For some reason, it was the towels that had me a little concerned. You told me to lie back on the bed and You fisted me. Then You said it was time to go for dinner, so I figured i would try to pee before we left (not an easy thing to do right after you cum). So i went into the bathroom and, to complicate matters, You joined me. i drank from Your cock (while trying to relax enough to pee!) and you added Your scent to my face, neck, and hair. i liked that. It made me feel like i belonged to You, like there was more of a connection between us. Do You think people could really smell it when they stood next to me? In a way, i hope they did and that it made them curious about what was going on.

    After dinner, we went back to Your house for a while…maybe that's when You filled the bag. Anyway, You fisted me again until i was ready to say, "Let's forget about Tina's and stay here." However, it was Your agenda we were following, and You said it was time to go. Despite my puffy, needy pussy, i managed to put myself somewhat back together and don those exasperating shoes. While You walked the dogs, i went to get the car (smoked a quick cigarette 😊) and came back to pick You up. i couldn't figure out what was taking You so long.

Anyway, i drove us to Tina's under Your direction, since i had no idea where i was going. The place seemed to be in an industrial area...looked like a warehouse or something. We went inside where everyone seemed to know You and seemed glad to see You.

Then You took me into the dungeon area, which was pretty big with quite a bit of equipment, but thankfully no one else was in there at the time. i didn't know what to do, so i was watching You intently for some kind of clue. When You told me to get undressed and sit on the base of the cross, i was actually quite grateful. Then You blindfolded me, handcuffed me in place, and i heard You walk away.

It seemed like You were gone for a long time. It was kind of disorienting since i didn't get a good look at my surroundings before being blindfolded. I thought i was alone in that big room, although i kept hearing little noises and wasn't real sure if anyone else was there or not. The handcuffs are always uncomfortable, digging into my wrists, and there was really no way of getting into a comfortable position with my arms around that rough wood, not to mention my bare ass sliding around on equally rough wood.

i must have been absorbed in fidgeting around when You came back in the room because i didn't hear You approach until You opened Your knife about an inch from my ear. i think it scared me so much because i wasn't sure it was You. i don't think You said anything, but i could sense it was You. Then i thought You walked away and suddenly the knife was opened right next to my ear again. (laughing) i had visions of several people standing there with open knives which, as You know, is a rather scary thing to me.

The thing is, though, that i trusted You completely and i wasn't scared... a little nervous and jumpy yes, but not scared. It was kind of strange, but the more i thought You weren't there, the more connected to You i felt. When You finally touched me and said something, i felt...something like joyful maybe, or relieved. i felt immediately and completely relaxed and wanted to do anything at all to please You. You uncuffed me, but left the blindfold on, and then told me to stand up and turn to face the cross. Then You started flogging and spanking me. You kept spanking my pussy, which was already sensitive from all the fisting, and it was really hurting. i was trying to get You to stop and, at the same time, i wanted You to keep going because my pussy was feeling all needy, but it was hurting too much. You kept going back & forth between flogging hard & light and spanking my ass and pussy. Finally, everything just ran together into one of those whole body orgasms that sends electricity all the way up to the back of my neck.

When Rob used to flog me, it was like being run over by a train. i would go out into space in a straight line and that was it. With You, it's like riding a roller coaster...speeding up and slowing down, with all kinds of unexpected turns. i always did like roller coasters...

To be continued.

Love,
Your slave puppy

Sun, 2 May 2004
sharon wrote:

Dear Master,

i forgot to tell You that i have a very noticeable "scratch" going from my chin down to my stomach. No one has said anything about it and i'm not sure how i would explain it if they did. Along with Your initials, it makes me think about You every time i look in the mirror. It's a visible reminder that i belong to You.

Have a wonderful day!

Love,
Your slave puppy

Steven writes:

I made the markings on puppy's chest and neck with my knife. Knife play is in the family of edge play. I like simple knife play. I've done cuttings, but they don't excite me unless the person I am playing with gets off on it. Other than that, it does nothing for me.

However, I do like to use my knife for a different sensation on her skin, as in scraping off wax, teasing her pussy and clit with the knife point, or masturbating her clit with the side of the blade. My main purpose in using a knife is to create fear and anxiety; and I like the reactions I get as her body stiffens and becomes quiet and still. I enjoy orchestrating control over those fearful emotions. I sometimes chain puppy up and run the point and the blade up and down her body, inner thighs, back, and ass, especially after a spanking when her flesh is tender. To get her attention, I may also use both the point and the blade around her face and neck, but not around the eyes. In this case, I scratched my initials on puppy's chest. For the next few days, it will remind her of what we were doing, before it fades away.

Sun, 2 May 2004
Steven wrote:

Dear puppy,

I'm happy you enjoyed the dinner and the dance afterwards. You are good company, fun to play with, and are learning to serve me in delightfully obedient ways.

Tina's is like a social club, with people hanging around, watching movies, and playing intermittently. The other Chicago club, GD2, is similar in that respect. It is only on special occasions or during regional events like Vicious Valentine, Black Rose, Beat Me in St. Louis, etc., that you will see a dungeon filled with people. People plan all year for those occasions and they show up in costume to play and party.

Most event dungeons are non-sexual. Penetration is not allowed by law, which limits the type of play people can do. BDSM in the public straight community is pretty much a non-sexual activity, which is not the case in the gay world. Now I have to contradict myself a little. There are both straight and gay people who consider BDSM to be non-sexual; there are people who consider it to be sexual at certain times; and there are others for whom it is very sexual. But in the public context, straight BDSM is a non-sexual sport.

On the other hand, the Bijou is very different. It is not BDSM-centered, although it gets its share of rough sex. The Bijou is more about anonymous sex. The men are very serious about satisfying their sexual hunger when they're cruising. There is no laughing; it's DICK TIME, and DICK TIME is serious business. When they want to socialize, they go down to the back lobby. As far as you being there, you don't make anyone feel uncomfortable. They were happy to see you sucking on my Dick – it makes their juices flow. The Bijou is all about sex and play. The men would have loved to see me spank, flog, and fist you. My dear puppy, those things will be coming soon. As far as Tue and Thurs, let's make it Thurs.

Sir

Sun, 2 May 2004
sharon wrote:

Dear Master,

    (smile) Yes, i suppose DICK TIME is serious business. It is, after all, what makes the world go round! Perhaps i was looking at the wrong place on their anatomy to gauge their happiness?

    i am happy You were pleased with the evening. i am still wearing a smile! The whole past week has been delightful!

    i think You may have irrevocably altered my diet. i have survived on fast food and chocolate for as long as i can remember. Now today i passed up the cake and cookies at the store and came home with pineapples, grapes, and strawberries, plus a whole fruit platter. See how good You are for me!

    i had a strange dream about You last night that i couldn't get out of my head for most of the day. i dreamed that You went with me to meet my parents, and that they really liked You, and that all of you got along fabulously. In the dream, i felt my father's approval of You and i was very happy. i don't know what that means. i've never really cared one way or the other whether my parents approved of anything i did, and i rarely tell them anything about what's going on in my life. It seems strange that something like that would pop up in a dream.

    Thursday seems soooo far away…i'm not sure if i can wait that long to see You.

Love,
Your slave puppy

Mon, 3 May 2004
sharon wrote:

Tina's Place: Part 3

Dear Master,

    i remember being a little wobbly in the knees by the time we were finished at the cross. You removed the blindfold and steadied me by the arm when i was stepping down from the platform, and You asked if i was okay. i was doing good, so You directed me over to that thing to kneel on. While walking over there, i noticed someone sitting not far away and staring at us. That surprised me because, according to the women at

Shadowfind, that is a real *faux pas* in a public dungeon. i thought it was kind of amusing...i was tempted to turn and bow or curtsy.

    i knelt on the bench and leaned forward onto the leather padding. It was actually quite comfortable...larger and softer than Yours, but there was nothing to hold on to. You had fisted me when i was standing at the cross and You did it again when i was kneeling on the bench...alternating with spanking and flogging. i remember the spanking sounded so loud in that room. i was having one orgasm after another and wishing You would fuck me.

    By that point, spanking my pussy wasn't hurting anymore...it was feeling good. Things were all running together and i felt like i could go on like that all night...but You stopped. You told me to get up, then led me over to a chair to sit down. i desperately needed You to fuck me, but You said such things weren't allowed there. So i got dressed and dazedly went to the ladies' room to put myself back together.

    I still must have been rather spaced out in the bathroom because i took my comb and makeup out of my purse, laid them on the sink, forgot about them, and then started digging in a half-panic through my purse to find them when they were right in front of me. It was one of those moments when you hope you're not on "Candid Camera"...it made me laugh out loud at myself.

    When i got back, You had almost everything put away and i felt bad for wandering off without helping. Then You took me into the lounge area, which was embarrassing because i felt like everyone was staring at me... it made me nervous. Of course, You were acting like nothing unusual had happened. Then You introduced me to Tina. He asked how long i've "been around" which, at the time, struck me as an odd question. i was tempted to tell him 44 years, but assumed that wasn't what he meant... i'm still not sure what he was asking.

    We left Tina's & i drove us back to Your house, which was a lot to ask from someone who had her head in the clouds... kind of like driving drunk. Then You took me on the tour of the Bijou. When we finally got up to Your bedroom, You fiiiiiinalllly fucked me, which made me verrrrrry happy.

    i remember You were talking about playing at the Bijou when You were fucking me. i never know how seriously to take the things You say when You're fucking me, but it sounded like You were serious about that plan.

Love,

Your slave puppy

Steven writes:

The House of Shadowfind was a bed and breakfast in Michigan that catered to the BDSM community. It was noted for its cleanliness and impeccable service administered by a staff of slaves well-trained in Victorian service. The house also had a well-equipped dungeon and a full library.

The weekend puppy stayed at Shadowfind, there was a group of women having a special weekend retreat at the house. They were letting their hair down, so to speak, talking freely and openly about Chicago's BDSM scene. Puppy remembers the conversations of that weekend, which formed her first impression of Chicago's public BDSM community. Shadowfind closed its doors in 2005.

Fri, 7 May 2004
sharon wrote:

Dear Master,

my pussy is feeling so good today... wishing i could serve You again tonight. i was enjoying myself so much this morning that i didn't want to get out of bed. i also seem to be a kaleidoscope of color in the most unusual places, considering where i remember the flogger falling. i had a marvelous time last night. Thank You.

i really liked wearing Your chain/collar. It made me feel very humble and submissive, very cared for, like i belonged to You. i wish i could wear it all the time, but You said i haven't done anything for it yet. i don't know what You meant by that. i will do anything You want.

i also liked the harness. It was surprisingly comfortable...rubbing my pussy whenever i walked...ingenious design! Every woman should have one!

The "outing" to the Bijou was fun and kind of scary at the same time. i was afraid to take my eyes off of You. i kept noticing people walking in behind You and then disappearing into the shadows. Then when You tied me facing the cross...every time You would pause and then come over and touch me, i kept thinking it was someone else coming over while You were looking the other way. It would take me a second to make sure it was You. It was like You were my lifeline or something... my protector. It's just such a weird feeling knowing people are watching like that. It's different than at Tina's. The Bijou seems more "dangerous." It must feel like that for the men who go there too.

When i was in the sling, i could feel people standing very close all around me, but i was afraid to look anywhere except at You. That was the first time i've been in a sling like that. It felt kind of awkward at first...until You focused my attention elsewhere. It was surreal having all those hands touching my body. Every so often, someone would turn away and i could hear them playing with each other right next to me. By the time You were done working Your magic on me, i managed to end up more off the sling than on it... and had forgotten all about the bystanders. my pussy is getting wet again just thinking about how You fisted me...i do love the way You do that. Then when You fuck me after that, it's like i can feel everything much more intensely... mmmm... gonna have to stop thinking about all this because i'm making myself all lonely and frustrated.

Anyway, the whole atmosphere at the Bijou kind of messes with one's mind...and then walking out of there with everyone watching...(laughing) after my performance in the sling, i didn't look at any faces this time!

i miss You.

Love,
Your slave puppy

Sat, 8 May 2004
sharon wrote:

Dear Master,

i hope You are enjoying this absolutely gorgeous day! i started out early this afternoon to shop for Mother's Day and stumbled upon a giant craft show and festivities on my way through the forest preserve. i never did make it to the mall. Now it sounds like everyone will be coming here for dinner tomorrow, so i guess i better figure out what to make... maybe shish-ke-babs on the grill... and maybe i'll go buy a patio set so everyone can sit out on the deck.

If i remember correctly, You said Your mother lives in Florida? Did You send her something for Mother's Day?

i haven't heard from my older son. i think he finished up with school on Friday, so they're probably partying this weekend. He was talking about going straight to New York City or San Francisco when school got out, so i doubt i'll see him until June when he starts working here. i'm doing a poor job of keeping up with his schedule anymore.

i miss You. i am thinking about You all the time...and dreaming about You too.

Love,
Your slave puppy

Sat, 8 May 2004
sharon wrote:

Dear Master,

What would You do if i showed up on Your doorstep with all my worldly possessions?

Love,
Your slave puppy

Sat, 8 May 2004
Steven wrote:

Gone fishing.

Thu, 13 May 2004
sharon wrote:

Dear Master,

Thank You for the lovely evening. my supper was delicious... an enchanting combination of textures and flavors. i hope You will pardon the fact that some of it dribbled off my chin... since there wasn't a napkin within my reach. The dogs seemed happy to clean it up though.

Love,
Your slave puppy

Steven writes:

When puppy came over that night, we were in the kitchen when I had her remove her clothes. I then put a harness on her with a dildo in her pussy and had her sit on a dog bed. I put a leather collar on her neck, handcuffed her hands behind her back, blindfolded her, and then I attached one end of the chain to her collar and the other end to a door handle. There was no place for her to go; all she could do was focus. I then fed all the animals and cleaned up. When I finished, I fed puppy fresh cut pineapple,

45

grapes, apple slices, and melon, and had her drink a little of me to add a different flavor.

Fri, 14 May 2004
sharon wrote:

Dear Master,

    Sitting on the floor with arms tied down and wearing a harness, handcuffs, and blindfold... i liked it... but i can't quite put my finger on exactly why. i felt helpless, humbled, completely focused on what i imagined You were doing and what You might do next. i felt kind of a loss of identity, a loss of control, but secure, relaxed and open...like being a child with no decisions and no responsibilities. All of these things come close but aren't exactly right.

    Kneeling has always sort of flipped a switch for me...symbolic of submission i guess...or of elevating the person i'm kneeling in front of...or a sign of respect maybe. Even if i kneel at a patient's feet in the process of taking care of them, it does something to me. It just seems like it's where i should be. It sounds weird that something like that could make me feel that way...maybe it has something to do with the indescribable expression on peoples' faces when i look up at them.

    Anyway, i was sitting on the floor like that, trying to listen for where You were and what You were doing. It surprised me when something was put in my mouth because i didn't hear or feel You approach. The taste and texture of the pineapple was greatly magnified for some reason...and for some reason i had difficulty chewing while blindfolded and with my hands tied. (i won't even try to explain that one!) When i heard You approach again, i opened my mouth expecting more cold, tart pineapple. Instead, my mouth was filled with Your warm, sweet cock...the taste and texture also being magnified. There couldn't have been more of a contrast, and switching back and forth seemed to magnify the flavor of both each time. It was like drinking cold pineapple juice alternating with warm tea. A unique culinary delight!

    Walking up Your winding stairs while bound and blindfolded is not an easy task. i was dependent on You for every step. i trusted that You wouldn't let me fall... which says a lot because i can't think of anyone else i would trust to do that. When i was sitting on Your bed, i felt like i should be doing something, so it was making me a little tense to hear You fixing the bed, etc. It seemed like there was an awful lot of activity going on. You had told me about the wax, but i was trying to figure out what else You were doing. i smelled a nice scent and figured You must have lit a candle, although i'm still not sure what that was because it seemed kind of sudden for a candle.

When things start moving a little faster, i think my mind must have checked out or something because i can't remember the order of things...everything just flows together like a collage. i remember when i was sitting on the edge of the bed, the dildo was pressing on just the right spot and i was wishing You would hurry up with whatever You were doing and come over and fuck me. When You told me to lie down, i was disoriented for some reason. i didn't know which way was which or where i was on the bed... kind of lost in space for a while.

The dildo, handcuffs, and straps were gone. i was floating, like in a dream... and You were doing anything You wanted. i was like a receptacle of sensation. At some point, You tied my hands and feet to the four corners of the bed and covered me with oil. i knew what was coming, but You moved so quietly that i was startled to feel the hot wax. It didn't burn instantly this time though. It was more like a spreading heat, but the more You poured on, the more it started to burn. It was like all of the nerves in my skin were standing at attention.

Then, if i remember correctly, right in the middle of the waxing, You all of a sudden applied the vibrator to my clit and i started to cum almost immediately. (laughing) It was like my body was ahead of my mind and i had to quick change direction and run to catch up with it. About the time i caught up, i think You went back to the waxing.

At some point when You were using the vibrator, i remember my clit felt like it was about the size of a grapefruit and even the touch of the air was almost too intense to handle.

It felt good when You were scraping the wax off with Your knife. i could have laid there for hours enjoying that, but You changed directions again and were already doing something else by the time my mind shifted gears and caught up... kind of like floating up into the sky and then suddenly finding yourself someplace else.

You are very handy with a speculum... You could teach a thing or two to some gynecologists. i think they store theirs in a freezer and they handle it like something found in a mechanic's toolbox. You, on the other hand, slipped the thing in my ass and i didn't even know what it was until You started to spin the thing that opens it up.

If i were to step back and look at the situation, it would seem kind of humiliating, but it didn't seem that way at the time. i was rather worried about how far You were going to go with it though. You keep alluding to the idea of fisting my ass and frankly, i don't see how that could be possible. i like the idea of being open for You though.

Anyway, it was a little uncomfortable at first, but You went slowly and i was trying very hard to relax, so it was okay. Every time it started feeling stretched to the limit, You stopped and fucked my ass which was actually quite soothing... and much more fun! Then when You put the speculum back in, it seemed more comfortable. At the end, it didn't hurt so much as it made my heart pound and i felt kind of nauseous and dizzy... kind of like having the bed spins when you've had too much to drink. I was glad You didn't push it any further.

Do You know that when You make love to me, it's like no one else i've ever known. You could teach a thing or two to all the rest of the men in this world on that subject too!

Love,
Your slave puppy

Thu, 20 May 2004
sharon wrote:

Dear Master,

i am finally back online! It seems my darling sons hooked up a router the wrong way so it was showing we had two IP addresses (whatever those are). So the Internet company took it upon themselves to turn one off...the only real one. There are about 20 cords attached to stuff on my desk and i have no idea what he did, but Don moved them all around and has the problem, in his words, "temporarily fixed."

The rest of my evening has been consumed with trying to set up online bill paying. After about 2 hours of listing everything, i lost it all because the web site was messed up and now will have to start over... another day. Hopefully the actual bill paying function works after all this trouble!

Thank You for the wonderful evening last night. Obviously, i'm no connoisseur of Japanese food, but i liked the *sushi* better at the other place. (laughing) Then again, maybe it was the *sake* that made it taste better. If we go to one of those places again, i need to take home a set of chopsticks to see (again) if i can figure out how to use the damn things. That kind of food appears easier to eat with the chopsticks than with a fork. my brother-in-law tried to teach me and my 3-year-old nephew how to use them once. my nephew figured it out right away. i didn't manage nearly as well.

    i do think it's funny to be walking down the street with a wet spot on the back of my skirt, but i'm glad You didn't say anything about it until we got back to Your house. i don't think those girls walking behind us paid any attention to it though. Personally, i was more concerned with what was dribbling down my leg when i stood up in the restaurant. It seems Your generosity with the lubricant had a devious purpose! In the future, i think i may have to remember to wear underwear with the shorter skirts...

    You let me fly last night. Thank You. i think You could have used that "cat" on me all night long. It was perfect. It felt like soft fire streaking across my skin, all up and down my body, in rhythm with the music. Before i met You, i was always kind of afraid of a cat. In fact, i did not like it at all. With You, it's like an energy (for lack of a better word) that flows back and forth. You mentioned something about "processing the pain." That is a perfect description of what was happening. It was traveling all over my body and as long as i didn't try to stop it, it kept taking me higher. The really neat thing is that i didn't end up feeling like i was beaten up...could fly without crashing so to speak. Thank You.

    It is storming really bad here so i think i better unplug some stuff before it gets hit by lightning.

i love You.
Your slave puppy

Steven writes:

    My home and office are in a four-story corner building, and the first floor has a storefront with two large windows facing Wells Street in Chicago. The front half of the store is used as a shipping and receiving room; the back half is my stock room. There are two entrances into the building. A single door to the right leads upstairs to the office, while the double doors on the left, between the two large bay windows, open into the shipping room. Inside the building, there is a door between the shipping room and the stairway going to the office.

    Before we went out for dinner, I took puppy into the shipping room where I had her bend over with her arms out, holding onto the shipping table, a few feet away from the large windows. I lifted her skirt, spanked her for about ten minutes, and then finished our little scene by lubricating her, fucking her with a dildo, and then fisting her. I did not clean her off. Instead, I had her suck on my cock for a few minutes before we walked down the street to have dinner. Afterwards we walked back to my place to play.

In reference to processing pain, everyone (bottom, submissive, or masochist) has a different pain threshold level. The ability to process pain involves concentrating from within oneself. It is the ability to accept and then embrace the sensation. If you allow it to, the pain can transfer you into the other world of forbidden pleasure, also known as "subspace." If you reject it or fight it, the sensations will soon become painful, unpleasant, and will evoke anger, distrust, and the need to escape, all at the same time. In other words, resisting the pain can result in a Bad Experience.

I have played with a few people who loved to fight, who craved the struggle with the pain. In these fighting scenes, the vocal exchange is often very intense. Puppy is not a fighter; she has learned to process the pain.

Sat, 22 May 2004
sharon wrote:

Dear Master,

Staying dry? It seems like every time i poke my head out the door it starts storming! i've been drenched three times today. i don't remember it ever raining this much in May.

i got an e-mail from Michael (previous Dom) today. He says he misses me and wants to get together again. He's been sending e-mails every couple of months. i haven't responded to any of them, so i'm not sure why he's still writing. i know he writes to people on Alt every day and figured he would have found someone by now. i actually feel kind of sorry for him. He's basically a good person in a very difficult situation. i guess that just shows that money can't buy happiness. In fact, money seems to be more like a prize for the runners-up in life. Some people spend their whole lives trying to get rich only to find that once they get there they have sacrificed everything of real value and are left with an empty shell... very sad.

In answer to Your question, i enjoyed the night of "simple fucking, fisting, and pissing." Those are the best parts! As i was trying to communicate before, i don't require an elaborately orchestrated "event." i am there to serve You in whatever way makes You happy at the time. Whatever makes You happy makes me happy... although i suppose i would be a little disappointed if there was no fucking at all. Also, i admire the fact that You have enough self-awareness to know when it's not a good idea to be wielding a whip, flogger, etc. In a way, i felt like i was giving You more during that "simple" evening... not sure exactly how to explain that.

When You fisted me before we went out for dinner the other night, i could hear people talking and laughing right outside the window. The thought ran through my head that i wonder if people can get arrested for doing something like that in plain view from a city street, even though they are playing inside of a building. (It's funny how the thought of getting arrested always crosses my mind when other people are around.) When You told me to bend over, i thought You were going to spank me. Then when You applied the lube, i thought i was going to be wearing the dildo and harness to dinner. Then when You fisted me, i thought let's just skip dinner and go back upstairs...though it doesn't seem possible to think so clearly while being fisted. When You stopped so abruptly, my thought was - DON'T STOP NOW!!

It took a few minutes to mentally regroup. i always seem to be about three steps behind whatever direction You're going in, and there's nothing to do but laugh about that. i must have had a dazed expression on my face. At that point, You probably could have walked me down the street completely naked and i wouldn't have cared one bit.

In the restaurant, You were talking about IML *(International Mr. Leather, an annual event in Chicago on Memorial Day weekend)*. It always makes me wonder what the waitress or people sitting nearby are thinking when You talk about stuff like that in a restaurant. i was kind of preoccupied though, with my pussy feeling very empty... and widely open. It felt like i was making a puddle on the seat. i actually looked at the chair when i got up and was relieved not to see a puddle... never thought about the back of my skirt...duh!

Along with my pussy-preoccupation, the food was being very uncooperative. i would have really appreciated it, at that point, if You would have just tied my hands behind my back and fed me. Although i don't recall learning this in college anatomy & physiology, i am convinced there is a switch in the female body that turns off one's brain whenever the pussy is penetrated, thus making one incapable of performing even the simplest tasks.

Anyway, i have no idea what i was doing in the restaurant, was having difficulty following what You were talking about, was hoping we would hurry up and get out of there, and was a wee bit concerned that You were going to do something to throw me hopelessly off-balance, and then who knows what would happen! (laughing) i assume You were aware of my flustered state of mind, and i appreciate the fact that You acted like there was nothing at all going on.

Love,
Your slave puppy

Steven writes:

At times, I enjoy playing with puppy before we go out because when I'm finished, she's like a deer caught in headlights. Fisting is on the top of the list of things puppy likes, followed by sucking my cock and drinking me. Before we go out, she is required to say "Master, may I help you relieve yourself." I also enjoy putting my scent on her and telling her that everyone who comes near to her will know that she belongs to me. Various forms of humiliation, single tail, flogging, and spanking also make puppy wet to the point of orgasm. She enjoys bondage as a form of meditation and anticipation. I incorporate some of these things in all of our play.

In public play, I usually have puppy lying on the floor naked, blindfolded, spread-eagle, and bound in ankle and wrist restraints and rope. I want her to feel as though the people around her are inspecting her. I want her to be self-conscious and embarrassed about being so exposed. It is somewhat humiliating to her at first, but then her excitement takes over and, after a few minutes, her pussy opens, glistening and very wet to the touch. I may walk away for a while, always watching her. I need her to focus on the room temperature, on her body, the sounds, her own thoughts, and the situation she is in. All of this is very exciting to me.

Sometimes I tie puppy to a chair, either naked or clothed, and blindfold her, and again walk away, always keeping an eye on her. Our public play is usually simple singletail, flogging, fisting, and spanking of her ass and pussy simultaneously in rhythm. When I spank her pussy, I may do it flat-fingered for more contact, but most of the time I cup my fingers to create suction and noise. When penetration is not allowed, I know she will have a gushing climax with a pussy and ass spanking. This is how we make love in a public play space.

Tue, 25 May 2004
sharon wrote:

Dear Master,

i hope Your day is going as well as mine! i've been working day and night for the past week on a proposal to get rid of the hospital's million dollar QA program they are so proud of. Then i did a presentation today for the CEO & VP's and they all agreed to it without a bit of argument. Everyone else had told me it would be impossible to get rid of that albatross. i think i was more shocked than anyone at the lack of resistance. So now each subsidiary of the hospital will have the opportunity to develop their own QA program, which will provide more useful information about their specific area at a fraction of the cost. Honestly though, i think in the past, people have used corporate resistance as an excuse for being lazy. There have been so many things i've been told "can't" be done since i started there and most of them have only taken a few minutes to resolve.

Also, i hired a new nurse today who will start on Thursday... just in the nick of time since i came within an inch of strangling one of my current nurses this morning for being so incredibly stupid. i am slowly thinning the ranks of the incompetent and am now getting some enthusiastic & committed people in place....just a few more nurses to let go and things will be looking pretty good.

You had me quite immobilized last night. i think i could get out of most bondage if i tried, but i definitely wasn't going anywhere last night... and no amount of squirming was making it any more comfortable. The chains were cold and unforgiving. You weren't going to let me go off into the clouds either. That was the first time i've been interrogated like that, in that kind of circumstance. It wasn't what i expected. i'm used to getting yelled at so that's what i thought You were going to do... more like a verbal attack that would make me feel defensive. Your interrogation reminded me of my father's when i was about 12-13 yrs old and got caught smoking. I couldn't come up with a word of excuse for myself then either. i think it's easier to get yelled at... it kind of puts up a wall between the yeller and yellee. Then you can yell at each other and neither one listens to the other, but both of you feel better just to get it out of your system...if that makes sense.

When You were interrogating me, i just wanted to touch You to let You know that i really do want to serve You. There wasn't anything i could say... no excuses. The blindfold was covering the tears in my eyes. Maybe You really are too nice to me and i don't know how to react when someone is so nice. Have You ever seen one of those things with the four steel balls hanging from strings. When you lift one of the balls and let it drop, the two in the middle stay still while the one on the other end flies up and it keeps going back & forth like that. That's the kind of relationship i've been in for the past 25+ years. When we come together, we bounce off of each other in opposite directions, never going in the same direction, never still or in motion at the same time. It's become kind of an ingrained reaction. i think that's why i have a hard time intuiting what You want.

Anyway, when You are nice to me, i keep expecting something bad to happen... and if i do something for You outside of the sexual arena, i have this illogical expectation that You're going to go off and do...i don't know what...it's illogical. The thing is that You are very consistent in how You react to things, which should make it easy to figure out what You want, but it's Your consistency that baffles me. i'm always trying to read between the lines when, in fact, You are quite straightforward. i always think You mean something other than what You're saying when that's probably not true.

When i think back to when i got started with D/s, a big thing that attracted me to it was that a Dominant person would always tell me what to do, so i wouldn't have to think or worry about what he wanted, or try to figure out what to do. i would be able to make him happy simply by obeying. Perhaps what people refer to as being a "doormat?"

i see women everywhere of whom nothing is expected of them except to take care of the house and family, look nice, have afternoon tea, and talk about nonsense. For the life of me, i can't figure out how they do it. i would love to spend my days cooking and cleaning, taking care of You, and fixing myself up to look nice for You. Instead i spend my days in the trenches dealing with things that aren't talked about in polite (or even impolite) company. A few weeks ago i got a call from a hysterical nurse who discovered maggots in a patient's wound, so i had to go out, calm everybody down, and clean the wounds myself. Last Wednesday, i got a call from the inpatient unit that a patient with superior vena cava syndrome had swelled up to the point that his face split open and green pus was gushing out. It made the nurse so sick she couldn't go in the room. i had to go over and try to preserve a shred of this man's dignity while his family watched him die.

i'm not saying i don't like what i do. It's just that i can't turn it off like a light switch when i leave work. It's like i have to go through a debriefing or something and just "be" and let things process through before I can leave the weight of the world for someone else to carry for awhile, before i can relax and have fun. When You talk to me, it's like i hang on every word You say because it's so drastically different than anything i hear the rest of the day. i become absorbed in everything You say because i don't have to solve Your problems, or tell You what to do, or make Your business a success. i don't have to think...just listen... and everything else disappears.

Actually doing something is a whole separate dimension that simply doesn't occur to me until You draw my attention to it. Then it's like i wake up and think, "What the hell am i doing sitting here on my ass?" Then i realize You've already taken care of the animals, etc., and everything is already done once again. Then i start backpedaling, trying to analyze what You're saying, always about three steps behind the program. It isn't until You fuck me that my body and mind are in the same place at the same time. Now that i've rambled on far too long, i have to get to bed... too much thinking.

Love,
Your slave puppy

Steven writes:

When puppy is chained to the bed, she is my prisoner. Depending on the scene, the physical restraint of bondage can put her into a wonderful state of meditation, peace, and tranquility. She can't move, and if she does start to fidget, she quickly gets very uncomfortable. She must stay centered and focused within herself, making it very easy to do various forms of interrogation scenes.

I had puppy sitting in the middle of my bed, totally immobilized by chains attached to various parts of her body. The chains are anchored to eyehooks in the floor all around my bed. She had four chains attached to metal rings on the belt around her waist and three chains attached to rings on the collar around her neck. Her legs were spread wide open by chains attached to ankle restraints and secured to the floor. To keep her from closing her thighs even an inch, I put thigh restraints on her and attached chains to them, also secured to the floor. Lastly, I had her spread out her arms and attached chains to the cuffs on her wrists.

Once all the chains were in place, I started to adjust the tension, adding and subtracting links with adjustable clips, keeping her off-balance in the center of the bed, and taking away all her freedom of movement. Then I used a vibrator on her clit and attached clothespins to various parts of her body. She could neither adjust her position nor escape from the pain/pleasure of what I was doing. She was mine to playfully torture as I pleased.

There are a growing number of people who enjoy Shibari, the erotic and romantic art of Japanese rope bondage. With Shibari, the aesthetics of the creation connects the participants beyond just BDSM bondage. It takes time and patience to learn this art and to create the beauty of rope artistry, depending on the type of bondage and the design of knots, loops, and tension. The time spent creating the bondage on someone creates the connection. The person creating the rope design loves to show his/her artistry, while the person being bound loves the time and attention being spent on them. The fact that the bottom/submissive is made beautiful in bondage heightens the captive experience.

I am not a rope artist. I don't care about the aesthetics; and I don't care to spend long periods of time setting up the bondage. I am not that patient, not to mention that I would hang myself with all the rope.

There is nothing pretty about chain. I like the cold, hard, heavy feel of chain, the quick adjustability of the tension, the immobility it produces, and the ease of undoing it all. Chain is unforgiving, feels more sadistic, and leaves my captive absolutely helpless.

Thu, 27 May 2004
sharon wrote:

Dear Master,

i am sorry about the spots on Your bed. It reminded me of a *Cat In The Hat* book i used to read to my kids in which a small pink spot ended up everywhere. In the future, You may have to confine me to floor space if i am there on day # 2. Also, i am sorry about not asking to use the bathroom. It's kind of embarrassing trying to contain the mess and i was trying not to make a big deal of it. You handle these things very nonchalantly, but it's still embarrassing for me.

i've been thinking about ways i can serve You, but last night seemed kind of strange…on a different plane. i'm not sure why. i couldn't seem to get out of work mode. i talked to our marketing manager today about those brochures, but she has her mind made up and is not willing to give up her pet project even though it's gotten out of hand. She's been working on this for a year and has so much time involved in it that the real cost of the thing is probably more like $50K. i don't have the heart to burst her bubble.

In regard to serving You, i think i need to "make" You sit down (and not get up) while i take care of the animals & clean up. Also, i can get the bed ready and again "make" You sit down while i get everything out that You want...and then i can put everything away again. Also, i can undress/dress You and i can "help" You if You need to use the bathroom.

Generally speaking, i guess i just need to ask You what i can do even though that seems kind of pushy to me. i guess i just need to get over the feeling that it's impolite to be messing with someone else's stuff unasked. It has always been a pet peeve of mine when people come to my house and take it upon themselves to clean up the kitchen after dinner or something...it just seems rude. After they leave, i always go back and redo things the way i want them done... maybe a little obsessive-compulsive?

Hmmm... how about if i think about what else i would like to do for You and write about that... tomorrow?

i love You.
Your slave puppy

Steven writes:

I have given puppy a few responsibilities and duties to take care of when she is with me. She's pretty good at doing most of them, even though she does tend to get lost in space. Taking care of me is difficult since there are so many things that I have to do such as feeding and walking the dogs, feeding the birds, planning the evening's events, thinking about the next day's projects, writing, etc. One of my businesses is open 24/7 and requires my attention at various times during the evening. My other business, which is located on the first two floors of the building where I live, closes at 6 p.m., but I have people who like to work later hours. I also have punk rock bands that practice in the basement of my building, so I hear their music until 10-11 p.m., then the building finally starts to quiet down. At times, I also get lost in my own mind.

Fri, 28 May 2004
sharon wrote:

Dear Master,

i hope You had a good day at IML, sold lots of books, and had lots of fun! i've been thinking about You all day.

Love,
Your slave puppy

Sat, 29 May 2004
Steven wrote:

Dear puppy,

    I am tired. It's been a long weekend so far at IML, and not as good as I would have liked it to be. I haven't told you when to come to the event because I don't have the time available to spend with you. I know that doesn't matter, but with the way the booth is laid out and with all the running around that I'm doing, you would just be waiting around. That doesn't mean that you can't come by; it would be lovely to see you. Now isn't that confusing?

    Someone approached me to give a demonstration class at Galleria Domain (GD2) – it's something to think about. How are you doing? I've been thinking about your premonition. It would be nice if you were right. Thank you for your thoughts.

Sir

Steven writes:

    Puppy did come to IML. As for the demonstration, being asked to give a class was a novel idea to me. What topic would I present? I considered topics such as the adult industry, the legal system, being in prison, sex clubs, or vaginal fisting. I liked the idea of doing a class on vaginal fisting – not a 101 class about safety and technique, but something on how I incorporate fisting when I play. I considered doing an audience participation in a supervised fisting gangbang...

Sun, 30 May 2004
sharon wrote:

Dear Master,

    i seriously thought about coming up there but figured Saturday would be Your busiest day and i would just be in the way. Then Dale came home and it didn't seem right to leave as soon as he got here. i took him out for dinner, had 2 glasses of wine, and ended up going to bed about 9:30. Now it's 3:30 a.m. and i'm wide awake. How about if i come up there on Mon afternoon to help You pack stuff up?

i miss You.

Love,
Your slave puppy

Sun, 30 May 2004
Steven wrote:

Dear puppy,

    Monday, around 1:30-2:00, is good. You can walk around the vending area. Dress is jeans, casual. We will start tearing down around 3:00-4:00. When we finish bringing everything back to the office, we'll go out for dinner and then back home to play.

Sir

Fri, 4 Jun 2004
sharon wrote:

IML 2004

Dear Master,

    IML was kind of like i thought it would be, except i didn't think it would be nearly that big. i did think more people would be (un)dressed in fetish clothing though.
    You didn't give me much (any?) direction on where to go when i got there. (laughing) i was wandering around like a "lost puppy" for quite a while. i went upstairs first since that seemed to be the direction everyone else was going. i asked someone where the booths were and the way he looked at me, i figured i must be in the wrong place. He couldn't seem to comprehend that i was there for IML, so he sent me back to the main floor where i wandered around some more. Someone else gave me some very complicated directions, which about all i grasped was that it was on a lower level. i ended up having to ask about 10 people before i finally got to the place where i had to show an I.D. (for the third time). i'm not sure what the purpose of all the identification was, but think i'll go with the fantasy that they didn't believe i was 18 yet.
    At that point, i just started following the guy in front of me and somehow ended up where all the vendors were. i had pictured a much, much smaller room where i would be able to see You right away. Instead, it seemed liked an endless maze of booths. i had visions of wandering around for hours before i would be able to find You. i started down what i thought was the main aisle and about half-way down, i saw what i thought were books in the next aisle, so i went over there only to find they were

actually videos or pictures or something. Then i turned around and there You were. my lucky day!

    i was worried i would just be in the way, but You seemed pleased to see me. i was still feeling quite lost in the commotion when You asked me to kneel... that helped. When You said You were going to show me around, i didn't know what You had in mind... wasn't sure what i was supposed to do. Of course, the instructions You had given me before had totally vacated my brain leaving no forwarding address. So i was just trying to watch You and follow Your lead, but i kept getting distracted by all the stuff on display, not to mention all the interesting-looking people walking around.

    i must say that the creators of all that stuff are quite imaginative people! One question... You said that the toilet seats on display were for scat play. i don't mean to sound too dumb, but how exactly does a scene like that go? The things were too short and small for anyone or anything to be underneath them... am i missing something? Also, i didn't grasp how the suits of armor are used in play...? Okay, so i have a few more questions. Have You ever used those latex outfits in play? They look like they could give someone heat stroke real quick. Oh, and i also found those elephant-sized cock pumps quite fascinating. i would have liked to check out that guy's cock when he took the thing off... looked like it would be quite painful. i thought the masks were neat... It would be fun to go to a party where everyone was wearing a mask and nothing else. i would also like to see someone (definitely not me!) take one of those giant-sized cocks in their ass... It would make having a baby seem like a picnic. i really find it impossible to believe that any human ass could accommodate such a thing.

    A lot of the stuff there looked like it could cause a lot of internal injuries. For example, as a nurse i know how much damage a Foley catheter can cause if inserted by someone who doesn't know what they're doing... i can't imagine inserting one of those metal probes into someone's penis without causing serious and permanent injury, not to mention a high risk of infection. And who in the world would ever agree to be a guinea pig for some sadist to practice on! Anyway, i could go on forever talking about all the paraphernalia at the show. There is apparently no end to what people will try.

    When we got back to Your booth, i was very happy to kneel at Your side. It seemed like You were doing a good business so while You were talking to customers, i was watching the people walk by. Aside from the goofy guy changing outfits every two minutes, there was one couple who was particularly intriguing... an older man with a younger man who was obviously his slave. They were holding hands and walking like they were headed somewhere in particular...like the slave was going to be punished or something. They were wearing normal street clothes, but i've never seen anyone who appeared to be so serious about and totally immersed in slavery. It was obvious that it was far more than play to them. i was wishing they would stop and talk to You, but they didn't. Very intriguing... they left an imprint on my mind.

One more question regarding the tour of the show... You started to tell me about the "hankie code" (at least that's what i think You called it) but then we got distracted. What is that all about? i remember hearing bits & pieces about it many years ago, but it was always people just jokingly making reference to it in general.

i was glad to have the opportunity to help pack stuff up... it made me feel somewhat useful. i've had a love affair with books for as long as i can remember, so it was hard to resist looking through any of them. i was a little amused at how Patrick was so particular about how they were arranged because i would be the same way if they were my books... and i thought i was the only one with such idiosyncrasies! (laughing) i am so ridiculous that i keep rearranging the books on my shelves so they appear to be more appealingly organized. Everything else can be a mess, but the books must be organized and neat!

When You sent me to get my car, i first of all got lost trying to find my way out of the place; then they brought me the wrong car; and then they gave me directions to the wrong loading dock. You must have thought i would never get there... and i thought the same thing! The fact that i actually found the right place was purely accidental... again my lucky day!

When we got back to Your house, everything seemed strangely quiet and peaceful. The dinner at Orso's was very nice. You mentioned something during dinner about having a connection with Guy Baldwin... something to do with a trial and maybe death... and i meant to ask You about that the other night. i'm curious why that particular connection came to Your mind. The reason i'm curious is because when i told You before that there was one thing, one fact, that i know and that You will need for Your business, the word that kept coming to my mind was "bereavement." It makes absolutely no sense to me. Does it mean anything to You?

Another strange thing is that about the time You were recovering from cancer was when i made a rather sudden career change and got involved with hospice. It was like a calling... in a very different direction from where i thought i was going. Actually, all of the dates i gave You were when my life took an unexpected turn in an unexpected direction, eventually leading me to where i am now. i always felt there was a reason for those things... like i was progressing toward some unknown destination. It's interesting that You were going through major changes at each of those same times...

    Okay, i've rambled on for long enough tonight. i will continue with the "catching up" tomorrow.

i miss You... i never got to taste You the other night...

Love,
Your slave puppy

Sat, 5 Jun 2004
sharon wrote:
Dear Master,

    Monday was a fun day. A three-day rainy weekend is entirely too long to be stuck in the house. i was so glad when You said to come & see You. After dinner we went back to Your house and now so much time and stuff has passed, i don't remember exactly how things went.

    You showed me Your new bullwhip. i was a little worried You were going to practice using it on my backside. When i was a kid, there were always real bullwhips and electric bull zappers around and my brother would torture me with them. Pain is not a sufficient word to describe what those electric things felt like. They would make a 2000 pound bull howl... would knock me right off my feet... which my brother found to be quite humorous. The whips i was familiar with were different though. i think the solid part was about 3-4 feet long & the whip part shorter, I guess because when you're dealing with a bull there is no time to take aim or worry about technique or you would be crushed. i'm getting sidetracked...sorry.

    When we went upstairs, i remember You had me suspended from the chains in the ceiling and You were using the floggers, etc. i was so relaxed... my body felt like melted chocolate... and when You came over by me, Your scent and touch was... incredible. You could have done absolutely anything with me and i would have been happy. When You let me down from the chains, You were going to fuck my ass but i couldn't seem to get in the right position... maybe a little too relaxed?

When we went back to Your bed, You had me sniff that stuff (poppers?)...i wonder if that had something to do with how relaxed i felt. i don't think it did much to relax my throat, but it did make my face feel extremely hot for a little while. Maybe it did relax my throat some though because i was able to take Your cock deep enough that it made my eyes water and my nose run... that was embarrassing. i think that's the biggest impediment to my ability to deep-throat... getting all snot-faced... not very attractive. Then, when i was all "snot-faced" You had me sit on Your cock and i was all out of sync because i was desperately needing a Kleenex. It must have been rather amusing to You. Thankfully, You flipped me over and fucked me, and it felt sooooo good... i will never get tired of how good it feels when You fuck me... and You always smell so good. Your scent alone is enough to make my pussy all wet and needy. It's funny how a person's natural scent can make such a difference... pheromones i guess... powerful stuff.

Love,
Your slave puppy

Steven writes:

This was puppy's first lesson (from me) in sucking cock. I gave puppy Jungle Juice Platinum (smoother on the nose, nice head build up). It is one of many poppers that are used within the gay community as a sexual enhancer. Poppers relax the throat and anal muscles, so for some people, getting fucked in the ass by a big dick or large object is made easier. Relaxing the throat muscles lets you take more of your partner's cock into your mouth and throat, hence face fucking. I have been selling poppers since 1970.

When it comes to having my cock sucked, I especially enjoy the thick mouth cum (mucus) that a good deep cock sucking produces. puppy continued to work on the art of cock sucking 2-3 times a week for about 5-6 weeks. The difference was fabulous. She now has great throat and jaw muscle control and can suck a dick with the best of them. puppy is doing her Master proud. puppy describes her cock sucking technique in detail later in this book.

Cocksucking and drinking from my cock have been referred to in many of puppy's letters throughout this book. These phrases have come to symbolize puppy separating from her work and family life and entering into my world of sexuality.

Sun, 6 Jun 2004
sharon wrote:

Dear Master,

What a beautiful day! i've been thinking about You all day... wishing i was there with You instead of here. It would be nice to spend the whole weekend with You sometime.
Wednesday... i enjoyed going with You to walk the dogs. i like walking, especially after being stuck in an office all day. Maybe that's something i could do for You? However, us "puppies" might wander off on an extended adventure. i think it would be fun to take them down along the lake shore. Do they like the water? Something else that would be fun to do sometime is go to the greyhound races. i somehow ended up in a discussion about that with a woman at the tailor's today... betting on the dog races. i'm not much of a gambler though... actually not at all. It would just be fun to watch them run.
Anyway, back to Wednesday. It's fun riding in Your cars. i always feel like everyone must be watching us go by. It's not every day that one sees a Rolls Royce driving down the street... at least not in any neighborhood i've ever lived in. (laughing) Sitting in the front seat, You had me using the vibrator and i couldn't stop cumming. Was i putting on a show for everyone going by?
Supper was nice. i was looking for the waiter to ask him to bring us some water when You got back... i didn't realize it was a "serve yourself" place. i'll confess that i was preoccupied looking around the store and not paying attention to what was going on in the restaurant until they called our number. Of course, things were a bit fuzzy across the room that night anyway without my glasses on. i really need to start paying better attention to stuff though.
It seemed like it got late fast, so we went over to the theater... where You really caught me by surprise when You sat down on the bench. For some reason, i wasn't exactly sure what You had in mind, but kneeling was kind of an automatic reflex. Then when i was down on the floor, i wasn't sure that's what You wanted. Rob used to always sit down just like that and expect me to kneel between his legs the same way, but i wasn't allowed to touch him. That's what threw me about it. If i thoughtlessly put my hands on his legs instead of behind my back, i would get punished. So when You sat down like that, i all of a sudden didn't know what to do with my hands. It sounds dumb, but there was a big conflict going on in my

mind at the time. In the past, You have always been standing when i kneel for You or else i have knelt at Your side. You never sat down like that before... i thought You were angry and were going to yell at me. Then when You looked away, i thought i had really screwed up. Then You smiled.

It's getting late...will write more tomorrow.

Love,
Your slave puppy

Wed, 9 Jun 2004
sharon wrote:

Dear Master,

    Good evening Sir! i had fun last night. Definitely think i need to keep a pair of gym shoes in my car though. i didn't realize we would be going that far when You asked if i had on comfortable walking shoes!
    i want You to know that i really appreciate that You didn't let the lack of keys ruin the evening. Most people would have gotten all bent out of shape over something like that. You, on the other hand, were able to improvise very well ☺!!
    i liked sitting outside later at night... absorbing the street atmosphere. It was fun, and a perfect evening for being outside. It's funny how everyone has to stop and comment on the dogs. That must be a city thing. Where i come from (in Indiana) You could walk the dogs all over the county and no one would pay attention. The dinner was very good. i haven't had Chinese food for a while, since i had gotten into kind of a rut about a year ago and was eating it all the time.
    The Bijou is definitely a unique experience! It adds such a mental twist to things knowing we are being watched by all these gay guys... and nobody is shy about watching, or even participating. i can't even begin to imagine something like that taking place in the straight community. There are all those private places in the back yard and yet people are crowding in to watch. It's such a strange feeling. Fortunately, You had me so distracted i didn't care who else was there!
    The whole evening seemed so sensual. Lying in the sling while You were fisting and fucking me...and there were hands all over me. (laughing) i was trying to keep my eyes closed so i wouldn't be all self-conscious, but i was also afraid if i opened my eyes it would all stop. It was

like a wonderful dream. When i did open my eyes a couple times, all i could see was You and all these arms. i couldn't see anyone's face except Yours. That's a good thing because if i ever meet any of them in the street, i won't know who they are and, therefore, won't get embarrassed. It was an experience i'm sure many, many women have fantasized about. i felt totally helpless...and cared for. i must also say that being in the sling is a very excellent position for fucking!!!!

i'm wondering if it felt as good to You as it did to me. It was like all of my weight was putting pressure between my legs...like all the blood was rushing to that spot... like my entire body consisted of one giant pussy...probably the reason for the high-pressure squirting... sorry if i got You wet...i had more than a few powerful orgasms in that sling! And You kept coming around to give me hugs & kisses... which made the whole thing absolutely perfect.

i am looking forward to serving You again tomorrow night... to see if i can distract You again.

Love,
Your slave puppy

Steven writes:

puppy's letter refers to a night we played at the Bijou. We had gone for a walk along the lake with the dogs and then had some dinner. When we got back, I realized I had left my keys in the house, so we walked over to the Bijou Theater building to get an office key from either Sydney (my daughter) or Margaret (one of my employees) who both live in apartments above the theater, but neither of them were home. Since we were at the Bijou and I would have to wait for them to get back, I decided to play with puppy. So I left the dogs in the lobby where my employees would watch them, and I took puppy inside to play for a while. I figured that by the time we were finished, Syd or Margaret would be home.

I took puppy through the theater and out into the back garden, which is a maze of tall bushes and wooden fences surrounded by the brick walls of the buildings next door. The garden is a place where people can play outdoors with some privacy and without fear of police. We played in a corner of the maze where the two outside walls were brick and the two inside walls were tall bushes and trees. The entrance to this space was a path between the bushes and one of the brick walls. Just outside the entry to this play space were more shrubs and another tree.

I had puppy extend her arms to the brick wall and bend over so her body was at a 90-degree angle. I lifted her dress up over her waist and started to caress her ass. I put my fingers from my free hand in my mouth for wetness so I could massage her pussy and clit, while my other hand lightly spanked her ass. After a short time, she spread her legs so I could spank her pussy and ass in unison. I moved her over to one of the low stone benches and told her to bend all the way over with her arms extended, supporting herself on the bench. Again I raised her dress up above her waist, so her ass was raised up in the air. I proceeded to put half my hand into her pussy while masturbating her clit and alternating with spanking her upturned ass.

When I was finished with this outdoor foreplay, I took puppy up to the second floor dungeon for a spanking and then fisted her in the sling. puppy had many orgasms that night and I had a raging hard-on throughout the night until I climaxed, a wonderful ending to a wonderful evening.

Sat, 12 Jun 2004
sharon wrote:

Dear Master,

How did the art fair go today? It turned out to be a beautiful day to be outside! Too bad i've been working at the computer all day trying to catch up on everything i didn't get done all week due to the personnel problems. i did interview two nurses yesterday and i hope to hire them both. i also picked up my new spectacles today (apparently they lied to me about the 4 weeks!) However, i'm having some difficulty seeing. One eye is supposed to be for distance and the other for near vision, but in order to see anything clearly, i have to close one eye which means i have zero depth perception. Hopefully, this straightens out before i have to drive somewhere!

i was still pretty wound up from that meeting when i got to Your house the other night. Hopefully, i've got everyone on the same page now so we'll see how long that lasts. i'm sorry You had to go out to get that parking ticket. i parked there because i was trying to keep You from having to go out in the rain. The best-laid plans of mice and (wo)men...

Soooo... moving on... How did i do on the positions? Probably a little sloppy... some room for improvement. After about, oh 100 attempts, i figure i'll have them perfected.

i'm wondering if You enjoy having Your cock sucked as much as i enjoy doing it? You taste so good! i also liked that suction cup thing on my clit... never tried anything like that before... i'm thinking it could be done a lot harder. (laughing) i'm sitting here wondering what would happen if You did the suction followed by the vibrator... very shocking i'm sure! You would probably have to peel me off the ceiling! That sideways fucking reminded me of a very nice position i tried many years ago where the man lays on his side and the woman lays on her back, sort of perpendicular to him, with her legs over top of him... and with contact in all the right spots... works very well... especially for a lazy woman! Maybe we could try that sometime?

Do You know You had me dripping so much it was running down my legs when i walked in the house that night? Fortunately no one else was awake because i probably had another huge wet spot on the back of that dress. i think i will have to remember not to wear that dress on the days i serve You...

i keep thinking about the other night at the Bijou. It seems so surreal... like a dream... lots of fun.

Missing You...

Love,
Your slave puppy

Sat, 12 Jun 2004
Steven wrote:

Dear puppy,

It has been a long hot weekend out in the sun with the dogs and 80,000 people. We did very well, better by far than any of the previous years. I enjoy talking to people who tell me they see me on the street walking the dogs, and people who make sure they stop by the booth every year. It's nice to see people I spoke to four or five years ago and who are now coming by with their children. I'm beat. I've been working thirty days straight. How is Mon and Wed for you?

Sir

Steven writes:

I am the proud owner of four greyhounds and I belong to a greyhound adoption group (website: www.greyhoundsonly.com). Some years back, I approached the Old Town Chamber of Commerce about having Greyhounds Only (GO) as part of the art fair. Now every year, the Old Town Chamber gives GO a double booth to promote adoption of the retired race dogs. In 2004, the Old Town Art Fair was ranked 19th in the country out of 300 street art fairs that were reviewed.

Summer 2004

Tue, 15 Jun 2004
sharon wrote:

Dear Master,

      i hope Your day is going well. i interviewed a couple more nurses today and found one who is even better than the one who turned down my job offer yesterday... and she can start on Monday. We just need to settle on a salary.

      It seems my son has booked us on a flight to Miami on Thursday afternoon. Nothing like giving me a little notice like i asked him to. So much for Father's Day. i haven't seen my father since Mother's Day and he's not going to be happy. We should get back Sunday afternoon after stopping off in Dallas on the way home.

      In case You're interested, i wasn't serious about the idea of using the suction and vibrator together. i can see i'll have to learn to keep my big mouth shut (or my fingers still). You must have been in the mood to torture me last night! my clit is still tingling... and there are some rather sharp pains on my backside whenever i sit or even lean against something! You have definitely been on my mind today! That cane is a wicked instrument. Maybe You could save it for when i've been really bad... or else i'll have to work on adding some more padding to my backside. All of this pain, but not a single mark... You are probably not believing that it hurt as much as it did. You must have been quite amused by all the squirming.

      Something else You were using was stinging a lot... must have been that horsehair flogger. The hood was a different experience... i think mostly because i could see myself in the mirror and it looked so strange... like it wasn't me... like it was some anonymous creature standing there, someone who i was observing from somewhere else. The hood was also very uncomfortable because it kept sliding back on my head and pushing my nose up. i was hoping it wasn't going to leave an abrasion under my nose... which would be rather hard to explain! i kept trying to relax and go off into subspace, but You kept bringing me back... as You said, for Your enjoyment, not mine. (smiling) i hope You were pleased. That's the part of all this i've never quite figured out... the more uncomfortable and out of control i am, the more i feel like i'm pleasing You instead of me. It's hard to explain, but in the end i feel better about it that way. There's probably some psychoanalytical explanation for that... something to explain what happens with the loss of control...

i got a letter today offering a $25,000 grant to do a study on end-of-life issues such as pain, the loss of control, and how people cope with it. It's all so intertwined with what goes on in a bdsm dungeon. i've often wanted to tell patients to mentally let go of their pain and go off into "subspace"... but the problem is how to explain it without telling them how i discovered it. It seems like there are scientific secrets that could be learned in a dungeon and applied to the pain so often inadequately managed in health care... like extracting the chemicals flowing through a submissive's body as she is being whipped and then using them to treat the pain of illness/disease/injury. So much of it is psychological... tied to the meaning of the pain. That's the whole concept behind using narcotic pain meds, such as morphine, that act on the central nervous system (brain).

Pain is actually felt/interpreted in the brain and the narcotics disconnect the mind and emotions from the pain. The pain is just as bad as it ever was, but the person doesn't care...as if the pain belongs to someone else. Except for the side effects, it works very well. Things like aspirin, Tylenol, and Motrin work at the site of the pain to actually relieve it (inflammation, etc.). i'm rambling...sorry ☺... don't mean to bore You. In any case, i don't have time to put a grant proposal together before the July 14 deadline, so science will just have to wait a little longer to discover the secrets of the dungeon!

See You soon!

All my love,
Your slave puppy

Steven writes:

The mirror puppy refers to when wearing the hood is in my 4th floor living room, which I also use as a dungeon. The dungeon is a large room (20 x 90 feet) next to my bedroom. We play in there quite a bit, so you will be reading about some of the dungeon scenes throughout this book. There are chains hanging from the ceiling, and facing one grouping of chains is a very large (4 x 11 feet) gold-gilded ornate mirror that leans against a wall. I placed the mirror and chains in such a way that the person chained up can view herself and watch what I am doing to her. There are also chains on a support post that extends from floor to ceiling, as well as chains that hang down from the ceiling in the center of the room. The dungeon has a spanking bench, pillory stock, other play equipment, lots of antiques, a billiard table, and large windows along the two outside walls which allow an abundance of light to enter the room, making the room bright and airy during the daytime.

I don't always do a scene in order for my bottom/submissive to go into subspace because that gets boring for me. Once I get them to their destination, they are happy as a lark and couldn't care less about the world around them as long as I continue to feed their subspace high. Instead of allowing them to stay in subspace, my enjoyment is in bestowing different sensations and in alternating punishment and pleasure. For example, I may paddle puppy's backside and then use a heavy flogger until her ass is sensitive and raw so when I administer the singletail, it creates a slicing, burning sensation. By this point, she's gone over to the other side and she's flying, so I stop the pain and start playing with her pussy, which often leads into fisting her. At times, I spank her ass or pussy while I'm fisting her to mix another kind of pleasure and pain. After she's had a few orgasms, I start all over again either with the singletail, flogger, paddle, or just spanking her with my hands.

For this kind of scene, I often attach puppy's wrist cuffs to the chains hanging from the ceiling so her arms are above her head and spread wide. At times, I like to put a belt with D-rings around her waist so I can attach another chain which is hanging from the ceiling directly in front of her. This chain goes in between her legs, through her pussy, and attaches to a D-ring on the belt in back of her. As I adjust the chain tighter, it lifts puppy up so she has to stand on her toes. I like leaving her there for a while because I like watching her struggle to get into a comfortable, or at least bearable, position. Then I'm ready to go to work, which is my pleasure.

Sat, 19 Jun 2004
sharon wrote:

Dear Master,

It seems like i wrote about the sling before... at least i intended to! Being in the sling at the Bijou is hard to describe because the whole atmosphere there is part of it. In a way, being in the sling reminds me of when i had my kids...being on the delivery table with my legs up in the stirrups, surrounded by people watching my pussy and the only face i could see was the doctor's between my widely spread knees. The sling is more fun though!

It amazes me how people seem to appear out of nowhere whenever i get in that thing. It kind of feels like being in a soft leather cocoon i guess... cozy and dark. i am aware of all the people standing close enough that i can hear them breathing, but i'm totally focused on You... You make me feel safe. i don't think i could ever do that with anyone else i've known. Being fisted in the sling... hmmm...makes my pussy wet just thinking about it. You were very gentle to start. Once You were inside of me, You swung me back & forth with Your fist in me, which was nice, relaxing... except there seems to be a certain spot that when You touch it, i just want You to start pounding into me hard – and the movement of the sling prevented that. So i was trying to stop the swinging and provide more resistance... a totally different maneuver than being fisted on the bed or elsewhere! (chuckle) And i'm sure it didn't resemble anything even remotely graceful!

i managed to pull myself up with my arms so all my weight was on the "stirrups" which were, at that point, closer to my crotch than my knees. But i still had no control over the darn thing. You were driving me crazy going hard and then easy... and i was desperately trying to swallow Your fist with my pussy, but the more i tried, the more the sling moved, and the more i defeated myself. It must have been quite amusing for the onlookers. You finally did whatever it is You do to cause a gushing orgasm... and then You started over again... and again... and again... and again... until long after i cared about controlling anything... and at which point even a light breeze on my pussy would have set me off on another orgasm.

Then You got me up, told me to get dressed, and i followed You out through the theater like absolutely nothing unusual ever happened... except for the silly grin on my face.

Love,
Your slave puppy

Steven writes:

Here are my thoughts about playing with puppy that evening. Men came out from the shadows, from all the dark unseen areas, to watch us and to fondle each other, and then some of them slipped back into the dark. The sling that puppy was in is about 23 years old. The leather is beautifully soft from all the lubrication mixed with sweat from all those years of sex play.

There are many types of exhibitionists. puppy is a quiet exhibitionist; she is not one who needs people to watch, and she doesn't need to be the center of attention in a crowd, but public play does excite her. She needs to be directed into this kind of play. She focuses on me, knowing that she is in a public place and she is vaguely aware of her surroundings. She knows our play is in public and that she is exposed - a humiliating situation which excites her. Her breath quietly quickens and she gets very wet. When I am ready for her to cum, she will repeatedly orgasm throughout the scene. At times, puppy ejaculates when she cums, which makes the play more delicious; and it makes me very hard.

Sun, 27 Jun 2004
sharon wrote:

Dear Master,

  i hope You're enjoying this beautiful weekend. Do You go to the Taste of Chicago? i went to two graduation open houses and a wedding yesterday...a nice day for all. i'm skipping an open house today though or i'll never catch up with stuff at home.

It never fails that the damn Internet refuses to function whenever i write my most "eloquent" letters... and it never sounds quite right when i try to re-compose them. In the letter that didn't go through last Friday, i talked about how good it was to see You again after the trip. It wasn't until i saw You that i felt like i was finally home. i've realized that i am happier when i'm with You than at any other time. i really missed You when i was in Florida. i liked crawling up the stairs to greet You... not easy with the dress & purse, but i think i have a solution for that next time. i also liked being chained & tied in the kitchen... and drinking my delicious supper. Thank You.

  i was pretty impressed with how much of Your cock i was eventually able to take in. i never thought i would be able to do that since i seem to have an extra strong gag reflex. The only problem was that by the time my throat was relaxed enough to do it, my sinuses were so full i couldn't breathe. In any case, You have done something that no one else has ever been able to do. Maybe next time it will be easier!

  i just noticed that my inner thighs are covered with bruises where You were nibbling, not too gently, on my flesh, so i'm hoping it stays fairly cool for the next few days since shorts will be out of the question. i was so preoccupied with Your cock that i was surprised to see any marks at all. Keeps me thinking about You...

Love,
Your slave puppy

Mon, 28 Jun 2004
sharon wrote:

Dear Master,

i heard from *(my first Master)* Rob again today... just one line: "you will make amends." He doesn't get it.

i miss You.

Love,
Your slave puppy

Wed, 30 Jun 2004
sharon wrote:

Dear Master,

(chuckle) Being the good student that i am, i feel like i should be practicing for the deep-throating lessons. But alas, nothing to practice on...
Despite getting so snot-faced, i am still quite impressed with my progress. The poppers are apparently a miracle drug. This is my big accomplishment for the year! or two... or four... Perhaps i should add deep-throating to my resume under "special skills." It actually felt good once my throat was relaxed enough. i can still feel it today, like the inside of my throat has been massaged. i'm wondering if my throat will get used to it like my ass did, making it easier each time.
i can understand the idea of more suction in the mouth, but it's so impossible to imagine what any of it feels like to a guy. i guess that's the advantage of gay guys – they know exactly what feels good to their partner.

Thinking about You always...

Love,
Your slave puppy

Fri, 2 Jul 2004
sharon wrote:

Dear Master,

i have so much fun when i'm with You. You are really expanding my horizons! i never thought i'd see the day when i would be strolling around naked in a men's sex club, or anywhere else for that matter. It wasn't so long ago that i was so self-conscious that i was embarrassed to be seen in public wearing a bathing suit for godsakes! When You talk about these things, i keep thinking You can't possibly be serious... or there's no way i could do whatever it is You're talking about. But You always make everything okay... fun... as long as i can keep You within eyesight. i can't imagine ever doing something like that with anyone but You. i truly do love every minute of the time i spend serving You. Such a lucky puppy i am!!!

i don't know what Your plans are for the holiday, but it looks like i will be able to take Monday off (finished the budget today!) and could spend the whole day/evening serving You if You would like.

Have a wonderful rest of the day!!

Love,
Your slave puppy

Steven writes:

Puppy is talking about yet another trip to the Bijou. This time, we walked through the theater to the back lounge where the bathrooms and soda machines are. There is a doorway to the left between the soda machines, and this door leads into an enclosed area around a spiral staircase, which goes up to the second floor playground. The area surrounding the staircase has a bench running along two of the walls and a row of lockers against another wall. The men can rent a locker if they want to put their clothes or valuables away while cruising. I told puppy to get undressed and put her things in one of the lockers. When she was naked, I had her follow me up the spiral stairs and down the hallway to the front dungeon area. As we walked, people parted. After playing for about two and half hours, we went back through the hallway and down the stairs to the lockers where puppy got dressed. Puppy was glassy-eyed with a grin plastered on her face as we walked out through the theater.

Sat, 3 Jul 2004
Steven wrote:

Dear puppy,

Thank you for the offer, but I need the time to clean up the office and get some writing done. I spent the day doing research; I think I did pretty well. I'll do the same tomorrow, so I won't be able to spend time with you. Enjoy the Holiday.

Sir

Steven writes:

My businesses are open 24/7 and have been for the last 25 years, so I have established work and play routines that work for me. My work does not have to be for my business; it also includes the creative projects that I do. Some people garden, others cook; I need to write about events in my life and also to research information in my world of sexuality (old magazines, history, films, movie posters, photographs, and the people that created the genre). I daydream about expanding my world, about the time when my business will encompass all forms of sexual information and sexual fantasies for people on the Internet and for those who contact my company. I absolutely love it.

Sat, 3 Jul 2004
sharon wrote:

Dear Master,

But it's a holiday – You're not supposed to be working on a holiday! In fact, i think there might be a law against working on a holiday. i may just have to come over and distract You in order to save You from possible arrest.

Love,
Your slave puppy

Sat, 3 Jul 2004
Steven wrote:

Dear puppy,

Thanks, but I need the quiet time with no phones and no business distractions. I have too many things to do, so I won't be able to give you much attention. I hope I don't get arrested – I was hoping that the times had changed – but it does have its upside in a bizarre way. I would get my picture (new mug shots) taken again. Good idea, new look for my column. Enjoy the day.

Sir

Sat, 3 Jul 2004
sharon wrote:

Dear Master,

  Aha! So that's why You've had so many arrests... You just wanted Your picture taken! There are easier ways You know!
  No need for new mug shots... i'm off tomorrow too. Surely You will be needing to relieve Yourself and will have no one there to assist You. i wouldn't want You to have to wait all the way until Tuesday!

Love,
Your slave puppy

Sun, 4 Jul 2004
sharon wrote:

Dear Master,

  i've been thinking about that movie (*Troy*) the other night. i can't figure out the thought process of why men so often allow themselves to be destroyed by a woman. What does it accomplish except to make them miserable...or dead... yet they keep doing it century after century. It just doesn't make sense to me...seems kind of foolish, in fact. Of course i don't understand why a woman would allow a man who she supposedly cared about to be destroyed, unless she never cared about him in the first place. Even then, it doesn't make sense. So many things that people do are beyond my comprehension.
  i've also been thinking that i need to go to boot camp for slaves with attention deficit disorder. You are a very patient Master, but i'm beginning to think there is no hope for me. i can't seem to get my head out of the clouds when i am with You... and i wouldn't want You to be thrown out of "The Masters' Club." Perhaps i need more structure... or punishment...for being neglectful...
  Now that i think about it though, puppies are not exactly known for paying attention... ☺ Can i use that as an excuse?

Love,
Your slave puppy

Sun, 4 Jul 2004
Steven wrote:

Dear puppy,

    In my opinion, there are insecure people out there who are needy and selfish. They get very obsessive and possessive with the other people around them (family, friends, and loved ones) because they don't have control of their own lives in the outside world. Then there are some people who have that fatal attraction towards each other in which the relationship is based on the negative extreme, and obsessive control of each other leads to destruction of the relationship. I would guess its basis is in passiveness and aggression. In truth, they're both aggressive in pushing each other's buttons. Each one maintains control over the other and feeds off the force that binds them together. I think some abusive relationships fall into this area. The problem is that they're so self absorbed that they don't think about the impact of their relationship on the other people in their lives. Basically there are a lot of wacky people out there, including President Bush.

    To improve upon your slavely sloppiness, correct your lazy faults, and improve your structure… teaching, correction, and discipline must be held off for another day. I'm too lost in what I am doing and don't want to stop.

Sir

Wed, 7 Jul 2004
sharon wrote:

Dear Master,

    Guess where i will be having dinner on Friday at 6:00 – Orso's! my brother-in-law called tonight to tell us where to meet them. He was giving me such bad directions on how to get there that i finally had to tell him i would find it on the net. The night is going to be very weird!

    Regarding what You said about not giving me enough attention if i had been there on Monday, i just want You to know that i'm not doing any of this for the attention. i get more attention than i need on a daily basis, which also means that i certainly understand the need for solitude. i just like being there… we don't have to do anything special. Your house is starting to feel more like home than my own… (chuckle) except i have a garage attached to my house that always has my spot open and is quite easy to park in now that i have a laser light to guide the process!

It felt very strange last night to be tied and "decorated" with flowers... like an object i guess... or a painting. And standing in front of the mirror...it looked like i was watching someone else... like with the hood. It was quite effective at transporting me to a different state of mind, although it's hard to describe what it did. i don't know how You come up with these things! Actually, i had the same feeling at one point when i was in the sling at the Bijou last time... like i was watching myself from a few feet away. Maybe it could be called an "out of body" experience... very peaceful.

It was also very strange with the whips last night... the lighter ones. It felt like i was being showered with light-filled crystals. It started at the top of my head, then went all the way down my body, over and over. i've never felt like that before. And it felt like i was standing in the bright sunshine... actually, it felt like i was swinging, like when i was a little kid going back & forth and stretching for the sky. i don't know what You did different, but You could have kept doing it all night.

You always make me feel so good...so relaxed. i hope i make You feel good as well.

Love,
Your slave puppy

Steven writes:

I was out of town for the weekend. My home is directly across the street from Orso's where puppy had dinner with her husband and in-laws.

Sat, 10 Jul 2004
sharon wrote:

Dear Master,

i don't know if You have computer access this weekend, but figure i'll write anyway. The show at Zanie's (after eating at Orso's) was decent last night. Some parts were very funny. Arthur and his brother were drinking before they got there which made things difficult before we even got into the restaurant. i was glad when the night was over.

That reminds me... i was standing in front of Your house last night waiting for the others to arrive and there were several (Asian) people standing there taking pictures of Your building from all angles, and they were trying to look through the windows on the first floor. Don't You think that's kind of odd? Do You suppose maybe they were looking for property to buy? Do You get that kind of thing very often?

Also, i was thinking about that woman You said You've been corresponding with who is over 6 feet tall. Are You sure she's a woman? The reason i'm asking is because Rob had me corresponding with a "woman" one time who we ended up meeting for coffee. She was over 6-foot tall and turned out to be a transsexual (or transvestite?...i'm not sure of the proper term). i wish i could have videotaped that meeting. Rob was trying to act so cool and open-minded, but it was obvious he thought she had the plague and that he was going to catch it by sitting across the table from her... so funny. i thought she was about the nicest and most intelligent woman we'd met and i thought it might be interesting to get together with her, but Rob said i wasn't ready for something like that... It still makes me laugh to think about it. i bet he went home and scrubbed himself for an hour to make sure nothing rubbed off on him.

Actually, i was kind of fascinated by the idea of having a sexual encounter with such a person who was really a man, but now in a woman's body... talk about mental gymnastics... messing with one's mind! Would that be classified as a hetero- or homosexual encounter? For me or for Rob? Her name was Kitty... i had kind of forgotten about her... or did i already tell You about her in *The Puppy Papers*? i would really like to read that whole thing before it goes to press, but You're probably right that i would want to edit everything... i guess it's better for it to be a surprise.

Anyway, the reason i was thinking about this woman is because You said You wanted her to serve me. i'm not sure what You meant by that. i know there is no way i would ever be able to flog or torture anyone... there is not a sadistic cell in my body. Rob always wanted me to top a woman and i can tell You that it definitely didn't work. It seems like i've told You this before. i guess i did okay with Marlene topping me, but for me to top another woman (or man) would make me really uptight... i wouldn't know what to do with them. So i'm just letting you know that it's not in me even though you haven't asked me to.

Okay, i've rambled long enough. i hope You're selling lots of books this weekend to make Your trip worthwhile. i miss You... couldn't quit thinking about You when i was in Your neighborhood last night... would much rather have been upstairs sucking Your cock. (laughing) When i went into the bathroom at Orso's, it wouldn't have surprised me one bit to see You walk through the door for my "after-dinner-drink." Your presence was there even though Your body was in Ohio.

Love,
Your slave puppy

Steven writes:

I was just finishing up our first book, *The Puppy Papers,* when puppy wrote me this email. She did not know which of her letters I had included in the book until after it was printed.

Fri, 16 Jul 2004
sharon wrote:

Dear Master,

Shall i assume that You would like me to serve You tomorrow night? i don't want to mess up again! ...though now that i'm thinking about it, i hope You weren't planning on me being there tonight ☺!

i think there must be a full moon this week. All of my staff are being incredibly annoying with their petty quarrels, trying to make each other look bad, and being generally lazy, disagreeable, and uncooperative. (Maybe they're having group PMS?) Now today, my new performance improvement coordinator informed me she is moving to Hawaii... in one week! One of the other nurses who started two weeks ago informed me yesterday that she's quitting because she doesn't want to work weekends. Who ever heard of a nurse that doesn't work weekends! i'm about ready to say the hell with it all and close the place down. i'm starting to think there is no one in this state who actually wants to work.

i hope Your week is going better than mine. You seem to be the only sane person in my life right now. Full-time slavery is looking better every day...

On a lighter note, i don't know how i managed to take in so much of Your cock the other night without the assistance of poppers. i never thought that would happen no matter how much i practiced. (i'll try not to break my arm patting myself on the back for such an accomplishment ☺). It's a miracle!! And i thank You so much for Your patience!

Also, i've been thinking about what You said that i'm not taking things serious enough. i am sorry about that. i do take serving You very seriously. It just seems like the more stressed out i am at work, the less serious i can be when i'm away from it... a paradoxical reaction i guess – the more frustrated i get, the more i have to laugh at myself. There seems to be a lot of people working in hospice that do the same thing. i guess it's how we keep from getting burned out by working with death & dying every day. Anyway, up until now, i've just been following Your lead and depending on You to set the tone of things. i've concluded that i need to take responsibility for shifting gears and getting myself in the right frame of mind... i'm not sure just how to do that, but i think it takes more than a few seconds to turn everything else off.

Now that i'm thinking about it though, that was the thing that fascinated me about bdsm in the beginning... the quick transition... a blindfold & bondage and i was instantly transported into another world...where time stood still... actually being present in the moment. i had never experienced anything like that before. Like last night, i didn't start to relax/focus until You tied me up. It's like the more You take away (movement, sight, speech, comfort...even breath)... it kind of makes me empty, so the only thing i'm thinking about is pleasing You... if that makes sense. i honestly don't think that makes me a "do-me-queen." It's more that i need You to help me make the transition (sort of stop the world from spinning) so i can be where i want to be...serving You.

Hmmmm... i guess if i could make the transition on my own, i would have no need for a Master... could just be a simple slut. Well, this line of thinking has taken me in a bit of a circle. Any advice?

Love,
Your slave puppy

Fri, 23 Jul 2004
sharon wrote:

Dear Master,

i was able to read Your articles on puppy play last night... very interesting.

For as many times as You've told me to get undressed, you'd think it wouldn't faze me anymore, but it always makes me feel momentarily... embarrassed, i guess... or off-balance...especially to be standing in Your kitchen naked while You are fully clothed. Actually, i guess it immediately and unavoidably puts me into a submissive mindset. It definitely feels better to be kneeling than standing there in the middle of the room. i think that removing my clothes, revealing my body so to speak, i always feel like anyone who sees my (far) less-than-perfect body is going to laugh. Anyway, once a few seconds pass, i'm good with it.

i really like the collar & leash. It does something to me... not sure what... maybe a feeling of being controlled...owned...available...humbled. It makes my pussy wet. You are so kind to provide soft pillows for all

Your puppies to sit on! Being tied there and with the blindfold & handcuffs, i am at Your mercy... You can do anything You want with me... and i feel ready & eager for anything You want to do. It's funny, but being in that position makes it easy to understand why dogs & cats always nudge or rub against you to get you to touch/pet/pay attention to them... it's a different perspective of the world.

  You put the blindfold on and then walked away and didn't say anything. You were being very quiet like i was no longer even there. i was waiting, expectantly, for... something. i think a blindfold must stimulate an imagination neuron in my brain. Then You said something to the dogs about what a useless slave You have to be sitting there while You do all the work & how that's not the way things are supposed to be. i started feeling guilty and wishing i could help You. This is when things started getting weird. All of a sudden i started on this sort of "journey to the center of the earth"... like an implosion.

  All of these scenes from throughout my life started playing over and over before my eyes, like a movie going in fast forward. Then it slowed down and settled on two things. One was when i was around 4 or 5 years old. i was quite a fussy eater at that age and my father would always fill my plate way too full with stuff i didn't like and then make me sit there until i ate everything (or more accurately, gagged it down). At this particular time, no matter how hard i tried, i just couldn't eat everything on my plate. It was Christmas time and my father said that if i didn't clean my plate, i wouldn't be able to participate in Christmas. i was sent to my room and could hear everyone else opening presents and having fun and i was forgotten. i was alone and no one came to get me the whole night.

  The other thing was when i was in the 4th grade. We had spent weeks preparing to put on a play and i was really excited about it. i only had a small part (a talking tree), but couldn't have been more excited if i were starring on Broadway. On the big day, my best friend and i were putting the final touches on the scenery when our teacher asked my friend a question. She gave an answer, but not loud enough for the teacher to hear. So the teacher asked again and, trying to be helpful, i repeated what my friend said loud enough for the teacher to hear. The teacher got angry, dragged me out into the hall, and told me i had to stay there for the rest of the day for being such a smart ass. i honestly had no idea what i had done wrong. The play was performed without me.

  i have no clue why these two things were going through my mind when i was sitting on Your kitchen floor, but they were so real it was like they were actually happening. The weird thing is that in the past whenever i have recalled either of those things, there were always strong emotions tied to them. The other night there were no emotions. They were just things that happened... meaningless... like they had happened to someone else. i have no idea if i was sitting there with these things going through my head for a few seconds or a few hours. You had not made a sound the entire time, and when i started hearing You move around, it was like i was coming out of a trance.

    You came over by me and put Your cock in my mouth and i was so... ready. You tasted so delicious. i don't think i've ever been in such a "submissive headspace" as i was at that moment. i was so hungry for You it's a wonder i didn't just melt into a puddle on the floor.

To be continued...

Love,
Your slave puppy

Sat, 24 Jul 2004
sharon wrote:

Dear Master,

    It seems i got a little sidetracked in the last letter...

    Being hand-fed is a complicated thing... a lot like the collar & leash. You are in complete control. For some reason, that feeling of being controlled flips a switch in me...turns me on (pun intended). i don't know if i'm going to eat or what might be put in my mouth. You don't ask if i'm hungry, what i want to eat, or if i've eaten enough, too little, or too much. (Now that i'm writing this, it seems strange that the episode with my father forcing me to eat had just gone through my mind when You started feeding me.)

    The pieces You feed me always seem huge and for some goofy reason, it seems much more difficult to chew when i can't see what i'm eating. It takes a few "chews" to figure out what's in my mouth. (chuckle) It might be wise to let me know when You're putting Your cock in my mouth so i don't accidentally bite it off before i figure out what it is! The taste of everything is magnified when You feed me like that, and it feels like i'm drooling all over myself, which i must have been because that's when the dogs came over and started licking my face & chest. It makes me feel like a helpless mess, totally dependent on You. The idea that it pleases

You to make me that way...for some reason, it excites me and makes me want to please You more.

Something else i want to mention...You were so gentle when You fed me. Your extraordinary gentleness and patience in the midst of everything else always amazes me. It demonstrates a very unusual amount of self-control on Your part, something i've never seen in the "vanilla" world... or in bdsm. The contrast between sadism & gentleness draws me to You...makes the connection...the dance. It's what makes me want to offer You myself, body, mind and soul, as Your slave. i am so lucky to have found You!!

To be continued...

Love,
Your slave puppy

Sun, 25 Jul 2004
sharon wrote:

Dear Master,

You removed the handcuffs and stood me up, still blindfolded, then led me with the collar & leash. At that point, i still had some sense of direction and an awareness of the obstacles that were likely to be in my path, and You were very careful to tell me when and where to step. You led me up the stairs and told me to lie down on the bed. Turning to lie on the bed is where i seem to get disoriented. Even though i'm sitting on the edge of the bed, i don't know what direction the bed goes or where i'm going to be when i actually lay down. As soon as i layed down, You left the room (i think). Then i started on another journey in my head.

i remember wishing i could somehow write down all the ingenious things i was thinking so i wouldn't forget them... and, of course, i can't remember any of them now. In any case, i ended up in a very beautiful place, high up in the mountains. i was looking down and could see it was raining down below and everything was a beautiful blue-green and misty-looking and this beautiful mist was rising up all around me and everything was incredibly still and soundless. (laughing) You'd think i was on drugs or something! Again, i don't know if i was laying there for seconds or hours, but that's where i was when You came back. It was a very different evening... all the waiting and silence.

You stood me up again and started leading me across the room. i had no idea where i was at in the room. i told You i had to pee and i thought You would take off the blindfold and let me go into the bathroom, but instead You left the blindfold on and led me to the toilet. Now, let me say that chewing or walking while blindfolded is nothing compared to trying to pee while blindfolded! i'm afraid i would be in deep trouble if i were blind! It definitely took some concentration to get my body to cooperate.

With such practical matters taken care of, You led me over to the chains hanging from the ceiling and indicated for me to hold on to them. Every time You led me somewhere, i kept thinking You were going to do something, but once again You left the room (i think). i don't think You were gone as long this time though. When You came back, You started using the single-tail, making hot lines all across my back & ass. It felt like all the muscles in my body had been tied in knots and You were slowly and methodically untying them all. i remember bending forward & stretching, and it felt like my whole body was crackling... coming back to life. You were switching between the single-tail, spanking, and a heavy flogger that felt like it had spikes on the ends (and with perfect timing i must add). i was so incredibly relaxed and heated up You could have done anything in the world with me.

Then You led me over to the chaise and told me to lie down. i can never seem to get my ass high enough in the air until the 3rd or 4th try. It felt so good when You fucked my ass... felt like i was so open and relaxed that i was sucking You in. The thing about ass-fucking, again, is that You are in complete control. It takes a whole lot of effort for me to move at all, and what little i can move seems to be more of a hindrance than a help. (chuckle) i'm not sure what muscles i need to work out to remedy that situation.

i like it when You bring Your legs up and actually sit on me...It seems to work better that way. Anyway, while You were fucking my ass, i had a powerful orgasm that had been building up the whole night. By the time You were done with me, i think i actually did melt into a puddle on the floor... okay, maybe i was just sprawled out on the chaise, incapable of voluntarily moving a muscle... i don't know for sure because i was still blindfolded.

Then You led me back to Your bedroom and fucked me... my reward. It always feels soooooo good to have You inside my pussy... i think i'll go to bed now and dream about You... or maybe take care of myself before i go to bed... and then dream about You.

Love,

Your slave puppy

Mon, 26 Jul 2004
sharon wrote:

Dear Master,

    i re-read Your articles on "Puppy Play" (with the lights on this time – much easier!) and since You said You wanted my comments/ questions, here goes (in no particular order)...
    i think barking is the most difficult thing You have asked of me. You're going to think this is really ridiculous, but the biggest reason it's so difficult is because i don't know how to do it. (For example: Is it "arf-arf," "ruff-ruff," "woof-woof," "bow-wow," or something else?) i always have to stop and think about how to do it... and will have to admit that it does make me feel quite foolish, hence the typically weak bark. i feel like i'm not "communicating" anything... just making noises out of context... or like i'm yelling at You, which doesn't seem right. Everything else with puppy play is much easier.
    Until i read Your article, i guess i never thought about what Your purpose is with the barking. You said that "barking is the final stage of submission." That statement gives me a whole different perspective on submission. It seems like i must have thought of it more as simply obeying and now i have to seriously question whether anything i've been doing is actually submission... or just me trying to please You the way i think You want to be pleased, if that makes sense... like i am the one determining what is or should be acceptable to You according to my own standards.
    Sheesh! Just when i thought everything was flowing, here i am sitting on the fence again! The point of all this is that i think anyone reading the article is going to be wondering what You really mean when You say "barking is the final stage of submission." i don't think they are going to understand the difference... that it's beyond simply controlling the sub/slave's behavior or communication... so hopefully You can explain it to them a helluva lot better than i can.

Love,
Your (perpetually fence-sitting ☺) slave puppy

Steven writes

    puppy is adorable. The barking is about submission and control; and how someone barks speaks volumes to me. puppy gets lost in her need to please me, to the point where she becomes unaware of how I want her to focus.

I do puppy play with puppy every once in a while, but have her bark for me more often. Barking and puppy play are not often mentioned in our e-mail exchanges because it is just part of what I do.

Tue, 27 Jul 2004
sharon wrote:

Dear Master,

    i am thinking about You this morning...wishing i could wake up to the taste of Your cock in my mouth...

See You soon.

Love,
Your slave puppy

Wed, 28 Jul 2004
sharon wrote:

Dear Master,

    You kind of threw me last night when You were talking about Your plans for another woman. Technically i don't have a problem with a situation like that. Life has taught me to extinguish any feelings of jealousy before they flare up... non-productive emotions that they are. In fact, i think i would be quite content to serve both You and a Mistress. However, i do want to point out that other women do not seem to like me. For some reason, they tend to go nuts when i'm around... like my very existence means i want to steal their husband/boyfriend... which is ridiculous.

    Women who i think are friends suddenly become hateful, angry, and freak out for no reason... or go to great lengths to cause me harm. It's not that i don't like women, it's just that experience has taught me not to trust them at all. Actually, it's more than that... women scare the hell out of me. So my concern (because it will happen) with the scenario You described is the question of what would happen to me when this person does her Jekyll-Hyde transformation... because i won't see it coming... i would be like a fly caught in the web of a spider... not the kind of predicament i want to find myself in.

    (chuckle) Of course, if i spent any time dwelling on risks or potentially negative consequences, i would have never met You in the first place. In fact, i probably wouldn't leave my house for fear of catastrophe. So once again, here i am talking in circles and i'm going to blame that on being a Libra. See how much better off You are that i don't do a lot of talking when i see You? This circular thinking could go on for hours and end up absolutely nowhere! i guess i will just leave all these things up to You and trust Your judgment... it's much easier that way.

Love,
Your slave puppy

Sat, 31 Jul 2004
sharon wrote:

Dear Master,

      i got my hair cut today ("shaped up" -- although she didn't seem to capture the vision 🙂) and my kids are hassling me that i look like a grandma. They tell me that i look ridiculous and should dye my hair white to match my "grandma" hairstyle. So after consultation, over three bottles of wine, they have decided that my image can be enhanced if i purchase a chopper for a mere $25,000 and convert my wardrobe to leather, chains, and boots. Now i'm thinking this could be fun. After all, if i'm ever going to own a chopper, now is the time... right? The neighbor tells me that the nearest Harley dealer is only 15 minutes away so i'm thinking i should check this out. Perhaps when You get Your bike restored we could go for a ride? The words are kind of swimming on the page at the present time, so i'm going to have to end this before i go seriously cross-eyed.

i miss You…wish i was there with You instead of here.

Love,
Your slave puppy

Sun, 1 Aug 2004
sharon wrote:

Dear Master,

      On my way home i was thinking about what i told you a few months ago that something big was going to happen in your life… something good. You thought it had to do with some unforeseen forced change in Your business, but i don't think You understood what i was trying to say. You are not going to lose Your business. It's going to go through some kind of funnel, like sand in an hour glass... and after that, it will be completely different... and You will be riding a "wave"... which, to my way of thinking, means it would be effortlessly successful. i don't think it has anything to do with the Bijou or the other thing You were talking about. Maybe it's some kind of new technology... i don't know.

i also don't know what it has to do with Your father or the woman i described. i'm sure You used to know her though... something happened, an accident, and You lost touch with her...You think she's gone but she's still here and she's been trying to get in touch with You again... she's always surrounded by flowers... and her eyes are very distinct-looking... like an amber or copper color...but somehow i don't think they were always that color... i wonder if she's blind.

Dang! The stem just broke off my glasses and i don't have a spare pair and it's too late to go get another one tonight... i need to find some super glue or something. Will write more later.

Love,
Your slave puppy

Fri, 6 Aug 2004
sharon wrote:

Dear Master,

i hope You're having a better day today & that You're enjoying Your birthday! i wish i could be there to help You celebrate. Did You do anything special? Half of Your present arrived today, so with any luck the rest will be here by the next time i see You. i want to bake You a birthday cake but can't figure out how to keep it from melting while sitting in the hot car all day... hmmmm... maybe something without frosting... what kind of cake do You like? i've been forever banned from singing "Happy Birthday" but thinking perhaps i could bark the song for You on this special occasion... it ought to make You laugh if nothing else!

For the event in Indy on Aug 27-29, i'm wondering when You're planning on leaving – Thursday night, Friday morning or Friday night? If i'm going to go, i'll need to put in a request by next week for the time off.

i want You to know i was in quite a foul mood before i arrived at Your house last night... in fact, i almost called to cancel. (chuckle) It's a good thing You didn't start whipping me right after i got there or You may have seen... let's just say an unexpected response. Your introspective mood was the perfect balance to my furious one. There's nothing more painful than being hurt by someone you trust... it takes a long, long time to heal... can't ever go back... and i've never known a person who did the hurting to ever admit it or apologize for it... just have to keep going and try to forget about it. i guess it makes a person more aware of the effect your own actions have on other people though.

i think that has a lot to do with why i've become more quiet as the years have passed... after having dealt with so many angry and irrational people that do stupid, selfish, and hateful things. i always wonder what seed is inside of them to cause them to do things like that…What pain or emptiness could cause people to lose touch with their own humanity?... What need was never filled?... What guilt is eating at them?... What attempt to reach out in love or kindness was rejected that makes people want to hurt someone else before they get hurt themselves? It's like a defense mechanism that's stuck in the "on" position and it prevents them from trusting anyone else or accepting kindness... and the more you try to help them, the more they lash out at you. They must feel very small and frightened on the inside.

There is a theorist (Erickson) who came up with this whole theory of human development across the lifespan. According to him, at each stage in one's life there is sort of a fork in the road where a person can either accomplish the required task successfully or it will have negative effects on any further development. The very first stage (birth to 2 years old) is called "trust vs. mistrust" and his theory is that, in this case, if a person doesn't learn to trust by the age of 2, it will be nearly impossible to learn it at a later point in time.

Interestingly, the final stage of development starts around the age of 50 and is called "integrity vs. despair." You said Your friend will probably die of stress if he doesn't resolve this thing, but according to Erickson, he will surely die of despair... a lack of integrity, meaning, and purpose in life... in other words, the loss of his spirit... nothing of himself (his pride and honor) to pass on to subsequent generations. i've seen these despairing people suffer horribly during the dying process. There is no medication strong enough to successfully relieve their fear and confusion and spiritual distress... the desperate look of terror in their eyes... it's the only symptom we are helpless to relieve. It's like a glimpse into hell itself. And they usually die all alone... very sad.

Wow, did i get sidetracked in that paragraph!! i started to tell You how stressed out i was last night and how You totally zapped the stress right out of me with that vibrator... must have taken a left turn in the thought process somewhere! In any case, i had a lovely time last night and i hope You were pleased... and at least somewhat distracted from everything else for a little while. 😊

i love You.

Your slave puppy

Steven writes:

The upcoming weekend puppy refers to is the annual GLLA (Great Lakes Leather Alliance) event where Patrick and I will be vending for Kinky Books.

My introspective mood that puppy talks about was due to a meeting I had that day with a once dear friend in order to resolve a very uncomfortable situation. This person is one of three people who were very close to me and who have betrayed me in devastating ways over the years. There were smaller, but significant, betrayals by 5 or 6 other people. Some of the smaller betrayals dealt with people who testified against me in court on behalf of the government. Basically they said whatever the government wanted them to say in exchange for lesser penalties for crimes which they themselves had committed, so truth was not an issue. Instead, their own self-preservation was paramount, at my expense.

Regarding the meeting in question, about two years ago I learned that a person I've been helping out financially has in return been stealing from me. I also realized he has not been truthful to me in years. I am so disappointed with him as well as in my judgment of his character. I'm annoyed and angry with myself for being stupidly blinded by the loyalty and respect I had for him.

This man has been an angry and unhappy person for the last 15 years, so when I confronted him with the documents proving his theft, his response was anger, and his attitude was, "So what?" He somehow felt entitled to steal from me and wondered how I would dare to question him. I have been dealing with this knowledge for the last two years while I'm trying to resolve the matter and cut him loose. In the near future, I plan to write about him and the others in a book that will be called *Betrayals*. For now, I live with my thoughts and feelings until I can resolve the situation, and I try not to let it interfere with the rest of my life.

Sun, 8 Aug 2004
sharon wrote:

Dear Master,

     i hope everything is going well for You. i am worried about Your frame of mind since i haven't heard from You in a couple days.

Love,
Your slave puppy

Sun, 8 Aug 2004
sharon wrote:

Dear Master,

     i know i told You about the sand in the hourglass before... like a funnel. It was the oddest thing of it all... but the other night on my way home, someone was holding the sand in their hand and the wind was blowing it, sifting it, and it looked just like the sand going through the hourglass. It was a very bright and clear picture that lasted only a few seconds... very purposeful, peaceful, and exciting at the same time.

     i haven't thought about any of this for quite awhile, but the woman's presence is always there at Your house... very comfortable. She's someone You already know. She's been in Your "dungeon" and in Your bedroom before. She looks out the window in Your bedroom and the light shines on her long, wavy hair... makes it look almost red. It seems like she knows You very well and is very comfortable around You. i don't know why You can't figure out who she is.

     The man is someone You see on the street, walking towards You, but he won't look at You. He keeps his head down when he walks by You. i think You know him too... but maybe You wouldn't recognize him? Or maybe forgot about him?

Love,
Your slave puppy

Mon, 9 Aug 2004
sharon wrote:

Dear Master,

     i saw the sand again the other night after i left Your house... like it was being sifted in the wind. i've been thinking about You all day. i've had this weird feeling for about the past week that something big is about to happen in Your life... something good... maybe like an opportunity or something... and whatever it is, it is already happening but no one knows about it... and whatever it is, the feeling keeps getting stronger... like it's about ready to break through the surface... like the final preparations are being made and then it will come to light. You probably think this sounds dumb, but i've had "premonitions" like this before and just when i think i'm about to lose my mind, something happens. It's gotten to the point where i've started paying attention to them... though i've never told anyone about them until after the fact... and not sure why i'm telling You this now. It just seems very important for some reason... very important to tell You to "wait"... but wait for what, i don't know...

After i wrote that last night, the feeling of urgency went away and then came back late this afternoon... like there are all these seemingly unrelated pieces to a puzzle and i can't figure out how they go together... like things are being moved around, arranged, but either You or i am too close to it to see the whole picture. i had a similar feeling for weeks before the 9-11 catastrophe, except then it was a feeling that something terrible/evil was going to happen. i kept thinking it had something to do with one of my kids. Then on 9-10, i was sitting outside at work when i had this sudden feeling that something happened, something was put in motion and there was no stopping it, that nothing more could be done about it. It left me feeling very sad. Then the next morning the twin towers were bombed... and it was also the day that Don was falsely accused of stealing that car.

Another time, i was driving my kids to church one morning when i suddenly had this powerful feeling that i should turn around and go back home. It was like there was something in the road blocking my path and it took some effort to get past it. As it turned out, Dale ended up falling and splitting his head open at church that morning, and he ended up at the hospital. It's all very strange, but things have happened often enough that i have learned to pay attention. i just have this feeling that something is happening that is going to take You in a direction You never thought of before...and it's going to be very good. Maybe You should try doing that class at Galleria Domain... it could be a door opening to other things.

There may be something i have that You will need... although i can't imagine what that would be. Do You remember shortly after we met when i said something about us coming from such different backgrounds, that it would seem impossible we would ever meet, and that it must be fate? That feeling has never left. It's like there is a specific reason our paths have crossed and it is part of a much larger picture. So many things

You've told me about Yourself and Your life have seemed strangely familiar, even though i have no conscious recollection of anything similar happening in my own life.

There is also a woman with long curly hair. She is very beautiful... and something about her eyes... either they are brown/amber or she wants them to be... and she likes flowers...roses...any color but red. And there is a man with long blond hair and a beard. He's always looking down because he has to tell You something and he doesn't want to or doesn't know how... and You need to make him tell You. It sounds crazy, but all these things are happening and they are all going to somehow come together and change everything for You... and it will be very good.

Love,
Your puppy

Mon, 9 Aug 2004
Steven wrote:
Dear puppy,

I have no idea who this woman is that you're seeing; I do hope I didn't piss her off. It would be nice having a kinky angel watching over me. As far as the man, again I don't know who he might be. Nothing is going to happen unless I make it happen, so hopefully what you are envisioning will be good forces guiding things along to positive conclusions.

Sir

Tue, 10 Aug 2004
sharon wrote:
Dear Master,

Don is leaving for school today and Dale will be leaving tomorrow, and I'm sitting here crying. Don is much more quiet and i guess he and i just have an unspoken connection. We have been through a lot together and he's the one who is always there... always the one to understand and forgive. He just seems so vulnerable to be on his own. i'm afraid he'll be hurt by thoughtless people... It's very hard to let him go.

Love,
Your slave puppy

Wed, 18 Aug 2004
sharon wrote:

Dear Master,

    Thank You for the lovely evening. Yesterday was one of those red-zone-stress-level days that You manage to dissolve so easily with Your magic touch. i think three days is about the maximum i can go without seeing You before the stress hits the danger zone.

    After reading the excerpts from *The Puppy Papers* last night, i've been thinking about how You've said that people (women) are sometimes scared off by Your profile on Alt and how that thought never even occurred to me when we first started corresponding. Right from the first letter You wrote, i knew You were someone special. You were like a breath of fresh air and not once have i ever had the slightest misgivings about You.

    i've been trying to think about reading *The Puppy Papers* from someone else's perspective and, as You said, that there will be many people who will buy the book and enjoy it, but that the book is not for everyone. There are people in this world who will not understand our relationship and they will think it's a bad thing, corrupt, deviant. i don't want that to happen. In fact, i don't want anyone else's opinions to enter into the relationship at all... good or bad. All i want is a private relationship with You. i'm worried that if people start buying the book or talking about it, that it will change everything and i will end up losing You. Maybe i'll have to buy all the books myself so that doesn't happen...

Love,
Your slave puppy

Steven writes:

    People who will read *The Puppy Papers* may be experienced or they may just be curious about the lifestyle. Others who will buy the book already practice the lifestyle to some extent and they may want to know how another person lives it. They may want to know how puppy's relationship started and then progressed, or they may want to compare their own stories to hers. Some people may buy the book because they want open and honest two-way communication in whatever type of relationship they're in. Others are exploring the lifestyle and want to learn how to open up and be able trust without fear. Some have had those same forbidden thoughts, but could never open up and expose themselves like puppy did in the book. They are afraid that family and friends would find out; they fear being judged and ridiculed, but they still harbor the fantasy.

Then there will be women who feel that puppy needs to be liberated, not realizing she is liberated, that she makes her own choices. People from the conservative "religious right" will judge harshly and condemn without mercy. Finally, there are people who will simply enjoy getting lost in a different type of story.

I didn't show puppy the manuscript for *The Puppy Papers* until after the book was printed because I didn't want her to change anything from what she had originally written.

Fri, 20 Aug 2004
sharon wrote:

Dear Master,

i just want to say for the official record that i really do think You have a perfect cock. i can't think of any better word to describe it... how about a "10"... smells good and tastes great too! And i think i should be the expert on this since i have examined it very closely...and thoroughly... and in depth... and repeatedly... yup, a perfect "10." And just so You know, i can't say that about any other cock i've examined... the closest they might come would be a 6-7... probably 6. And in case You're interested in any other unsolicited opinions, i also think You have a perfect ass and chest and shoulders/arms, and when You lay on Your back and i trace Your profile with my fingers... i often wonder how any one person could be so perfectly put together.

Do You think so many women would have wanted to play with You over the years if all i'm saying were not true? It's just too bad that i can't have the pleasure of tasting You and feeling You inside of me every day...mmmmm... but alas, another long and empty weekend ahead of me.

Missing You already.

Love,
Your slave puppy

Sat, 21 Aug 2004
Steven wrote:

Dear puppy,

Let's leave Friday afternoon about 12:00-1:00, so we'll get there around 4:00-4:30. See you Monday and Wednesday.

Sir

Steven writes:

This is the weekend we're going to the GLLA (Great Lakes Leather Alliance) event in Indianapolis. It will be puppy's first pan-sexual event, and our first weekend away together.

Sun, 22 Aug 2004
sharon wrote:

Dear Master,

Yes, Monday & Wednesday are good. It will give me a chance to pack a suitcase on Thursday night. I can't get off until noon on Friday, but we should still be able to beat the traffic. The southbound Dan Ryan is a parking lot once rush hour starts.
See You soon.

Love,
Your slave puppy

Thu, 26 Aug 2004
sharon wrote:

Dear Master,

The "mummification" wasn't like i expected. The strangest thing was when You were wrapping my arms and hands. When my hands were completely covered and non-recognizable, it was like i lost my identity. It reminded me of when i looked in the mirror while wearing the hood.

(chuckle) While mummified, i went off on this whole deep meditation about identity and how we really identify ourselves more by our hands than our faces. If you think about it, you only see your own face in the mirror a few seconds or minutes a day, whereas you always see your own hands. It's sort of like you know you are you because those are your hands in front of you. It sounds dumb now, but it was quite a revelation last night... the relationship between one's hands and one's identity.

i had all these "genius" thoughts about all that and then got to thinking about why this feeling of losing my identity was so... unique... not bad or frightening, just odd. i couldn't relax enough to just let it happen, couldn't just leave my identity behind and go off into space to become just an anonymous object. Taking away my hands so completely was very strange. Monday, with the tape, i could still move my hands a little and could still see the shape of them, but last night, i couldn't move them at all. They looked like sticks or tree branches or something foreign that didn't belong to me.

Another part of the experience was that when my body was wrapped up, my face became extra, extra sensitive, which i probably could have predicted. The funny thing though was that while the rest of my body didn't feel anything, both times my pussy felt like it was on fire and gushing all over the place... to the point i could hardly stand it. i don't know why that was the only thing i could feel.

It was so nice when you opened up the wrapping around my pussy so You could relieve my predicament. The only problem was that when You used the vibrator, i couldn't move or spread my legs, so it was torture and pleasure at the same time. And speaking of exposed parts, the first time, when my nipples were exposed... well, it left me quite helpless and vulnerable to Your sadistic inclinations... which didn't help the pussy predicament by any means. Being totally wrapped was definitely "safer" from my perspective ☺!!

Overall, i'm not sure if mummification is something i like. i like feeling Your body against mine... i like touching and being touched. It seemed like the wrapping separated me from You.

(snicker) And then when You unwrapped me, i felt like a flower spreading its petals to the sun…really i did!

See You soon!

Love,
Your slave puppy

sharon writes:

Sir had told me how He gets annoyed with shallow women who say that a BDSM experience makes them feel like "a flower spreading its petals to the sun." He expects better communication than that, but i just couldn't resist the opportunity to be so shallow. After being wrapped from head to toe in saran wrap, i couldn't think of a better description for my experience.

Mon, 30 Aug 2004
sharon wrote:

Dear Master,

    The weekend with You was wonderful, except it was over too quickly. i was looking forward to spending the weekend with You and hadn't really thought much about what the actual event would be like. i guess i figured the people and vendors would be similar to IML and they were, only on a smaller scale.

    There seemed to be more "amateurs" at GLLA though, couples newer to the "scene" who were there to learn something. i didn't see too many (if any) of the more "hardcore" leather men attending any of the classes. Definitely a dichotomy of people... interesting just to watch.

    It seemed like the classes gave a very limited view of things...no depth...just scratching the surface. Maybe panel discussions would work better to provide a variety of viewpoints and get more people involved... or circle discussions over coffee. Most of the professional conferences I go to are like that too. Everything seems to be on an introductory level. I guess it's unavoidable due to the short time allowed for the classes.

    i can certainly understand why You're impressed with Tammy Jo. She is one of very few women i saw there that i wouldn't mind getting to know a little better. She seemed to really care about people and wasn't just there to make herself larger than life. The lifestyle seems to be very natural for her and not just a venue for rebellion against society.

    i don't have anything against blue hair, tattoos, multiple piercings, etc, but they are just outside adornments. They don't tell you anything about the real person. This is just my opinion, but i always feel like people who adorn themselves to the extreme are not happy with themselves on the inside and are trying to make up for it... to make themselves over on the outside... perhaps to make themselves feel worthy of something in some way... or it's like they are trying to cover up an emptiness, or pain, or feeling of inadequacy or something. It seems like they're trying too hard to be different. It's funny because i don't get that feeling from the cross dressers. They seem to be fulfilling an inner need and to find meaning/pleasure/fun in what they're doing. i guess i'm just not an exhibitionist... in that way... but to each his own. After all, they are all adults... and variety is what makes the world go round! Actually, i wonder what they all thought of us... the "conservative" looking ones.

The atmosphere was relaxed and comfortable. People were polite, well-mannered and, aside from outward appearances, rather conservative i thought. i didn't see any rowdiness or drunkenness or people getting out of hand. i was comfortable being there. It's nice that there are people of a variety of ages who attend these things.

People didn't go out of their way to talk to us, but when they did they were very nice, almost shy, respectful, not pushy or demanding. i think, socially, i would get along with the gay men better than the others. When i was in college and later working in the hospitals, i would have these wonderful friendships with guys and then find out after we were friends for awhile that they were gay... they just seem to be more fun.

Playing the first night... it was a good thing there weren't a lot of people around when You put the blindfold on me because i wasn't really aware that we were actually being watched. i knew other people were there, but i thought they were involved in their own scenes... not just standing there watching us. i was surprised the next day when several people recognized me and said they liked the way we played and liked how we connected during the scene. It's kind of odd that i didn't feel self-conscious walking around the place naked. i guess i was focused on You and just shut everything else out. As long as i know You're right there, i'm okay.

i was also glad i was still dressed when You tied me to the chair. It kind of got things started slowly. It must have been amusing to watch me jump when You opened Your knife next to my ear... not once, but twice... even though i knew it was coming, especially the second time.

i like when You use Your knife... never thought i would say that! When You run it across my throat, the thought that goes through my mind is that if it would make You happy, i would be happy to let You slit my throat… sort of like an extension of offering You my body, mind, and soul. Do You suppose that's a common thought under the circumstances? It puts me in a different frame of mind than anything else. Once You do that, there is no question You can do anything else You want with me... not that there is ever any question in the first place!

The cross was too small. i like the one at the Bijou better... it has some substance to it! i'm not sure if You were keeping me from going "over the edge" or if i was having difficulty relaxing, but every time i would start to "float," something would bring me back. It seems Your goal was to make me cum all over the place rather than send me off in the clouds... and it seems You were successful in Your endeavor!

It seemed like we didn't play very long and it didn't seem natural to get dressed right away... kind of an abrupt end to the play. i think these dungeons need a place where people can go fuck once they get themselves all lathered up. It's very frustrating to have a throbbing pussy and nothing to fill it up. Overall, i liked playing in public. It was nice for something different, but i wouldn't want to do it on a routine basis. i like just the two of us at Your house better.

To be continued...

Love,
Your slave puppy

Steven writes:

This was puppy's first alternative lifestyle weekend event. Everything was new to her – all the different sexualities, fetishes, and costumes. Prior to this weekend, she had never thought about going to a class on any subject in BDSM. I asked her to write her thoughts and opinions about the weekend. What I enjoy and appreciate about puppy is her willingness to let me in to her private thoughts and opinions. She does not inflict them on others; she always stays mindful and judges people as individuals. She does not have a mean bone in her body. I also have to mention that she doesn't realize how much of a sexual exhibitionist she is.

Tue, 31 Aug 2004
sharon wrote:

Dear Master,

Playing the second night... so nice that penetration was allowed after all!! i wasn't sure what You were going to do when You told me to lay on the towel. i must confess that i was rather self-conscious being sprawled out on the floor and being fisted while everyone watched. i was trying to control myself and You were not cooperating with my efforts. Back at the cross, i was still trying to control myself and You were still not cooperating with my efforts. And once again, You knew just what to do to achieve Your goal... making me act like some hopelessly horny slut! Talk about a dance! You took me exactly where You wanted me to go... even though You had to work a little harder to get there... whipping all the resistance out of me ☺. And when You were done, i wanted so much to suck Your cock, but i didn't know if You would let me do it there, or if it was "allowed." Again, it seemed like an abrupt end to everything. i was sooooo ready to be fucked... and feeling rather deprived until we got back up to the room. Poor little me!

Love,
Your slave puppy

Tue, 31 Aug 2004
sharon wrote:

Dear Master,

     i was awake yesterday morning for at least an hour if not two hours before You woke up, and was having a lot of difficulty keeping my distance when i really wanted to be dining on Your cock. Did i seem unusually eager when You finally told me to do just that?

     i'm sorry if i was crowding You when You were trying to sleep. Normally, i like a lot of room to stretch out when i'm sleeping and don't like to be touched at all, but it feels so good to be cuddled up next to You. i kept trying to give You space and kept finding myself crowding You again... like i was being pulled by a magnet. Thank You for not tying me to the opposite bedpost. It probably sounds dumb, but i think the thing i was most looking forward to about the weekend was being able to sleep next to You and wake up next to You in the morning. The simple pleasures in life!

     About the classes... there were two things brought up by both Tammy Jo and Garrett that got me thinking. One was the idea that there are different categories of slaves and the other was the idea of control and giving slaves responsibilities for things without telling them exactly what to do all the time. Neither of these are new ideas and we've talked about both of them before. You said that i am a "sex slave" and that is no doubt true, but i want to be more than that for You.

     So i keep thinking i need to help You domestically... housework, et al. However, there are two problems with that: #1 is that i've been running a household for 26 years and when i'm taking care of the domestic chores, i am the one in control and that is what i don't want. Frankly, i am weary of the domestic stuff. If there was nothing else going on in my life, i could probably get back into the "Suzy homemaker" stuff, but it wouldn't take long before it would start driving me crazy. Honestly, i would prefer to have a maid myself and not have to deal with it at all... just tired of it. A spotless house doesn't mean anything to me anymore. i would be happy to

do that stuff for You, but it just wouldn't give me a lot of satisfaction in serving.
So does that make me useless for anything but sex? It shouldn't. i want to be able to serve You doing something where i can be creative, something challenging, something i can put my heart and soul into. i really get off on doing things perfectly (obsessed?) but domestic service isn't one of them. So i don't know... am i a submissive or a slave? Is there some category of slave other than the domestic variety that would be of help to You? i want to be Your slave; i want You to own me; i want to please and serve You; but at the same time i want to serve You by doing something i can do well and with enthusiasm... beyond sex, which i am, of course, most enthusiastic about!
Will finish this later... need to think some more on this.

Love,
Your slave puppy

Steven writes:

puppy is not a domestic slave. It's funny that she doesn't realize that I am already using her talents. In my business, I try to cultivate people's strong points. I want the best out of them; I want them to be able to make decisions, positive ones, from the knowledge that comes after making mistakes. That's how we learn. I want them to take responsibility, to achieve goals, and to get satisfaction from a job well done. I have puppy writing her thoughts, feelings and opinions so I can create a living chronicle of her life in loose diary form. I also plan on having puppy help me organize future book projects, like my next book (here comes the plug) *The Destruction of the Moral Fabric of America*, which you will read about later on in this book.

I have instructed puppy that when she sleeps with me, whenever she wakes up, may it be in the middle of the night or in the morning, she is to suck on my dick. I want to feel that warm, moist, erotic sensation.

Wed, 1 Sep 2004
sharon wrote:

Dear Master,

Your correspondence with Guy Baldwin was very interesting... and oddly familiar. What do You suppose it means that death and dying have played such a big part in his life and in Your life and they are also the focus of mine... although very different experiences for each of us. Do You suppose our paths have crossed for a reason? i've always believed that each of us is put on this earth for a particular purpose and all the things happening to us are leading us to discover that purpose. There is something strangely familiar in that correspondence that i can't quite put my finger on. If You don't mind, i would like to read it again.

    i was reading more of *The Puppy Papers* tonight and got as far as Rob's letters. i had kind of forgotten about him wanting me to send him other people's correspondence all the time. So i guess i don't need to feel too bad about sending his correspondence to someone else!

    The caning last night... it felt kind of like a massage until the very end when You were focusing on my most tender parts. i guess it doesn't matter how much "flesh" a person has for that kind of caning. i think it would have felt good just to go up & down my spine. i've also concluded that, other than my pussy, my thighs are the most erogenous zone on my body. How funny to discover that at my age!

    i've been thinking about the submissive vs. slave idea. It seems like i've written about this in the past... perhaps if i keep reading the book, i'll find what my conclusions were then! i like the secretary category that Tammy Jo talked about. However, i'm not so sure You'd want me as a full-time secretary... i would probably drive You crazy with my perfectionism and over-productivity... although it might be beneficial if You needed any book editing done. i also like the idea of personal service (valet?)... but i am no doubt rather rough around the edges in that area... i'm pretty sure i slept through the Emily Post classes.

    Anyway, i think all the defining of differences between a sub and a slave is purely subjective. i want to be Your slave and if You want me to be Your slave, that's all that matters. Who cares what anyone else has to say about it. It would be nice to do something to settle the question once and for all.

    While writing this, i just got a call from Dale saying there is a "giant" hurricane heading straight for his apartment. He sounded a bit worried, but says he's not leaving town. He also says he's been living on Tostitos, macaroni & cheese, and olives since he got there. Nothing like causing your mother to worry! Between the lines, he did sound a bit homesick though. He also says it's a whole lot of work cleaning up after himself... poor thing!

    Shall i assume You want me to serve You tomorrow night? i will plan on it unless i hear differently.

Love,
Your slave puppy

Fri, 3 Sep 2004
sharon wrote:

Dear Master,

i had the weirdest experience last night. i must have been dreaming about You and rolled over without waking up. i thought i was sleeping next to You and reached over to stroke Your cock. i was getting all heated up and snuggling close to You, and then You started kissing me... only it wasn't You! In my delusional state, i didn't know who was in bed with me! Scared me half to death, but i couldn't seem to fully wake up. Then i was dreaming that You were fucking me, but You kept changing back & forth into Arthur and then back to Yourself. All day i wasn't sure if anything really happened or if it was all a dream. i found out this evening it was apparently real... and that i was unusually enthusiastic... though i'm still not sure what all happened or what i said. Do You suppose that could be classified as my first M-F-M threesome? A very strange experience indeed!

Love,
Your slave puppy

Fri, 3 Sep 2004
Steven wrote:

Dear puppy,

Midnight, twilight-zone sex may be the next big thing. You are in the forefront of sexuality.

Sir

Sun, 5 Sep 2004
sharon wrote:

Dear Master,

i re-read the last part of *The Puppy Papers* tonight and only found a couple things:

p. 294 - 1st full paragraph, line 8 - change "dysfunc-tional" to "dysfunctional"

p. 329 - line 8 - change "dis-appointing" to "disappointing"

last line in same paragraph - change "direc-tions" to "directions"

Also, i referred to Rob's letters on p. 367 - but they probably fit into the story better where You have them.

It always amazes me to go back and read something i've written in the past. i don't know about anyone else, but i'm fascinated enough to read the whole book again... (chuckle) and to find out what happens next (in the sequel)! It seems like when i was writing all that, i was going through some kind of inner journey that's hard to comprehend with just one reading. Going over the last part again, i saw much i didn't see the first time. It was good for me to write about everything... would have never done it if You hadn't "pushed" me. Thank You.

It's hard to explain what it's like to see my own thoughts in print... just as they occurred...without form or forethought... exactly as things happened. Actually, i've realized there are a couple other people i played with that i never wrote about. Do You really think people won't believe it's really true? It's so hard to imagine reading it from someone else's perspective...

i love You & miss You.

Your slave puppy

Steven writes:

I included this email to show how involved puppy is in her collaboration with me, in all of our book projects, in getting everything as perfect as it can be. I needed her thoughts about the *The Puppy Papers* so I could make *Puppy's Tales* (PP2) better.

Mon, 6 Sep 2004
sharon wrote:

Dear Master,

It seems like such a long time since i've seen You...i miss You.

i hope You've been enjoying this long weekend. i've only been called out once so far & that shouldn't have happened except the nurse couldn't see a phone number that was posted right in front of her face. Of course, after i drove all the way there, my badge wouldn't work to get in the door & then my car wouldn't start, so the whole thing took about four hours. Hopefully, tonight will be as quiet as the day.

i heard from Don in Florida today. He was disappointed at the lack of hurricane action in his neighborhood... only a couple trees down and no other damage. They had a three-day "hurricane party" at their apartment that did more damage than the storm itself.

i also heard from Dale, my "genius" son, who has been running 105 fever for five days and didn't know enough to go see a doctor. He tells me that owning a BMW is the best thing that ever happened to him. He says that thanks to the car, he is now dating a Colts cheerleader and also has a long line of "chicks" wanting to go out with him. i'm not quite sure how this "mandatory" car is helping with his education and job prospects though... unless all these girls are investment bankers.

See You soon!

Love,
Your slave puppy

Mon, 6 Sep 2004
Steven wrote:

Dear puppy,

Attached is the first review on *The Puppy Papers* from a tough critic. She liked it. See you on Tue and Thur.

Sir

Note to reader: The Puppy Papers review is located in the Appendix.

Mon, 6 Sep 2004
sharon wrote:

Dear Master,

Is this a good review? Were my earlier experiences so bad that someone should feel sorry for me? That was certainly <u>not</u> what i intended to communicate. Is that what You think about it too? i am very, very disappointed that it came across that way.

Love,
Your slave puppy

P.S. None of this is directed at You... just venting.

Mon, 6 Sep 2004
Steven wrote:

Dear puppy,

You're having opening night jitters. Don't be so hard on yourself. She was commenting on what you had to endure and the people who you met, no one connecting with you or seeing you for who you are, only for what they wanted from you. Yours is a journey many people go through. It's just that you have a wonderful ability to express this better than most. This will make people who read the book, stop, look and listen, instead of following blindly in the hope that everything will turn out all right when it might not. This is what she saw.

  The letters you wrote and how you wrote them made her see your experiences. Most people who read the book will relate to the different experiences or will be fascinated by them. Women who are married, have children, who work, who are looking for a master or wanting a better sexual life, will relate. You convey your experiences beautifully and with such openness. It is always strange to have others critique, judge, review, or give an opinion of your work and life. That's the price you pay for being an artist, taking a chance, exposing yourself. There will be some people who dislike it; others will love it.

  Tammy Jo is a Dominant, so she viewed the book through a Dominant woman's eyes. Her upbringing was very different than yours. She also doesn't use the Internet to meet people. She meets people at the university where she works, so her experiences are different. With all that said, she liked the story, the uniqueness of style, and the honesty of your writing. You should be proud; you have written a very good and unique book. I am very proud of you.

Sir

Mon, 6 Sep 2004
sharon wrote:

Dear Master,

  Thank You for Your kind words. Am i being thin-skinned? i guess i was just surprised at what she got from the book, though it shouldn't have been surprising. Every day i deal with people who hear what they want to hear, whether or not it has any resemblance to what was said. The advantage of writing over speaking is that you have proof of what you said... meaningless to the "hearer," but at least you know for yourself that you're not losing your mind. The nice thing about communicating by touch is that it's rarely misinterpreted... and it can express what words are so inadequate in doing.

i don't think You've put Yourself "out there" in the same way i did in this book. Most of the things i told You in those e-mails are things i've never told anyone else. Also, it was not at all my intention to make anyone else look bad or to garner pity for myself. Stuff just happened... it wasn't life or death serious, and no harm came from any of it. It was fun... exploring, learning, growing, experimenting. Why should anyone feel sorry for me? Am i supposed to feel wounded because someone else doesn't fit a certain textbook definition of the perfect Dom/Master/Top/friend/lover/partner, etc, etc. People are who they are...and who am i to say that someone else's way of doing things is right or wrong, good or bad. i'm just grateful that all people are not the same. What a boring world that would be. i have no idea where i'm going with all this ranting... except to say that pity is something i really detest. i am in no way, shape, or form a victim and there is nothing anyone can do to make me feel like one. The end!

Love & hugs,
Your slave puppy

Mon, 6 Sep 2004
Steven wrote:

Dear puppy,

You told your story. It's like a million other stories, but you are able to express yourself and write about it much better than most. You have never exposed yourself to this kind of criticism; very few people have. Your telling of your life is being reviewed and judged by others. They're asking themselves these questions: Does it tell a story? How does it compare to other stories like it? Does it hold my interest? Does it communicate? Do I relate to it? Could I do something like this? Could I communicate, tell all, like she does? Could I be so trusting like she is? Is the story any good?

How do you think it feels for people of all talents in the theater, movies, literature, or song to create a piece of work and have someone say it's no good, or that they should not be on the stage, or what in god's name made anyone produce this tripe? The other side is: It's ok; it could have been better, it's good, very good, brilliant, interesting, intriguing. *The Puppy Papers* is all these things to different readers.

Everyone who views a painting, sees a play, or reads a book comes away with a different experience in feelings and thoughts than the next person. What we have expressed in our/your story is real life. People will have many different opinions, but they will all find it an interesting read, not a laborious or tedious read. Some Dominants may like it and others won't. Most submissive women will love it, others will like it, and some won't like it at all. There will be jealousy, envy, and praise. You have created a real, unflinching, undoctored story of life, which is unique in any art form. You did it in words; you were open and honest. You created a work of literature. It's not Shakespeare, but it is a true lifestyle story. There is nothing out there to compare it to and, as such, it will be very hard to duplicate no matter how hard someone tries. It is unique for all others to be judged against. Congratulations.

Sir

P.S. People are voyeurs and you gave them a chance to lose themselves in your life. Also the format of the book is new and creative. You are breaking new ground, a visionary ahead of your time. When readers tell you how interesting your book is, you will be very proud of your work.

Wed, 15 Sep 2004
sharon wrote:

Dear Master,

i have spent the past four hours on the phone with my kids. One tells me he's found paradise on the beach in Florida and the other tells me he's found paradise on Wall Street. Now if i can just avoid bankruptcy paying for all this paradise, i will be a very contented puppy! Both are very excited about what they're doing though, so i guess i don't have anything better to spend my money on. Ahh...to be twenty-something and have the world in the palm of your hand... makes my head spin just listening to them talk!

i hope You are enjoying this "invigorating" weather!

See You soon!
i miss You.

Ysp

Fall 2004

Sat, 18 Sep 2004
sharon wrote:

Dear Master,

    i drank quite a bit of You last night...yum ☺... it has been a while. Since i've been practicing the deep-throating, i'm never quite sure how to proceed once i have Your cock in my mouth. If You are in my throat when You decide to feed me, i seem to inhale it which results in coughing and an inability to breathe. So not knowing what You have in mind or when, i don't know how far to take You in. Oh, the complexities of being a slave!

    i liked that You kept stopping to feed me in the middle of other things. It kind of put me in a "ready" frame of mind (or mindlessness). Moving so quickly from one thing to another creates a rare state (for me) of non-thinking... just being there to please You. It's hard to explain, but when You are demanding one thing after another, it puts me in a good place. Besides that, kneeling in front of You with Your cock in my mouth is my favorite place to be... except when You are fucking me and i can feel Your whole body against mine. i'm thinking it would be much nicer if i was there serving You now instead of writing about it!

    The puppy play does the same thing to my mind. Hurrying to pick up the flowers... i kept wanting to stop and get myself into a "puppy" frame of mind, but You were already heading in the other direction so i had to hurry to keep up. Between the flowers, smacking my ass, barking, feeding me, and then fucking me on the dog bed... (laughing) i guess it's beyond any frame of mind... like becoming an object. i never thought about puppy play this way before, but it's like pushing me over the edge with the whips... to a peaceful place... where You could do absolutely anything You want with me.

    And then before i could get my senses together, we were off to the Bijou. i was off in la-la-land and You were talking about Your business or something. i don't know how You do that. (laughing) After taking my dress off & putting it back on so many times, i was ready to just rip all the damn buttons off of it and leave it open because it was requiring way too much concentration.

    Walking around the Bijou is always a strange experience because all these faceless people just appear out of nowhere; and it seems like they're always hurrying in the other direction from the way we're walking so we end up passing a whole line of them... surreal... like something in a dream. Of course, i'm always hurrying to try to keep up with You so i don't get lost in the maze!

There were two scents at the Bijou that, for some reason, really stood out. One was when we first walked through the door, and i don't know why i never noticed it before. It was an earthy, musky scent. It was familiar, like something from the distant past, but i couldn't figure out what it was. Then the cross had the scent of fresh cologne mixed with sweat, like someone else was there, superimposed on me, and experiencing the same thing i was... like a spiritual presence...an unseen "ghost" who was also present and being whipped in another dimension.

You could have whipped me all night on that cross. There was no threshold of pain to cross over. i was already there. Fortunately, You knew when to quit though since i would have stayed there until my skin was shredded. i don't remember being so "weak in the knees" before...helpless. If You hadn't lifted me into the sling, i don't think i could have gotten into it... my brain couldn't seem to tell my muscles how to work in the right direction.

When You were fisting me, i was completely unaware of anything else. Again, it would have been wonderful if You would have kept going all night... except You would have had to carry me out of the place... and drive me home ☺. The idea that there might have been other people in the room watching all this never even crossed my mind.

Walking back to Your house and then up all the stairs to Your bedroom was a challenge. It feels sooooooo good when You make love to me... thinking about all this has my pussy dripping... and ready for whatever You have in mind for tonight.

See You soon.

i love You,

Your slave puppy

Sun, 19 Sep 2004
sharon wrote:

Dear Master,

i tend to smoke more after working all day... it seems to help me process the day's issues... but the reason You didn't smell any smoke on me was probably because i was able to shower and change clothes right before i left home. Maybe i should start taking a shower when i arrive at Your house instead of before i leave!

You seemed different last night. Is there something You're not telling me?

You asked what i thought about the open house at the Leather Rose... It's nice for people who like a social atmosphere. It didn't do anything special for me, but then i've never really felt the need to belong to a social group... i prefer one-on-one. In general, the clubs seem to have more of a social atmosphere than a sensual one. Of course, maybe i'm spoiled... the play space at Your house is by far the nicest and most sensual one i've seen. Maybe You should invite the owners of L.R. to play with us at Your house (and the Bijou) so they can better envision the possibilities. That might be fun...

i love You.

Your slave puppy

Wed, 22 Sep 2004
Steven wrote:

Dear puppy,

You have to remember that my place is not a public club. I do not invite 100 guests over when we play, but maybe we'll do 50 to see how you handle it. On second thought, you would do rather well.

What has been on my mind lately has nothing to do with you. I have told you a few things. As you know, I've decided this is the year that I'm getting rid of the ongoing negative drama from the past. So between the lawyers, the government, the court cases, and a long thieving relationship, I expect to be a little exhausted and preoccupied at times. I have made the decision to resolve my problems. These issues will take a little time to resolve, but will eventually become yesterday's news.

You seemed a little taken aback when I mentioned that I play with others. I told you when we first met that I play, and have always played, with others. There is no need to always mention it; I will not throw it in your face.

Sir

Thu, 23 Sep 2004
sharon wrote:

Dear Master,

      i know You've had a lot on Your mind and i know You play with other people. Will You promise to tell me explicitly when You get bored or unhappy with me? You have seemed... preoccupied? different?...for a while, but it never even occurred to me that You were playing with someone else. i can be kind of dense sometimes. i also understand the need for contemplation and solitude at times and i don't want to interfere or intrude in that sacred place. i just want You to be happy... and if/when You ever need some space, i just need You to tell me in Your usual honest way.

Love,
Your slave puppy

Thu, 23 Sep 2004
Steven wrote:

Dear puppy,

      I have always played with others; I have mentioned it a few times. I don't want to create jealousy and drama. But again, what has been going on lately has nothing to do with you. You have been a godsend in bringing me back to a positive reality, to the better and more important things in life.

Sir

Thu, 23 Sep 2004
sharon wrote:

Dear Master,

      i don't know how a person can be so tired and not be able to fall asleep. If this insomnia goes on much longer, i'm going to become delirious. (laughing) i've always said if i didn't have to eat or sleep i could get a lot more done... this will teach me to be more careful about what i ask for!

      It's okay. i want You to talk about anything You want, anything that makes You happy. Your consistent honesty and straightforwardness makes me try to be as honest and straightforward as possible in return. i just don't have things sorted out as well as You do, so i ramble.

      Writing is my way of processing things... always has been. What is very clear to You is still fuzzy to me. i am trying to figure things out as i go along. i need You to keep talking to me about everything and anything. If it brings things to the surface, then they can be dealt with... which is better and healthier than keeping them buried inside. Please don't avoid talking about things because You think they might upset me.

i love You.

Your slave puppy

Sat, 25 Sep 2004
sharon wrote:

Dear Master,

  i don't think i can go away for a whole week without You 😊. So i've come up with an idea 🌐! You could take a week of vacation and join me in Washington. The room is already paid for, and You could be the inspiration for my speech, and i could wake You up every morning by feasting on Your cock, and You could relax in the spa or something while i am at meetings, and i could serve You every day, and we could do some sightseeing (if You like that kind of thing), and i would be a very, very happy puppy! And hopefully You would be a very, very happy Master! Now is this a genius plan or what! You haven't had a vacation for as long as i've known You, so You are definitely in need of one... and they tell me Washington is beautiful this time of year. Can i make a plane reservation for You Sir?

Love,
Your slave puppy

Sat, 25 Sep 2004
Steven wrote:

Dear puppy,

  Thank you for the invitation and for your wonderful thoughts, but I can't make it. Do well and enjoy your trip. I will miss you.

Sir

Sun, 26 Sep 2004
sharon wrote:

Dear Master,

i've realized that the one who is different this week isn't You; it's me. i'm feeling really down... discombobulated... for no particular reason... except i haven't been able to sleep all week... wired, frustrated, too many people wanting a piece of me and not enough hours in a day i guess... feeling insecure, ugly, can't do anything right...generally feeling sorry for myself, crying for no reason... and just tired. Anyway, i don't think it has anything to do with You, but i've been reading things into Your words/actions that aren't really there and then creating problems in my own mind that don't exist anywhere else. i'm sorry. You are the one dealing with all the big problems and i'm the one wallowing in senseless self-pity. i don't like feeling this way. i keep telling myself to snap out of it, but apparently it's a dark cloud that will pass in its own good time. i feel like i'm lost in the dark and don't know which way is which. Maybe my body chemistry is out of whack and i need to start eating better. In any case, i hope You will be patient with me until my sanity returns. i just want You to know it isn't You or anything You're doing that has me feeling this way... and i'm sorry if it came across that way.

Love,
Your slave puppy

Sun, 26 Sep 2004
sharon wrote:

Dear Master,

Okay, here's my story: i love You. i've never loved anyone like this before. i would walk away from the rest of my life in a minute if i thought that's what You wanted. i will do anything in the world for You and be anything You want me to be. But You've always said You "can't take care of anyone right now," and that You like Your solitude, and that You have all these things You need to take care of, etc... and i understand all that, so i am very careful to give You plenty of space. But i've always thought (fantasized?) that someday, when You are ready, i would be Your full-time slave or submissive or partner, or whatever You want to call it. The thing is that i seem to need You more than You need me. i am not "jealous" of anyone else You play with, but at the same time, i am not interested in serving anyone else... only You. Anything i would do with anyone else would only be to please You.

      My past relationships are just that. my relationship with my husband is basically non-existent since i've known You, like two strangers leading separate lives who happen to reside in the same house. The only time i am really happy is when i am there with You, and when i'm not there i am always thinking about You and wishing i was there. So i am confused when You talk about looking for a "primary" person in Your life, because You are the Primary Person in my life. That is why i was so surprised when You said You were seeing someone else... because i have been so focused on You that i haven't even thought of anyone else... out of touch with reality i guess. Then You said when/if You should find this "primary person," i would continue to serve you both. i don't understand. i would come over to "entertain" You for a couple hours and then You would shoo me out the door so You could spend the rest of the night with her? It seems to me that would quickly become a chore for You both and i would be eliminated. i don't want to lose You. You are the best thing that has ever happened to me. i don't know what i would ever do without You.

      The thing is that i'm sure the hundreds of other women You've known have all felt the same way i do and they are all history, so why should i be any different... i'm not. You have been very open and honest about all this right from the start and nothing You've said recently is anything new. It's just that i feel like You are slipping away from me and i want to hang on to You, but i know that clinging will only push You away. So i've got all this stuff going in circles in my head and getting bigger and bigger and i don't know what to do about it. i am so afraid of losing You.

I love you,

Your slave puppy

P.S. You said You have come to love me but not in the same way i love You. How does a Master love a slave? As a friend, a teacher, a father, or something else? None of that seems quite right since we are, in fact, having sex. Also, how is a slave supposed to love her Master? Have i gone off in the wrong direction?

Sun, 26 Sep 2004
Steven wrote:

Dear Puppy,

Are you getting nervous because you're going away for a week? Don't. Everything is all right between us. I will be here when you get back. I do not want to be the cause of your breakup with your husband. NOW ISN'T THAT A STUPID THING FOR ME TO SAY. If you should break up with him, I will not leave you. The trip to GLLA was to take you to an event and spend the weekend with you. I wanted to get to know you a little better away from everything else. But my reasons were not the same as yours and that is what I have learned about women. I have told you my thoughts on this before. You women dream and fantasize about what you would like to happen, how you want things and the person you're with to be. Then that fantasy becomes your reality and you get disappointed if the dream/fantasy does not happen, even if it's absolutely unrealistic. As for men, we're just dumb. As for being a Dom/Master to a sub or slave who chooses to be with me, there is only one way, my way.

I have grown to have a love for you, but I do not love you the same as you love me. I love you as my slave; I respect you as my slave and as a person. I like and enjoy your company and servitude. Our bond is our compatibility. We met because you were looking for a Master. As a Master, I am selfish by society's standards. In my world of consensual agreement, I feel my philosophy of life and my morals, standards and principles are consistent. What I practice is more caring, understanding, and respectful than what is practiced in the outside world. If you did not feel the same way, you would not be with me.

I have told you from the beginning that I play with others; I'm a single man. When I met you, I was playing with two other women once or twice a week. I still play, but the bottoms have changed, but not you, puppy. I am not monogamous, never have been. If that is what you are now looking for, I am not the right fit. As far as play is concerned, I have not asked you to join me with any of the others, but I will when I feel it's appropriate. They just want play time and that is all I want from them. This is always discussed up front as I did with you. This is my arrangement from the beginning. No, I am not looking to shoo you out the door. I haven't done that yet; but remember you do have to go to work in the morning and you have a husband at home.

As for a primary partner, I would like one. I am looking for someone who will accept my life, my business, you, and of course who will dance with me. If that person feels three is a crowd, then that person leaves. I am Master of my life, my world. For whatever reason, all the women I have been with for longer periods of time have tried to change me. It's always funny to me how excited they are in the beginning for the forbidden fruit, to enter my world, to come to my party, to dance. As we got to know each other more than superficially, as they got more involved, the reality of the existing relationship wasn't what they wanted any more. They wanted things to change. They wanted less rough sex play; they wanted to set limits; they wanted my life to conform to their needs. My world was unmentionable and they could not tell their friends or family about it for fear of judgment and consequences. They wanted a more serious, acceptable, conventional relationship. I have no idea who the fuck they thought they were talking to. I was not about to change my life, my business, my history, or pretend to be someone other than who I am. That's why I tell everyone up front about myself, my life, what I do for a living, but not much of my history at first – I've found that's a little too much for people to comprehend.

I've told you that you're a big part of my life and you come with me into any other relationships, if that should be your choosing. My partner (if that should happen) will be your Mistress, and together we would form our household, our family. If being my slave is what you want, but you do not want to be part of a group/family/house, then you have to tell me that. You have to do what is right and comfortable for you.

As far as US slipping apart, where are you getting that notion? I tell you my thoughts and talk to you about private matters. You are my slave and confidante. You are important to me, puppy. We have been together and growing for almost a year. We collaborate; we've created a book, and we will create others. I enjoy the creativity that we have together.

Enough said, have a wonderful conference. Knockum dead with your presentation. See you when you get back.

Sir

P.S. If you get a chance, email me and tell me how things are going.

Steven writes:

What I'm writing here does not refer to anything that puppy wrote. This is for you, the reader. I'm not an accountant or an insurance agent, and I don't work in a large corporation. My business is sex – live, in books, on film, DVD, audio, etc. My sex businesses are open 24/7, which means that I provide sexual services 24/7. My sex club has not closed for one minute in 25 years. At home, I research gay films, sexual history, etc., and I often write throughout the night. I started my businesses because I like my dick, I love to play, and I enjoy providing people with the opportunity to have pleasure. I've had 21 obscenity arrests, numerous busts for being a keeper of a house of prostitution, and I don't know how many other ridiculous charges, along with numerous bench and jury trials. I'll stop here before I run out of space. I think you get the point.

As far as who I play with, there must be a physical and mental attraction for me. I play with women who want to be controlled in the bedroom and there is no struggle for who is in control outside of the bedroom. If it's going to be a long-term relationship, not just topping and bottoming during a play scene, then the dominant and submissive dynamics of the relationship are set in stone. The women I play with are either single, in a relationship, or married. As far as relationships with married women are concerned, I do not solicit these women, but I have not shied away from those who have contacted or solicited me.

I do not tell puppy anything specific about the others. I let her know some things, but no details. Why don't I say anything more? Why should I create jealousy? That would be asking for trouble. I meet, date, and play with other women. I feel that bringing another woman/man/couple into a scene first requires compatibility and attraction. The idea of the scene would have to erotically excite me for me to bring another woman/man/couple into a scene with puppy. I'm not interested in "the more the merrier." I also have to say that, as I'm getting older, some of my habits are changing. I feel more of a need to write and work at my business than when I was younger.

Sun, 26 Sep 2004
sharon wrote:

Dear Master,

And you men are always so rational, reasonable, logical, sane, etc... that's why we women need you☺! i know i'm being over-emotional and ridiculous and making a mountain out of a molehill, or rather, making a mountain out of nothing at all. i'm sorry. Maybe i am just nervous about the trip & presentation. It's just that i watch You very closely when we're together and i am (or at least try to be) very attuned to Your moods. When i said You seemed different, i thought it had something to do with Your "friend" who was stealing from You or some other court case or business deal. i was worried that something bad had happened. Also, i wasn't able to get any sleep all week, and now i think i'm catching a cold, and i'm not looking forward to spending a week in a hotel all by myself, and i have so many things to take care of at work that i shouldn't be going anywhere because i know things will be all screwed up when i get back. Sheesh... makes me tired just writing all that. It would be so nice to just curl up on my puppy bed & sleep for a week... so, so tired. Thank You for Your patience and kind words. my sanity will return. It's just too much to comprehend right now.

     i doubt i will have access to a computer this week, but i will have my cell phone. i'll try to call You some evening. i'll be fine... the sun will come up tomorrow.

i love You.

Your slave puppy

Thu, 30 Sep 2004
Steven wrote:

Hello Natasha,

     It was lovely seeing and talking to you last night. Let me know about Tuesday at 7:00, if that will work for you.

Steven

Thu, 30 Sep 2004
Natasha wrote:

Hi Steven:

     It was a great meeting yesterday. I hope that we are still meeting tomorrow. My cell phone is ____.

Talk to you later,
Natasha

Steven writes:

     I contacted Natasha on the Internet, and she responded back. We sent a few emails to each other and then we exchanged phone numbers. She told me she never played outside of her relationships, but at this point, her sexual life was at a standstill. She felt there had to be something on the other side of the sexual mountain. I took this to mean she was having a mid-life sexual awakening. So she threw caution to the wind, got a little crazy, and joined an alternative web site on a whim, which is how we met.

I read her brief profile, emailed her, and she responded. On the second email, I told her about puppy and that I am not monogamous. I did not want to waste her time or mine if she felt this was a problem. She did not. After conversing for a while, I felt I wanted to bring Natasha into my scenes with puppy. Remember, this is for my gratification; it's good to be the King.

Fri, 1 Oct 2004
Natasha wrote:
Hi Steven:

I was out of office the whole day yesterday and did not have chance to write to you. It was wonderful evening. I started to read the book you gave me.

You know, when I lived in Soviet Union, many books were prohibited. I was given this book written by Boris Pasternak by a friend to read. I remember that I was riding a metro in Moscow, reading *Doctor Zhivago*. The book had another cover, covering the title, and I was making sure that nobody was peeking inside. The book was exciting and the sense of forbidden fruit was also exciting.

So yesterday I went to see a doctor (just regular check-up) and while waiting in a full waiting room, I had your book in a cover reading it. The book was exciting and the sense of forbidden fruit was also exciting.

The book is great. I did not finish it yet. At some places I had to laugh. Like when she said that she was amazed that you two have met because of different lives you have lived. This is exactly what I told you last night. The other was her fear of knives. Actually, that scared me too.

The other thing that I started to realize – how ignorant I am about that side of life. I am scared, but I want to explore this novel life. I realize that I was lucky to meet you. I do want to meet. My calendar tells me that Tuesday October 5 was taken a long time ago. Could we meet another day? Puppy is an amazing woman!

Talk to you later,
Natasha

Steven writes:

At our second meeting, I had given Natasha *The Puppy Papers* to read so she would have an understanding of what I do, who I play with, what I want in communication, mindset, and sexuality. I'm very proud of the book.

Sat, 2 Oct 2004
Steven wrote:

Hello Natasha,

How is everything with you? I'm glad you like the book. It seems like a long time from when we last met. Would you like to meet Wednesday over dinner or coffee? I want you to be sure about getting together. I was also thinking, would Saturday be better for you instead of Friday so you don't have to rush after work? My place at 6:30?

Steven

Mon, 4 Oct 2004
Natasha wrote:

Hi Steven:

Thank you for your letters. I finished reading the book. In fact, yesterday I stayed at home most of the day just to read it. It is a great read, very interesting and human. I would like to buy this book. I have the feeling that it should have a lot of interest from people. I will be happy to meet you on Wednesday. When and where? Also I agree Saturday is better. I'll be there at 6:30.

Talk to you later,
Natasha

Mon, 4 Oct 2004
Steven wrote:

Natasha,

I am happy you liked the book. It's a different type of story, written in a different style. Please, the book is my present to you. For Wednesday night, how is 7:00, my home? We'll go for dinner, talk about your thoughts, and I will answer all of your questions. If all goes well, we'll get together on Saturday.

You are entering a wonderful new world. I do hope it is making you smile, blush, and your pussy moist.

Steven

Steven writes:

In speaking with Natasha, I learned that she had no experience in BDSM. She was just becoming aware of her inner sexual self, and only vaguely aware of her submissive side. Her thoughts and fantasies revolved around a threesome. She also enjoyed watching. I learned that she has to think and analyze everything and put things into their proper categories. Natasha is many things, including a medical doctor, professor, and a scientist who runs her own research lab. I found that the way she communicated was the opposite of puppy. puppy is quiet when she is with me, but when she is at a computer she writes these open, honest, detailed letters. Natasha said very little in her letters, but when we were together she was never at a loss for words – funny and loaded with information, but never letting me know much about who she really was.

Now I have a date to play with a newbie. I had her read *The Puppy Papers* and some of my articles. I want to meet with her again to talk. I don't want her to get involved in anything she would be uncomfortable with. When she said, "Sure let's do it," it brought a smile to my face. I wanted her first scene to be easy, simple and erotic, something she would always remember. I wanted the picture to be etched and burned into her memory.

Mon, 4 Oct 2004
sharon wrote:

Dear Master,

It's cold here in the Midwest! my house is freezing and i don't know how to program the goofy high-tech thermostat to get some heat. Arthur never showed up last night, so i'm sitting here freezing and wrapped in blankets. i see this morning in the daylight that it appears he went on a spending spree at the local K-mart. We have this very nice new house and he's determined to fill it with wall-to-wall trash... very annoying... especially since he's color blind.

my period started last night, so under normal circumstances it should be done by Thursday or Friday, but the last few months it's been messed up and dragging on for an extra 2-3 days. i really need to see a doc to get that annoyance fixed but haven't had the time. In any case, it should be minimal by Friday, if that day works best for You and... You didn't tell me her name.

Also, what is it that i'm supposed to be teaching her? i'm not exactly a star pupil when it comes to protocols & such. Perhaps i could be "exhibit A"... what *not* to do?

i miss You.

Love,
Your slave puppy

Wed, 6 Oct 2004
Steven wrote:

Dear puppy,

This weather is invigorating, at least under warm soft blankets. Martha is still at K-mart.

Her name is Natasha. She was born in Russia and has been in the states about 13 years, or so she told me. Good sense of humor. What she will learn from you will be through attitude and example. You need and should go to the doctor, but you won't.

Sir

Wed, 6 Oct 2004
sharon wrote:

Dear Master,

The medical director i hired a couple months ago is Russian. He always comes to morning team meetings looking like he's been partying all night. He claims Russians are the only ones who know how to party... "hot-blooded" he says... hmmm.

Are You saying i'm a non-compliant patient? i'm just procrastinating because i dread the thought of trying to find a good doctor or dentist in Illinois, and particularly gynecologists around here who don't take into consideration that people work during the day. i thought it would be easier to get an evening appointment closer to the city, but apparently people in rural areas are the only ones with jobs.

The sun is warming the house quite nicely...at least i can no longer see my breath anyway!

Have a wonderful day!

Love,
Your slave puppy

Sun, 10 Oct 2004
sharon wrote:

Dear Master,

    i went to my parents' house for dinner today and spent the afternoon listening to my father carry on about how great George Bush is. By the time i got home this evening, he had already sent e-mails to further his arguments. There couldn't possibly be two people of more opposite opinions than You and him. i'm thinking it would be interesting to get the two of you together to debate the issues... though it may cause him to have a stroke. i don't think his blood pressure has come down yet and i only pointed out a couple little inconsistencies in his thinking. He definitely has his feathers ruffled.

    i thought last night went rather well. i liked watching the muscles in Your ass, legs, and back when You were fucking someone else. Each time You thrust into her, my pussy got wetter... a phenomenon! But i will start at the beginning...

    i tried not to think about the evening beforehand, so i had no preconceived ideas about what would or should happen... works better that way for me. For some reason, i did vaguely picture her to be smaller and to have longer hair though. i was at peak horniness (which is normally the case at the end of my period) so that helped. It also helped that i was tied and blindfolded when You brought her upstairs... kept me from being too nervous. You came back with her so quickly, i'm wondering if she was already waiting downstairs while You were tying me down? i am always so oblivious to such things... head in the clouds i guess.

    You were driving me crazy fiddling with my clit while You were talking to her... and it was so frustrating having my legs tied together. Then You quit, which was even more frustrating! i was trying to be so patient while You told her to get undressed, etc., but all i wanted You to do was fuck me. i could hear You kissing her & stuff and i figured You would forget about me like Rob did. (i don't mean to bring him up, but he was my only experience with this kind of thing). my needy/greedy cunt was feeling a bit deprived of Your attention. Then i could hear You spanking her, and her gasping each time, and i was a little worried she was going to freak out or something; and the evening would be over before it got started. i was wishing You were spanking me instead of her... since i would appreciate it more 🌐 and so she would be okay with things. i expected to be bound and helpless for quite a while and was surprised when You untied me so soon.

Natasha was on the bed, bound and blindfolded, and You stood up on the bed and had me suck Your cock right in front of her. When you took the blindfold off her, the wide-eyed expression on her face was priceless. i don't think she believed what she was seeing. You put her in another world...i wonder if she will ever forget that picture.

You tasted so good, but I was so grateful when You had me stop and told me to lay back on the bed and You fisted me. i completely forgot she was there... until You so abruptly stopped, leaving my pussy so very empty, and went back to her... very frustrating again. i wanted soooo much for You to fuck me. i appreciated it immensely when You told me to suck Your cock while You played with her. When You told me to play with her nipples, i was kind of hesitant because i didn't want to hurt or upset her, but she seemed to be okay with it. It seemed to help her get into it more. She has a nice body.

i don't remember the exact order of things, but i started to relax more after that. i guess i started to trust You more that You weren't going to forget about me. i didn't feel like i had served my purpose and was just in the way. Oddly, it also helped me to relax when You were explaining things to her. Anyway, when we were formally introduced, she seemed to be okay with everything and i figured that was the end of her first "experience."

Then, i was surprised (and happy) when You said something about using the single-tail on me. When we went in the other room, You tied me to the chains and then left the room, so i tried starting a conversation with her to help make her feel more comfortable. She didn't make a sound. (laughing) i think she *was* literally speechless! i looked over my shoulder at her and her eyes were as big as saucers, so i figured i would leave her be. i just relaxed and got into the music.

When You came back, i was so dang horny, all You would have had to do was touch me and i would have been cumming all over the place. i wanted You to whip me long and hard, but You kept teasing me. Fisting provided some relief, but i wanted You to keep going harder...with both the fisting and the whips. When You took me down, i wanted You to throw me over the chaise and fuck me hard. But i figured she had already seen more than she bargained for, so i resigned myself to the idea that the evening's "events" were over...little did I know the night was not over.

It was nice to sit & chat a little to make sure she was okay with everything... and i do appreciate the fact that i am not the only one You cause to be speechless 😊! i was verrry happy when You said it was Your turn and verrry happy to be the recipient of Your cock... and verrry disappointed when You stopped fucking me and started fucking her...which brings me back to where i started. You looked absolutely delicious when You were fucking her. You have such a sexy ass! Every time You thrust into her, i could feel it in my pussy. And then, for a perfect ending, You came back to me, because my most satisfying orgasm is the one that is simultaneous with Yours. Sooo... i guess all is good in subland...and You are a Master of the threesome! i know the evening was all about her first experience, but You managed to make me feel part of it and to feel good about it too. Thank You. You are very kind.

i love You.

Your slave puppy

Steven writes:

For a few days beforehand, I thought about how I wanted the scene with puppy and Natasha to play out, the sensations, the timing and rhythm. I wanted the scene to be easy, simple, and erotic, something Natasha would always remember, and a scene puppy would thoroughly enjoy. I wanted puppy to be relaxed but excited about the unknown.

Here's how the evening went from my perspective: puppy came over an hour before Natasha was to arrive. We went up to my bedroom where I had her undress in the middle of the room and stand there with her hands behind her head, elbows back, which pushed out her breasts. She stayed in that position while I got most of the things ready that I would need for the night.

After about twenty minutes, I had puppy go over and lie down on the bed. I blindfolded her, put wrist and ankle restraints on her, and tightly chained her outstretched arms and legs. The chains were secured to the floor at the four corners of the bed, so puppy was spread open and exposed. I put on *Mystere* from Cirque Du Soleil, so puppy could relax and meditate, and then left her there to go and get Natasha, who was waiting for me outside. When I met Natasha, I told her that if she felt any pressure, we wouldn't go forward. She blushed and said she wanted to go ahead with the evening, so we went up the stairs to my home. Natasha was blushing and laughing nervously. I said nothing to her about puppy.

Natasha is tall, slim to average, with large breasts. puppy is tall, very slim, with small breasts. I'm not big on breasts unless they do something, meaning they have to have sensitivity as an erotic zone for the woman. They make clothes look good, and look lovely when firm and perky; other than that, I have no fantasy about them unless they can make the woman wet or I can enjoy myself in making the woman dance during breast play.

Another thing, I am not a big man so I don't fit well with big women. What I find attractive is white teeth, a wonderful smile, neckline, and shoulders; I also want to see the spine on her back. I love slim legs going to a nice ass and an attractive, self-assured, sensual gait. Very important is a little space between the upper thighs by the pussy because that's a good cock fit for me. This overall look is very erotic, very sexy to me.

When Natasha came into the room, she saw puppy and she couldn't turn her head away. She took off her coat and I had her sit on the bed next to puppy, who was chained, naked, and exposed. As I spoke to Natasha, I started playing with puppy's pussy with my left hand, never taking my eyes off Natasha. Natasha was mesmerized. puppy was struggling to get herself in a comfortable sexual position; her clit was swollen; and she was soaking wet.

I stopped playing with puppy and had Natasha take off her clothes and sit cross-legged on the bed. I handcuffed her hands behind her back and then blindfolded her. All the while I was talking to her about what I was doing. I started playing with her body to see where she was erotically sensitive and to determine where I could switch to slight pain with a pinch here and there. I alternated between gentle and rough. I wanted to know what reactions I could get from her body. I wanted to hear her, watch her breathing, and watch her jump from mild, unexpected pain.

After a few minutes, I stopped playing with Natasha and turned to puppy who was still laying next to us. I started spanking puppy's pussy and pinching her nipples. As I was doing this, I talked to her which always excites her. She was starved for attention. I also wanted my words to create an image for Natasha. When I play or have sex, I talk about what I am doing, what I want to do, what they will do for me, and what I want them to do for me. I ask questions and get responses. I don't yell; I don't denigrate; I control. I want to know their fears, their pleasures, and their dark fantasies. After a while, when I ask, they bark for me.

I released puppy from the chains and had her kneel on the bed in front of Natasha. I took off my clothes and stood on the bed next to Natasha with puppy facing my cock. I was deliciously hard (of course, this is just my opinion). I then had puppy suck on my cock until she started to open up and deep throat me. I felt her thick mouth cum covering my cock.

I asked puppy if she liked sucking my dick, she took my dick out of her mouth and said "very much." Then I took the blindfold off Natasha. My dick in puppy's mouth was no more than a few inches away from her face. Natasha was mesmerized. She was breathing very hard and staring as puppy swallowed my dick. That is an image she will never forget. The opening scene was working out flawlessly.

After a few minutes, I put the blindfold back on Natasha and got off the bed. I then felt her pussy and she jumped a little. I started to pull on her pubic hairs and her body came to me. I was talking to her the entire time. I turned my attention to puppy; I needed to fist her to orgasm. Seeing that Natasha was a voyeur was good; I wouldn't have to work so hard now that her erotic imagination was helping me. We were all in sync, connected, and I was directing the rhythm.

I took the blindfold off Natasha with my free hand while I was fisting puppy. I think if I would have asked Natasha at that moment what her name was, it might have taken her a few minutes to remember. She had never seen vaginal fisting before or even imagined it. She was stunned and wide-eyed. As for puppy, she didn't want my fist to leave her pussy. When puppy had an orgasm, I stopped, asked them both how they were doing, and then went to the bathroom to wash up. They told me they were doing well.

When I came back, we moved into the dungeon room. Puppy was eager for a single-tail, a spanking, and another release. I wanted to see Natasha's reaction as she watched a flogging and single-tail scene. I was getting what I wanted; I was able to take both women into the other side of life and have such control over their erotic beings that it was awe-inspiring. I was totally focused on them and, at the same time, I was descending inward into my own world of Top space.

Puppy is a delight to play with. She is always ready and gets herself involved in the scene. I played with her on the spanking bench and then took her over to a wooden post that goes from the floor to the ceiling with chains hanging down the sides. I secured her arms to the chains and then alternated between flogging, single-tail, and a double spanking of puppy's pussy and ass. She gushed in my hand. Then I started the process all over again, allowing the rhythm of the lashes, spanking and single-tail on her body to take her into her other world of subspace. It was time to fist her again while she was standing, suspended by chains, with her legs open wide. puppy swallowed my hand and braced herself for another orgasm.

When I stopped, I went over to Natasha who was sitting a few feet away on the chaise lounge and fed her my cock. This soothed and relaxed me before I went back to fisting puppy to another orgasm; which came very quickly. I stood back and looked at my slave and my new sub; they were each lost in their own Disneyland.

I released puppy from the chains and sat her on the chaise lounge while the three of us talked for a few moments. Puppy had no idea what I was saying, and Natasha was blushing as I asked her some questions about the evening thus far. Enough chit-chat, I needed to be taken care of. We went back into the bedroom and I told them both to get into position. Puppy immediately got on her back with her legs spread wide open; and Natasha followed.

I started playing with puppy's pussy, opening her up with my fingers. She was in a wonderful rhythm. Then I entered her, talking and thrusting, always adjusting my rhythm to her body movements and tension. She had a few small orgasms and then a powerful one. Natasha had moved over and was caressing my back. I left puppy, then blindfolded Natasha and went to clean my dick. When I came back, puppy's eyes followed me as I went over to mount Natasha. I spat on my dick and started to spank her clit with it (I love doing that) while talking to her about fucking puppy. Did you like watching? Are you enjoying yourself? How does my dick taste? How does my dick feel? As I looked at Natasha, my ego told me she was doing well.

I entered Natasha while I was sitting straight up so I could play with and pinch her nipples. When I was ready, I started to thrust into her while guiding her, talking to her, and telling her I needed her cum all over my dick. I took the blindfold off by her third climax and allowed her to have a few more powerful full-body cums. Then I moved off of Natasha and had puppy clean my dick with her mouth. When she was finished, she laid back and I mounted her again. I told Natasha to move over and play with my balls as I was thrusting into puppy, who came quickly a few times. Then I had puppy play with my nipples.

My nipples are my erotic zone; I need them played with rough and hard. Do that to me and I will stay hard forever until I have a deep orgasm. I have no problem fucking top or bottom, upside down, or right side up, but I will always wind up on top in the missionary position for my orgasm because I love to have my nipples played with, pulled, and twisted. I demand this and I let my partners know when they're not doing it right. If they persist in doing it wrong, I will spank them while I'm inside of them. I may pull and twist their nipples to make my point. I will have my pleasure. For me, this position gets them as involved in my orgasm as I am involved in theirs.

I worked hard for four hours to orchestrate and achieve a depth of concentration and connection, while keeping the pain, pleasure and erotic levels high, the sexual tension electric, being aware at all times of their emotional, mental and erotic states, and managing to conduct all of this into a symphony that climaxed to perfection. This was my masterpiece. I was Master of my universe.

Mon, 11 Oct 2004
Steven wrote:

Hello Natasha,

I'm happy that you enjoyed yourself. Isn't it nice to smile about good things? Would you like to get together with me again on Wednesday night? I am being selfish. I will be out of town this coming weekend and I would like to talk more about all of this with you. When we get together on Wednesday, please be prepared to tell me what you thought of that night and how you felt the next morning. What thoughts are exciting to you now, a few days later? It was lovely being with you Saturday night.

Steven

Mon, 11 Oct 2004
Natasha wrote:

Dear Steven:

Saturday was wonderful, unbelievable. I have never experienced anything like that. I do not know how to think about it except that I hope that it will continue. Next morning... I felt great, energized, happy, embarrassed. You are a great person and great lover. I will be in the lab most of the next week. I would love to meet you this Wednesday.

Yours
Natasha

Wed, 13 Oct 2004
sharon wrote:

Dear Master,

It was sooo nice to finally serve You last night... and so nice to look forward to serving You three times this week! i've been thinking about Your essay request and find it necessary to start by reverting to college term paper mode 😈...

> collar: A band, strip, or chain worn about the neck; an indication of control; a token of subservience.
> *Webster's Ninth New Collegiate Dictionary*

... i don't know how helpful that is! To me, a collar is a symbol, somewhat like a wedding ring, except it symbolizes a different kind of relationship... the control and subservience part, as above. To me, it would mean that You accept me as Your slave...find me worthy?...and it would also symbolize my commitment/devotion to serving You, my Master. It is a "mark" of Your ownership that i would feel proud and honored to wear, while at the same time humble and grateful. i assume it would also carry certain expectations that You would define.

i'm having trouble coming up with the words to describe how it made me feel when You suggested the idea, so will have to settle for "very happy." Actually, i wanted to wear Your collar almost from the time i first met You, but i'm glad it didn't happen that way because it means more now... more than just playing, more than just pretending that i am Your property. i think it would be a step towards a deeper level of trust, serving, connection... kind of like a signpost on a longer journey. In light of my emotional crisis a couple weeks ago, i think it would also make me feel more secure in knowing my place in the larger scheme of things.

i've been thinking about what You said about loving me as your slave. It really means a lot to me that You would so patiently take the time and effort to explain what is really unexplainable. i don't need or expect You to love me in any certain way. Your honesty and willingness to talk about it means much, much more to me than anything else. i've never known anyone else who even attempted to be honest about what they're thinking/feeling... most people just say whatever they think you want to hear (which is meaningless) so this is new territory for me. i trust that You will guide the way because i'm following You!

i love You.

Your slave puppy

Fri, 15 Oct 2004

sharon wrote:

Dear Master,

     i can't promise You that i can quit smoking. i can try, but i've tried many times before and haven't been able to...

Love,
Your slave puppy

Steven writes:

     I do not like smoking. If you're a non-smoker, it makes kissing unpleasant. One of the things I like to do when kissing is to gently fill up her lungs with my breath as well as suck the breath from her lungs. With smokers, that brings up smoke or something smoke-related that leaves a harsh lingering taste in my mouth.

Sun, 24 Oct 2004
sharon wrote:

Dear Master,

     Arthur found and read *The Puppy Papers*. i need to talk to You ASAP. i will call You from work.

Love,
Your slave puppy

Steven writes:

     Puppy had spent the weekend with me in North Carolina at the Together in Leather event. She flew back home on Sunday night; when she arrived home, Arthur confronted her with the book.

sharon writes:

     The weekend with Sir was wonderful. We had spent a lot of time talking and I was feeling very good about our relationship. I was still wearing a huge smile on my face when I walked through the door at home. Arthur had done a great job of cleaning the house while I was gone and he greeted me at the door when I came in. He asked how the weekend went and offered me a glass of wine. I accepted the wine and sat on the couch while he went to pour it. As he handed me the glass, he calmly said he had found the book, read it, and recognized my picture as well as some of the details of the story. He wanted to know if it was true.

I'm sure my heart stopped beating. The idea of denying everything flashed through my mind, but I couldn't do it. So in a fraction of a second, I watched my entire life crumble before my eyes. I never wanted to hurt him. He was a good husband and devoted to me. I don't know how to explain it, but I just needed something more.

Mon, 25 Oct 2004
sharon wrote:

Dear Master,

If i have to choose, i will choose You.

Love,
Your slave puppy

Steven writes:

  I can't say I was surprised. I just didn't figure she would leave the book laying around for him to find in order to signal the end of their marriage. People leave notes, receipts in their pockets, and all kinds of telltale signs, but not a 400-page book outlining every detail of your infidelity. I told puppy this was her way of letting him know their marriage was over. She denied it. I told her, "If you didn't want him to know, the book wouldn't have been within a hundred miles of your home." She did what was best; it was now out in the open. I told her I wasn't going anywhere and that we would deal with the situation. She and Arthur would be all right. It would just take a little time to get over the hurt.

Mon, 25 Oct 2004
Steven wrote:

Dear puppy,

  How are you doing? You certainly have made a decision on what the truth is in your life. I can't say I'm surprised. I am not going anywhere; I'm just a little taken aback on how it was done. A little Hollywood, wouldn't you say? How is Arthur doing with all this? There are a few things you have to do so things don't get even more messy or painful, to avoid rubbing salt in the wound. Delete all of our email correspondence and get the book out of the house.

Sir

Mon, 25 Oct 2004
sharon wrote:

Dear Master

    i just deleted all the e-mails. Have to leave for a Dr. appointment now. i will do something with the book when i get home.

Love
Ysp

Mon, 25 Oct 2004
sharon wrote:

Dear Master,

    The book is out of the house... in my car...and i will take it with me to work tomorrow.
    The doctor said there is nothing seriously wrong. He figures my hormones are screwed up & causing excess bleeding (which would also explain all the emotional stuff of late). About 10+ years ago, a Dr. told me the only thing that could control heavy, excessive and prolonged menstrual bleeding (a.k.a. menorrhagia) which does not respond to medication, was a hysterectomy, which i refused. Now they've come up with a laser procedure that can be done as an outpatient. In 40% of the cases, this procedure will stop periods altogether, and in the other 60% of cases it greatly reduces them. He gave me a hormone shot today which is supposed to start a "normal" period within 24 hrs. Then he said it's up to me if and when i want the other thing done. No periods sounds wonderful – a miracle procedure, in my opinion. i think i will have it done as soon as possible.
    i will let You know how things go later tonight on the home front.

Love,
Your slave puppy

Tue, 26 Oct 2004
Steven wrote:

Dear puppy,

    Don't leave the book in your office. You never know who will go through your desk. The procedure sounds good. How soon is soon? Any recuperation time? Let me know what is happening with your husband. A side note: If he liked the book, would he do a review of it? Smile, only joking.

Sir

Wed, 27 Oct 2004
sharon wrote:

Dear Master,

      Thank You for last night. Your patience and understanding are enormously appreciated. i felt much more sane & happy on the way home... like a weight had been lifted. Please let Natasha know what the crying was about and that it had nothing to do with her. It had to have made her feel uncomfortable, so please tell her i'm sorry. You may also tell her i think she looks very good in a collar. In fact, i think You are very good for her... her whole appearance seemed to be transformed since the last time i saw her.

      Arthur was fine when i got home last night. He came out to the living room to talk for a few minutes... asked me how my day was, which is the first time i remember him asking that question. i told him about a couple things that happened at work and then he went to bed. i had always led him to believe i was working on the nights i was with You and for the time being, i think he wants to continue that charade. As i said before, i think he is only able to comprehend reality in small doses at a time.

      i do think it's important for me to continue as before so he understands that none of this is going to change what i'm doing... so he doesn't get the false idea that things are going to work out. i don't think it's going to take very long, but i think it's better to give him a little time to come to terms with everything than to shove it down his throat... at least any more than it already has been. i don't hate him, and i don't want to hurt him. It's just that he needs to understand & accept that it's over and he needs to be able to move on with his life.

      my thoughts seem to be more clear today, so maybe i'll try to explain things better to him tonight... depending on his frame of mind. i'll let You know how it goes.

i love You.

Your slave puppy

Steven writes:

Now that everything was out in the open, puppy felt terrible, but she made the decision that she wasn't going to change her routine and give a false impression that their marriage could work when it hadn't worked for years.

Wed, 27 Oct 2004
Natasha wrote:

Dear Steven,

It was a wonderful evening yesterday. I enjoyed every moment of it. I hope Sharon will be okay, she was upset. Sorry I forgot to bring the book you gave me. I read it. I will bring it back next time.

Yours,
Natasha

Steven writes:

The second time we all got together, I started the evening the same way as I did the first time. I wanted familiarity and voyeurism for Natasha before I changed the program. When puppy came over that night, she greeted me; I embraced her; and then I had her sit down on the floor while we talked. I wanted to make sure she was all right; it had been a tough couple of days. She smiled and said she was looking forward to the evening.

I led her up to my bedroom and told her to remove her clothes and lay on the bed while I put on some music. I fastened wrist restraints on her and then chained the restraints to the hooks in the floor on both sides of the bed near the headboard. I bent her knees, spread her legs wide, bound her thighs with rope, and then attached the rope to another set of hooks in the floor near the headboard. Puppy was on her back with her arms outstretched, legs securely up, and her pussy wide open. Then I blindfolded her and left her there to contemplate the navel of a flea while I went to get Natasha, who was waiting outside.

When I saw Natasha, I told her to take off her coat and leave it in the shipping room. I went up the stairs. When she came back from the shipping room, I told her to crawl up the stairs to me. When she reached me, I had her open my pants, take out my cock, and put it in her mouth. She was now mine.

After a few minutes, I told her to put my dick back into my pants and we went up to the bedroom where puppy was lying on her back, naked and bound, legs up and spread wide, ready to be entered. Natasha couldn't keep her eyes off of puppy. I told Natasha to take off her clothes and kneel down to greet me. After she offered me her body and mind, I then had Natasha lie down next to puppy on the bed. I blindfolded her and tightly tied her to the bed. She could clearly hear everything that I would be doing to puppy, but couldn't see it.

I brought out candles and massage oil and after lighting the candles, I rubbed oil on the bodies of both women (to make it easier to remove the wax). Then I started to drip hot wax on their bodies, their inner thighs, bellies, breasts, shoulders, and necks, stopping every so often to run the pointed tip of my knife over their bodies, from their chins down to their inner thighs. I used the point or side of the blade on their clits, causing them to nervously hold their breath and stiffen their bodies. I love to generate the twinge of fear and tension in them; it is empowering to me and terrifyingly erotic to them. I spent the next half hour removing the wax with my knife, which is a different sensation and very relaxing.

After toweling both women down, I had puppy get on all fours for a fisting. She was delighted, devoured my hand, and had a nice cum. Then I had her get into the missionary position while I untied Natasha. I had Natasha put on a latex glove and told her I was going to guide her in fisting puppy. Natasha was very surprised by my request, but she put on the glove and oiled up. I fisted puppy first. When I came out, I guided and worked Natasha's hand into puppy's pussy. First mine; then hers. I repeated this rhythm for a while and she did just fine. I let her fist fuck puppy for a little while, then I had her come out and I went in. Puppy was gushing.

Fisting is not only sexually fascinating, but it is also empowering to the fister. To the person being fisted, it's both spiritually and physically erotic. Most women are not concerned about a really long dick, but width is important. The length from your fist to your wrist is about 5-8 inches, and the diameter at the fist's widest point is about 3-5 inches, entering the mouth of the cunt. Inside puppy's cunt, my hand gradually forms into a fist, giving her the full feeling that she loves. When fisting puppy, I follow her rhythm and movements, making sure my thumb knuckle massages her G-spot, located on the inside above her clit. It is soft, gets spongy, fills with cum, and then when puppy has a powerful orgasm, she squirts. I may also masturbate or spank her clit with my free hand.

When I was finished, I untied puppy and we all went into the living room for some puppy play. Puppy went first so Natasha could see what was expected of her, and then Natasha followed. I felt and saw the connection with Natasha after our first scene, so I knew she would go along with my program. After puppy demonstrated how to crawl and pick up the flowers with her teeth, she sat down and I called Natasha over. I told Natasha to get down on all fours, and she responded without hesitancy. I held her head on my thigh, thanked her, and told her she was my good girl. When I asked her if she was okay, she said "yes," so I played with her for a short time. When finished, I told her to bark for me, which she did with enthusiasm. Natasha crawled over to the chaise and climbed up on it. At this point, everyone was deeply involved mentally, physically, and emotionally in the scene.

I then led puppy to the chains hanging from the exposed ceiling beams and attached her wrist restraints to them. (These are different chains than those on the wooden post.) A few feet away from where these chains hang is a 10-by-4-foot ornate mirror with a gold-gilded frame. puppy can view herself in the mirror and see what I am doing to her. I started flogging and spanking her, stopping at various times to have Natasha come over and suck on my cock for a few moments, which puppy could view in the mirror.

I played with puppy for half an hour before I took her down and brought her over to the chaise. Puppy had gone into her other world (subspace), so I took Natasha, whose eyes never left me, over to the chains and attached her to them. I used three floggers on her. The first was a kangaroo flogger, which is like paper and tickles the flesh. I swung it hard, wanting to make a loud noise, hitting her without hurting. The noise of the lashes would put her in another place. Then I switched to a lamb flogger that massages the surface of the skin and muscles, and then a deer flogger, which goes a bit deeper and leaves a woman withering, if for no other reason than that her imagination has gone wild. I am not altogether gentle with a flogger; I use a baseball swing that I like to think resembles Babe Ruth. A little later I switched to a singetail, and then kept alternating sensations for the next 20 minutes.

Natasha reacted gracefully to the singletail. I got more of a reaction with the flogging, but had her jumping and squirming from twisting her nipples, and had her screaming out loud from the spanking. Spanking was the most painful to her. It didn't take much to get Natasha to scream; she is very different than puppy.

We were new to each other, but Natasha had given me total control over her mind and body. I had to pay more attention, be more aware of what I was doing and where she was going. She was allowing me to push her little by little, and I wanted her to want more. I stayed connected with her by telling her how much she was pleasing me and how beautiful she looked, alternating different levels of pain sensations with the pleasures of pussy play, and always connecting with a firm voice.

I never forgot puppy when I was playing with Natasha. I never forgot Natasha when I was playing with puppy. At that point the energy was kinetic; the power was overwhelming; I was OZ.

Puppy had seemed to be doing fine, but now as I looked over, I saw her quietly crying. I stopped, went over to her and held her. She said she was doing fine and that it was just a needed release from all of the recent tension. I went back to Natasha and put a blindfold on her so she would not be aware that puppy was crying. I had puppy kneel by my side as I continued to play with Natasha. Every so often puppy took my dick in her mouth, looked up at me, and smiled.

After a while, I stopped and guided a blindfolded Natasha into the bedroom where I wanted to finish the play. Puppy got a wet towel and washed my cock, and then I fed Natasha. At this point, she was in another world. I needed to fuck them both and kept alternating from one to the other every few minutes, always cleaning off my dick in between the two. Natasha barked loudly when I told her to speak to me, and she had her most violent climax after watching me take puppy's ass.

When I finished, we all laid on the bed for a while, quietly talking. When I asked Natasha how she was doing, she responded, "I'm speechless," and "It was wonderful." I smiled; I was pleased with myself; and I was hungry, so we all got dressed and went out for a late dinner.

At the restaurant, we talked about the evening and about ourselves. Well, Natasha did most of the talking. Puppy was quiet and attentive as usual, and every so often she entered the conversation. I asked Natasha again how she felt about the evening. She said she had never experienced anything like this before and never imagined herself doing this. I asked her what she liked. She said she liked it all, but then stated that she never thought of herself as submissive. She didn't understand it, but she liked the feeling when she was with me. She found it very erotically stimulating to be bound and to be told what to do. It made her nervous to be punished and she didn't know why she liked it. She said it was much more intense than making love. I reminded her that she was making love, my way. She liked to be made to crawl, fetch the flowers, and bark. It was humiliating and exciting to her.

Another thing she really enjoyed was watching puppy. Natasha couldn't believe how sexual puppy was and how she was able to get so deeply involved within herself.

I asked her if she realized how much trust she also had in me, how much power she had also given over to me. She said she didn't believe it either, that she never thought about it, but she just knew it was right. She was excited and wanted me to take control. She was blushing and answered my questions with a nervous laughter. Puppy was smiling.

I learned that Natasha liked the singletail, enjoyed the flogging, did not like spankings, and loved watching puppy and I. She enjoyed being bound, being told what to do in the bedroom, liked being dominated sexually, and enjoyed mild humiliation, such as crawling, puppy play, being told to get into position on her back with legs spread and waiting, her submissive greeting to me when we first meet, standing naked and blindfolded in the middle of a room, barking for me in play and in sex, having her hair pulled, and being asked sexual questions during sex. The list goes on. She had never given such control of herself to anyone, and this was something she wanted to explore further.

I normally play one-on-one. I have played with two and three women (bottoms/subs) at a time in the past, but not often. Pairing up people who are compatible, who play sexually, and who like this kind of scene is not easy. A good scene is hard work and will last three to five hours. People have fantasies about rough sexuality and group play, but often have a difficult time handling the reality of it. I am excellent at my craft, may it be with one or more people. I feel there aren't many others who are as good as I am - that's my ego talking, the adrenalin that comes from control.

I love the work when it goes well; it puts me in such a controlling trance (Topspace). When it doesn't go well, I work my ass off around the rough spots to bring the scene to a satisfying conclusion. I have learned to keep tempo and involvement and to play to the bottoms'/subs' strengths. If there is more than one submissive, I understand the part that each one will have in the scene. I have also found that the older I get, the better I am at BDSM play because of experience and an increasing ability to plan, connect, understand, communicate, orchestrate, and direct.

Thu, 28 Oct 2004
sharon wrote:
Dear Master,

i think the brochure said 3-7 days before you can resume "normal sexual activities," but it would be worth it if it solved the whole problem... much better than 6-8 weeks to recover after regular surgery! It can be done as soon as they get the pap smear results back, which should be any day. i will just have to call them & they should be able to schedule it within a couple days. i'm thinking the sooner the better because it's really a huge annoyance.

Actually, Arthur said i should make a fortune off the book. When i finally relented & told him what i was paid, he said i should see a lawyer to have the contract nullified because i was taken advantage of... but don't worry, that's not going to happen. He said the book is extremely erotic and every man's fantasy, extremely well written, and that no one will be able to put it down once they start reading it. He also said he thinks i should keep writing that kind of thing... only not make it so personal/real. i actually think he would write a review, but i'm certainly never going to ask him!

He is being civilized tonight. He moved all of his stuff into the downstairs bedroom. He doesn't want to do anything until after the holidays because the kids will be home for Thanksgiving and we already have the plans & plane tickets to Florida for Christmas... won't that be fun☺. He is adamant that he doesn't want this to interfere with what the kids are doing. He wants to try working things out, but i am just not interested. i don't think we'll make it that long. From his perspective, i don't know how he can stand to look at me, but he really has nowhere else to go and neither do i. i will probably wait a few days and then try talking to a lawyer for advice... or maybe You can advise me on some things since i have no clue how to proceed with this.

Thank You for all Your words of wisdom this morning. It was a huge help.

i love You.

Your slave puppy

Thu, 28 Oct 2004
sharon wrote:

Dear Master,

i miss You. Are You sure You don't want me to serve You tonight?

Our hospice chaplain just came in to see me... said the holy spirit told him i needed a blessing today. Is that creepy or what? Maybe the good karma will start from this moment on! i am now blessed!!!

Love,
Your slave puppy

Thu, 28 Oct 2004
Steven wrote:

Hello puppy,

Glad all went well when you got home. The emotional upheaval and the uncertainty in the beginning is difficult, but things will work out fine. Here is a note from Natasha asking if you're all right. It must have been very strange for her in the middle of all the SM and sexual activity to see you crying. I'll see you tonight.

Sir

Thu, 28 Oct 2004
sharon wrote:

Dear Master

Yes, she is politely asking about it. Please tell her as much or as little as You want. She read the book, so i'm sure she will grasp the significance of what you will be telling her... i'll be there, but may be a little later than normal. We're kicking off a new program tomorrow & trying to finish up on the last minute details.

See You soon!

Love,
Your slave puppy

Steven writes:

When I spoke with Natasha and told her about puppy's situation at home (her husband finding and reading the book), I said, "I really think he gets the whole picture. He may not quite understand it, but he gets it." Natasha looked at me with disbelief and said with her usual off beat humor, "Are you sure?"

I asked puppy what her thoughts were about Natasha and the time we all spent together.

Fri, 29 Oct 2004
sharon wrote:

Dear Master

    Do You suppose there is actually a logical thought somewhere in the tangled up mess that used to be my brain?
    i haven't thought much about Natasha. She seems nice enough, pleasant... not manipulative or jealous. Her manner of speaking is kind of amusing. i don't feel any sort of connection with her, but it's probably better that way, for now anyway. i certainly don't need any more drama in my life right now. i guess i don't have any feelings one way or the other about her being there. i don't think she comprehends what kind of world she has entered into. She is experimenting and looking for romance and fun... taking a "walk on the wild side." You are making her very happy and there's nothing in the world wrong with that.
    i am so weary of thinking about relationship issues. Arthur's only concern seems to be that i'm going to take his money or go on a spending spree or something. He went through the checkbook, bank statements and bills last night for the first time in his life. Then he went up to the bank today to check the balances in the accounts. i feel like telling him to take all his precious money & assets and shove them up his ass. He definitely has an agenda & i suspect he has already talked to a lawyer. i guess i better call that lawyer in the morning. This is all getting quite depressing.

i miss You.

Love,
Your slave puppy

Sat, 30 Oct 2004
sharon wrote:

Dear Master,

    Thank You for last night. You always make me feel so much better. i guess i have a tendency to avoid reality... and obviously You are not going to let me do that. Now, as if i didn't already have an over-abundance of drama in my life, i got the results of my pap smear today and it was abnormal, so i have to go in next Friday for another biopsy. The report did not sound like it's cancer, but they can't do the other procedure until they get the results back from the biopsy, which will take about 10 days for a total of 17 days... very frustrating. i don't have the patience to be a patient. Also, my father got the results back from his biopsy. There is no evidence of prostate cancer, so that's a good thing.

Arthur was fine when i got home last night. He asked me how my day went & asked if he could move back in to the bedroom with me. i think he is farther out of touch with reality than i am. i guess we have spent the past 26+ years avoiding reality and it has become a habit. i think he would actually like to pretend like nothing happened and to go back to the way we were... living separate lives under the same roof. That's what has me so confused. i feel like he ought to be really angry with me, but instead, i think he would be agreeable to anything i want to do as long as it doesn't disrupt his life. It has me kind of stuck... like it would be easier to wait until a more convenient time, like after i get my physical issues fixed and after the holidays. Am i being stupid?

The whole facade has already been going on so long, would it really make any difference to wait a couple months if he's going to be civilized about things? Now that i'm thinking about it though, the whole thing would probably get me depressed, so it's better to just get it over with. It's hard to decide what to do while at the same time worrying about my health though. You were making perfect sense last night... maybe i just need a daily dose of reality.

Do You remember when i talked before about being on a path leading nowhere and that it was time to change paths? It sounds so simple to say, but it wasn't an easy thing to do then either... guess i just have to make the leap. After all, it turned out very well the last time since that's when i met You... and it would be soooo pleasurable to taste Your cock every day...

i love You.

Your slave puppy

Sat, 30 Oct 2004
Steven wrote:

Dear puppy,

    I do believe that in the next few months, life will continue as before, but with less stress than prior to Arthur reading the book. His reaction is normal. You have both lived in your own worlds, separate and apart, but still had routines together. Even though there wasn't a lot there as relationships go, you could still count on the familiarity and comfortableness of what you both established as a marriage. That's gone now, and that's what he's reacting to.

As far as a lawyer, I suggest someone who won't start a "War of the Roses," which would be stupid. The only reason people fight is to hurt each other or to get as much money as they can. The divorce becomes their entire existence. These people need a life. The only ones who benefit from the fighting are the lawyers, and there are lawyers who will create a war to run up their fees. Your money is best staying with you and Arthur, so get an attorney who will work with you both, who will look after both of your interests, not just their own interests. This may not be easy to do.

Right now it is best that you don't think about anything else until you get the results back from the doctor and you are well physically. See you on Tues. BRING THE BOOK WITH YOU.

Sir

Sun, 31 Oct 2004
sharon wrote:

Dear Master,

In response to Your question, T-I-L (Together in Leather) was smaller than i thought it would be... though there did seem to be quite a few people at the contest. i think the people there were more real than the ones in Indy. It seemed to be more of a lifestyle for them rather than just playing. They seemed to be more interested in every day life and relationships rather than specific technical skills. Some of the people seemed very experienced and others seemed quite new to it all.

It was kind of different sitting there selling books. i'm used to sitting at tables like that at health fairs & professional conferences, but i didn't feel very comfortable promoting a book that i wrote myself, although i was starting to get used to the idea by the end of the weekend. A lot of people thought the book was about puppy play. It hadn't occurred to me that the title would be misleading. i thought the one guy there, who is apparently a 24-hour puppy, was kind of weird. The "puppy" seemed really into it, but you'd think the master would get bored with it after a very short time. i think i'd have to question the mental status of someone so totally into being a puppy all the time... but what do i know. It seems to work for them.

There seemed to be quite a few poly relationships there...Masters with multiple slaves. i'm not sure what to think about them... i guess each group had it's own style. The first class i went to was a group of 3 slaves and their master. The thing i remember about the class was that they talked about each person in the group having a unique role to play, and if the roles were not clearly defined and separated, the whole thing would fall apart. There was also a formal ranking of the three, based on how long they had been part of the group. my mind is kind of foggy about what else they talked about, but it was an interesting class and well presented.

    The second class was presented by a woman with the last name of Dee. She was excellent. i think her presentation went over most people's heads, but she spoke in terms i could understand better than the other presenters... a familiar language and terms i guess. She has a background in health care. i'm glad You saved her handout because i'd like to look at it again.

    The class by Mr. McGeorge was good... but it seemed rather impersonal...like he treated his slaves like employees...very business-like. Now that i'm thinking about it, none of the people talking about poly-relationships talked much, if any, about the sexual aspect of the relationships. It was more like living in a commune with each person having their own job to do... not so different than a normal family, or at least any group of adults living under the same roof.

    i think that's why i liked the second class better. She talked about defining an individual relationship between a Master and slave within the context of a larger group. Her approach to things just made more sense to me... like it would end up in a more satisfying arrangement for all.

    i thoroughly enjoyed spending time with Jack and Patrick. Their relationship works very well. They are both interesting people & a lot of fun. i also think there is much i could learn from Patrick. He seems to know just what to do in every situation.

    Thank You for listening last night. Everything was spinning in circles in my head and i didn't know what to do. i guess i got scared and i panicked and wanted to run away from it all. Thank You for not letting me do something stupid.

Love,
Your slave puppy

Steven writes:

    This letter refers to the weekend that Arthur read *The Puppy Papers* and confronted puppy when she arrived home on Sunday night. We had gone to an event in North Carolina on October 22-24, 2004, called

"Together in Leather" (T.I.L.) with Jack and Patrick. Jack Rinella is an author and writes a column in *Gay Chicago Magazine* called "Leatherviews." Patrick is Jack's slave and he also works for me and is my partner in Kinkybooks.com. The event is put together by slavette and her Master/husband Scott; and it is for people more involved in the relationship aspect of the BDSM lifestyle. Patrick and I went there to vend for Kinkybooks. Jack gave two workshops and did a book-signing at our booth. Puppy went as an author to sign her book and to attend a few classes.

Wed, 3 Nov 2004
sharon wrote:

Dear Master,

     i just want to thank You for last night... it seems like it had been forever since i felt You inside of me... You felt soooooooooooo good. Thank You.

i hope You have a wonderful day!!!

Love,
Your slave puppy

Thu, 4 Nov 2004
Steven wrote:

Dear puppy,

     Are you all right? You seem to be out of sorts. I'm going to make an easy night of it. See you tonight.

Sir

Thu, 4 Nov 2004
sharon wrote:

Dear Master,

     Yes Sir, i'm fine (ruff, ruff 😊). Have been quite busy at work and i just have a minute between meetings right now. Happy to have You back home. i am looking forward to serving You tonight. See You soon!

Love,
Your slave puppy

Thu, 4 Nov 2004
Steven wrote:

Dear puppy

Sir
      Thanks for the bark. Now I know you're OK.

Fri, 5 Nov 2004
sharon wrote:

Dear Master,

      In case You're interested, Arthur has purchased *The Puppy Papers* from 3 local bookstores and is keeping them in a safe deposit box for "evidence." The bookstores apparently just order them from Amazon.

Your slave puppy

Sat, 6 Nov 2004
sharon wrote:

Dear Master,

      i was knocked a little off-balance with the news flash yesterday & think i forgot to tell You that the surgery is tentatively scheduled for the 19th of November, pending the results of the biopsy, of course. Since i am now 45, i'll have to have an EKG beforehand. If i had done this before my birthday a couple weeks ago, i could have skipped the EKG part. Apparently, a person's body totally falls apart the day they turn 45 ☺. It must be time to start all those healthy habits that "old" people take up... exercising, eating right, quitting smoking, et al... sounds borrrring.

      i got into an argument with Arthur last night and made him put $10K back into the checking account. He then asked me if i was a sex addict; and he's been on a drinking binge ever since. This whole thing is getting sooooooooooooooo depressing, but i'm trying very hard to remain civilized until after the surgery & Thanksgiving since both kids will be home for the holiday, and i would rather not have to explain everything to the entire family right now.

      Arthur has been making a point of not being here more than a few minutes when i'm here, so it's looking like there isn't going to be any discussion of property. Anyway, he's been speaking to his friends at work and they've been telling him all kinds of outrageous stories, so he's running in circles trying to hide everything, opening accounts with other addresses, racing to get the mail before i do, etc, etc. i went out in the garage to get something tonight and he came running after me... i guess he thought i was going to look in his car and find out his "secrets." Sheesh... gives me a headache. Well, i hope You're enjoying the weekend.

i miss You.

Love,
Ysp

Sun, 7 Nov 2004
Steven wrote:

Dear puppy,

You've had a full weekend. Where do I start?

The puppy papers: Amazon still has copies and so does a distributor. The book is out there, but I doubt that local bookstores in your area would order it. I can't get the few bookstores who would carry it in Chicago to order it. As far as you being a sex addict, I don't think so. Arthur being an alcoholic, which he does not want to acknowledge, is a problem. His drinking and emotional bullshit is going to cause you unbearable stress and the longer you wait to see an attorney, the more problems you are going to have. I will say no more on the matter.

When will you be getting the biopsy results back? If you're thinking about getting healthy you must be sick. Again delete all messages. You do not need any more problems.

Sir

Sun, 7 Nov 2004
sharon wrote:

Dear Master,

i was going to send You a welcome home message before You got back, but You "beat" me! my parents dropped by unexpectedly this evening and just left a few minutes ago, so this is my first chance to write. i hope You had a fun and relaxing weekend.

Arthur showed me the receipts for the books. He said he just went in the stores, asked for the book, and they looked it up on the computer and ordered it right then... i am assuming from Amazon, but he doesn't know that.

The biopsy results should be back by Friday. i'm not too worried about the biopsy at this point though, since the doc said it didn't look bad clinically.

And no, i am not sick. It's just that a month ago i wouldn't have needed an EKG before the surgery... like the risk of a heart attack suddenly multiplies on the day of your 45th birthday? Things like that just annoy me.

The whole marriage/divorce/lawyers/sex addiction, etc. etc. issue... i am procrastinating because of the health issues on the table right now. i know it's stupid not to have already talked to a lawyer, but i know that the whole thing is going to blow up in my face when i do, and even if it costs me, i'm hoping to limp along until after the surgery because i really, really, really don't want anything else to interfere with getting that done ASAP. Please feel free to continue lecturing me about it though because i do tend to have an unrealistically optimistic outlook on things like that... need to be frequently reminded that not everyone shares that optimism.

i have been missing You tremendously while You were gone.

Love & kisses,
Your slave puppy

Sun, 7 Nov 2004
Steven wrote:

Dear puppy,

I enjoyed myself at Black Rose, but I'm happy to be back home. Important – going to an attorney means you will be starting the process; so you will have protection. Remember puppy, by the time you find an attorney you like, hire him, and get him the information to file, weeks can go by, so do it tomorrow. The dust will settle in a little while. Right now, Arthur's blowing hot and cold; he has to work through it and so do you.

Well, from what you've told me I guess your husband is the biggest buyer of the book. I gave away 15, sold 19 to Amazon, sold 19 at N.C., and have 1100 to go. It looks like the big time. See you Tuesday.

Sir

Steven writes:

I had gone to Black Rose in Maryland that weekend. It is one of the larger lifestyle events in the U.S. I went to hear certain people speak and to look over the vendor area. Patrick and I wanted to vend there for Kinkybooks, but for some reason things had gotten screwed up in their acceptance committee, so we didn't get in. To keep myself busy at night, I volunteered as a DM (Dungeon Monitor). I think this is the last year I'm going alone.

Mon, 8 Nov 2004
sharon wrote:

Dear Master,

Yes, (laughing) it had already occurred to me that he is Your best customer!

Love,
Your slave puppy

Mon, 8 Nov 2004
Steven wrote:

Dear puppy,

I have to tell you the consequences of delaying. This is very real and it does affect others. Delaying is not an option. You are going to put me at risk. Your husband is going to dwell on it. By the time you call, make an appointment, see the attorney and he files the divorce papers, four to five weeks will have passed. If you wait until December, it will happen in January or maybe February.

If your husband decides to blab about the book to family, it will be embarrassing at first. Rest assured it will happen, and you and I will just have to live with it. But do not wait around stupidly unless you are going to reconcile with him.

Sir

Mon, 8 Nov 2004
sharon wrote:

Dear Master,

Okay. i have just talked to two law firms. One lawyer was a man who thinks everything has to be done immediately – filing, injunctions, etc. etc... i have no idea what he was talking about and he's very expensive. The other was a woman, who told me to relax, that my rights would be protected, and she would explain everything to me...and she is about 1/3 of the cost. She seems to be much nicer, though i don't know if that's a good thing for a divorce lawyer. However, i need someone to explain things to me and not get all hyper about it. So i have an appointment with her at 5:00 this evening.

And i feel much better now!!

Love,
Your slave puppy

Mon, 8 Nov 2004
Steven wrote:
Dear puppy,

Have you met with the attorney? What happened?

Sir

Mon, 8 Nov 2004
sharon wrote:
Dear Master,

You are the sunshine in my life.

It is a husband and wife team. i met with the husband who is also very nice. i can't remember everything he said, but he gave me lots of reading material. All i know is if i shed one more tear over this whole damn thing i may have to shoot myself. Ridiculous! i hate emotional women.

Basically, he said there is no rush because everything Arthur "dissipates" will come back out of his half of the settlement...i.e., when the house is sold. He said that Arthur can't be forced to move out of the house unless there is physical abuse. He thinks i should move out to preserve my emotional health. He thinks i am too worried about the small stuff... little things like money, assets, property, etc. He doesn't think maintenance is involved, but if it is, i would be the one paying it... this year, for the first time ever, i will make more than Arthur. Isn't that a kick in the tush! Anyway, for a no-fault divorce and because there are no minor children involved, we have to be separated for at least 6 months (can live in the same house, but without sexual relations). If I was in no rush, it would take a year to be done with it. Or i can file on the grounds of mental cruelty and if he doesn't contest anything, it could be done in 2 weeks. However, if he should dissipate assets, it is basically the same thing as contesting. If he contests either the fault or no-fault, it could take 2 years.

    The lawyer thinks i should wait until after the surgery to file. He said the divorce should be straightforward and that my health is more important... too many stresses at the same time. i told him about the book, but he didn't seem too interested in it. He said stuff like that hardly even matters when it comes to custody of children... though i just told him it was an erotic book, nothing else.

    i probably have the above info all confused, but will read all the stuff he gave me. When he found out that Arthur had an alcohol problem, he described the whole marriage from start to finish, and he was pretty much on-target. He pointed out all the ways an alcoholic manipulates people....it was like he'd known Arthur all his life. He's been manipulating me even when i thought i had everything under control. i guess i've been deceiving myself professing to be emotionally detached from the situation.

    Sooooo... i don't know if i'm any better off than before... but i guess it's at least a step in the right direction.

Love,
Your slave puppy

Tue, 9 Nov 2004
Steven wrote:

Dear puppy,

    Congratulations. You are, by far, much better off. They are absolutely right--this is a simple, uncomplicated, straightforward divorce. These people sound good. Are you going to use them? If so, you will have a protector. Six months will go by very quickly for no fault, so figure out when you last had sex with him.

    Alcoholism is that pink elephant in the middle of the room that nobody wants to see. It was good they told you that. When I first met you and you told me about his problem, I told you he was in control. I lived with it with my son, except I didn't tolerate it. I got him into rehab and then I went to weekly meetings for 2 years to learn about addictions. You're doing good.

Sir

Mon, 8 Nov 2004
sharon wrote:

Dear Master,

From what i am reading here (with eyes now crossed), everything depends on his cooperation. If he is not completely cooperative, it will take at least 2 years, and drive us both into bankruptcy. Which brings me back to where i started... trying to keep him from going psycho. It seems to me i could give him everything or i could give the lawyer everything, with neither being an appealing option. It all gives me a headache... seems like a no-win situation... depressing. After all these years, i had finally gotten to the point where i didn't have to watch the pennies and now i'll have to start all over. Not sure if i'm up to it...

i have absolutely no idea when i last had sex with him... could have been weeks or months ago... not a very memorable event i guess. Going to bed now... very tired.

Love,
Your slave puppy

Wed, 10 Nov 2004
sharon wrote:

Dear Master,

i hope You had a good day and didn't have to spend Your whole day waiting in the doctor's office. my day was much better, thanks to You. i don't know how my thinking keeps getting so befuddled... i feel like i'm on a roller coaster. Maybe i need to start calling You for a pep talk every time the bottom falls out. You are very patient with me. Thank You.

i've been thinking all day about Your question regarding what i expect (want? plan?) to happen in the future (i don't remember exactly how You said it). For some reason, i can't think about the future. It's almost like it would jinx everything. So much depends on what happens in the next few weeks. i'm just trying to take one day at a time. i would love to be Your full-time slave with collar & branding and everything else You talked about, but it's like if i think about it too much, i'll wake up and find out it's only a dream; and if it is only a dream, i don't want to wake up. Does that make any sense? It doesn't seem possible that it could really happen in real life. i've been here for so long wishing i was somewhere else that i think i've lost track of what's real and what is a dream.

i am looking forward to serving You tomorrow.

i love You.
See You soon!

Your slave puppy

Fri, 12 Nov 2004
sharon wrote:

Dear Master,

    Good morning Sir! i just thought i'd let You know i got the biopsy results this morning. It showed "dysphasia" which is not cancer, but cells that will turn into cancer within the next 10 years. So, they want to do a procedure called "cryotherapy" which freezes (kills) the cells of the cervix. So i can go ahead with the other surgery next Friday and then i have this cryotherapy scheduled for December 10. Sounds like an awful lot of cell-killing going on, but still better than having major surgery.

    Now that i'm thinking about it, I don't know why they can't do both at the same time... hmmm, will have to call them back to find out. Anyway, i guess it's good news...just seems like things are being dragged out for a long time. i have to get the EKG tomorrow morning at 7:00, so i might be needing a nap by the time i get to Your house. ☺

Have a wonderful day!

Love,
Your slave puppy

Fri, 12 Nov 2004
Steven wrote:

Hello puppy,

    Just an aging thing. Your worst fears are over.

Sir

Fri, 12 Nov 2004

sharon wrote:

Dear Master,

Yes, i was thinking this afternoon that this must be my 100,000 mile tune-up... then i should be good to go for another 45 years! i hope You had a better day today...not feeling so blue. The sunshine helps a lot, and it's supposed to be a beautifully sunny weekend... and You will have TWO submissive women wanting to fulfill Your every desire. What more could a Master want! i know that being able to serve You tomorrow will make my weekend much brighter! It will be so nice when i can be Your full-time slave...
  i miss You already and it hasn't even been 24 hours.

Love,
Your slave puppy

Sun, 14 Nov 2004
sharon wrote:

Dear Master,

Are You out enjoying the sunshine or sitting in front of Your computer? i'm wondering when i will get to read Your work? Will i get a "sneak preview" or will i have to buy a copy from Amazon?

i felt kind of uncomfortable last night. Natasha was lying there so still, i thought she was upset about something. How can You tell whether she's okay or not? i am being distracted worrying about her... don't know what kind of head space she's in. It seems like she comes & goes unexpectedly... makes me kind of nervous. In the end, she always seems good with everything, but how can You tell during the middle of things where she's at?

The bondage... like i said, i didn't like being tied to the post... it was extremely uncomfortable, but i figured i deserved it for being such a slothful slave, or i would have done some whining. You would have sympathy for a whining slave, wouldn't You? ☺ One thing about bondage though, i am always very eager to show my appreciation for being let loose!

Last night wasn't nearly as uncomfortable but i couldn't seem to relax. It's kind of a strange response, but what i really wanted to do was pound my head hard against the back of the chair... not sure what that means. It just seemed like it would feel good... would somehow relieve some stress. i was wishing You would come over and let me suck on Your cock... i didn't get much opportunity for that last night 😩...and i was soooo hungry. Come to think of it, i should have offered to help You relieve Yourself before we went out. Why can't i think of these things at the right time!!!!!!!!!! 😩😩😩 Such a failure as a slave. Why do You even put up with me? You ought to just tie me to that post and leave me there for a week.

i love You & will try to do better.
Your slave puppy

Sun, 14 Nov 2004
Steven wrote:

Dear puppy,

    Natasha is entering our world and she is not here to judge it. All of this is very new to her. She is trying to understand and intellectualize all of the feelings she's having. She's trying to understand where they are coming from, if they have always been there; and if they have always been there, then why has she suppressed them? Why haven't they come up before?

    Submission equals weakness, or so she thinks. It confuses her, and that's where her mind goes when she withdraws, to that questioning place. She's having a hard time balancing her wonderful erotic feelings with her submission. I do know she is getting very excited about it all. She doesn't know what to expect, what will happen to her, what will happen to you, or what she will be made to do. I can tell by her eyes, her breathing, and her stillness that she is a voyeur. Being next to us, being close enough to touch, taste and smell is beyond her wildest dreams. She's lost in it.

    But as for me, I am not getting the feedback I need and want. She is not communicating back to me what she likes and wants or why, except to say that she likes it all. I need more.

    My dear puppy, I have punished you once or twice before, but I told you what I was punishing you for. This time I did not want to tell you that you were being punished for not paying closer attention to my needs and what is expected of you. If I told you why I was punishing you, you would have persevered. I changed the rules. Under normal bondage, I would not have secured the rope around your neck to the post. I would have put it around your mouth and eyes and forehead. Another thing is happening that I was going to tell you about on Tuesday – I think I am getting into a rope bondage phase which may last for a few weeks, or maybe not.

Sir

Steven writes:

I had tied puppy to the wooden post with rope around her legs and body, and with her arms in back of her and wrapped around the beam. I also secured a rope around her neck to the post. If anything had happened, it would not have caused any damage, but you always have to be careful. I never left her alone in this type of bondage.

Sun, 14 Nov 2004
sharon wrote:

Dear Master,

(chuckle) Maybe i should work it out with Natasha for her to give me a thumb's up or something so i know she's okay. And yes, i had the same thought in the restaurant last night that she is trying to intellectualize everything. However, i think Your lifestyle would have been too much for me to comprehend in the beginning, too. Plus, it's extra difficult for her because of the language/culture thing. It would probably help a lot if You asked her specific questions and had her write out her answers... it gives a person time to sort out their thoughts and try to make sense of them. None of this fits into any neat category of experience that a person can relate to.

Also, i don't know what Your plan is, but if You want the three of us to continue, it might be helpful for her and i to get together to talk by ourselves sometime. She seems rather skittish of her own thoughts/feelings and may need to hear from another woman who's been there, done that. It may be less embarrassing to confide in another woman than in the person who is the object of her lust 😊.

After avoiding me for a week, Arthur finally decided to talk to me tonight. He asked if i was going to give up my lifestyle and i said no. Then he said he can't live like this any more and the marriage is over. He is really hurting, and i'm feeling really bad for him. He said the only thing left is to figure out the financial stuff, and it sounds like he's going to be reasonable about everything. Of course, he tried to make me feel guilty by saying he's supposed to be laid off in 3 weeks and that he's going to need knee surgery this winter. He also said he's going to stay in a hotel when the kids are home because he won't be able to face them... coward. He said i can tell them anything i want but he will never tell them the real reason. So i guess i will have to tell them by myself and just be grateful that he's not going to try to destroy my relationship with them. He also said he will take me for the surgery on Friday, but that i need to get my own insurance from work as soon as possible.

It sounds like he thinks it will only take a couple weeks to get a divorce and i wasn't going to argue with him. i figured he'd be reasonable if i backed off and let him process things, but i didn't think it would happen quite this quickly. It seemed to get the message across when i quit wearing my wedding ring.

So anyway, this is a bigger step of progress than going to see a lawyer. At least we can both agree that the marriage is over and that no one is going to try to fix it or take revenge... and i didn't even shed a tear... now that's progress!! He left to "go for a ride" and is really hurting, but i guess that's inevitable. i just wish no one had to be hurt... but i guess, in the long run, it's better to get it over with and move on.

i am scheduled for a mammogram Thursday at 5:00. If it's anything like the EKG, it could be midnight before i get out of there. So i'm wondering if i could see You on Monday & Wednesday this week instead of Tuesday & Thursday?

And... it wasn't too difficult to figure out i was being punished. Like i said before, i deserved it. i am sorry and i WILL do better in the future.

Love,
Your slave puppy

Mon, 15 Nov 2004
sharon wrote:

Dear Master,

Are You practicing some tortuous knot-tying techniques tonight? i'm thinking i will need to be verrrrrry attentive if i want to keep breathing during Your bondage phase!

i hope You had a good day and that You're making lots of progress on Your book. i am feeling really good today, like a big weight has been lifted off my back. i am starting to get (dare i say) excited about this divorce. i was thinking on the way home today about how i'm going to celebrate and decided i'm going to take ballet lessons. That probably

169

sounds ridiculous, but it's something i've always wanted to do. When i was a kid i begged my parents every day for at least 10 years to take ballet lessons and they wouldn't allow it. Of course, at this point, it may have to be geriatric ballet to start with, but it's the point of the matter that counts!

Arthur is being a real bitch today so i'm trying not to look too cheerful because me smiling really seems to irritate him... dancing around on my toes probably wouldn't cheer him up either. So anyway, as soon as it's all over with, i'm going shopping for a pink tutu & signing up for a class!

i miss You and am looking forward to serving (and tasting) You tomorrow night... feeling especially horny today and it will be a very long day tomorrow until i see You... how will i ever survive!!

Love,
Your slave puppy

Tue, 16 Nov 2004
Natasha wrote:

Dear Steven:

I had a wonderful time on Saturday night.

Yours,
Natasha

Tue, 16 Nov 2004
Steven wrote:

Hello Natasha

I am sorry I did not get back to you the other day. I am feeling very tired from this cold. There's something important I need from you and that is feedback on your thoughts and feelings. I know it is difficult since with your culture and upbringing, as you have said, you didn't openly discuss private, personal matters, but I do. If it is convenient for you, let's get together Friday night at 7:00.

Steven

Wed, 17 Nov 2004
sharon wrote:

Dear Master,

Good evening Sir! i hope You got some rest last night and are feeling better today. Though i must say You had more color in Your face by the time i left last night. Could it possibly be that You were not feeling well because You missed me? 😁

Well, Arthur and i had the big discussion tonight... and i'm still shaking. He responded pretty much as i thought he would. Said he put more into the marriage than i did so he should get more out of it... financially. He was angry about giving me half of his pension and tried to claim that most of the bills we have are mine. He tried to get me to feel sorry for him and he wants to blame me for everything. However, since he is quite the stingy guy, he agreed that paying one lawyer would be sufficient.

So the bottom line is, he agreed to split everything in half equally, but said he doesn't want any of the household stuff...but i expect he'll change his mind on that. He is supposed to inherit some land from his parents and i told him i don't want any part of that. He wants me to make a list of all the bills for his approval and he wants me to file for the divorce within the next 2 days. He wants to be done with everything by January because he is going to go to Milwaukee to work...for how long i don't know.

He also had me cancel his flight to Florida at Christmas and is really trying to make me feel guilty about that because i still intend to go. He also wants me to wear my wedding ring until the divorce is final... he said that hurt him more than anything. So anyway, he's going back & forth between being sane & being angry and i'm just trying to let the angry go over my head. At least he agrees it's over and wants to move on with his life. So i'll contact the lawyer tomorrow to see where we go from here. Right now i feel like i'm dreaming, that none of this is real.

Soooo... would You, by chance, like to go to Florida for a few days in December? Fort Lauderdale isn't too far from Your mother. i bet she would love to see You!

Also, You told me last night to write about something today and i haven't got the faintest idea what that was... could You please refresh my memory, Sir?

Love,
Your slave puppy

Fri, 19 Nov 2004

sharon wrote:

Dear Master,

i just watched an Oprah show called "Secret Sex in the Suburbs"... actually Arthur was watching it and told me to watch with him. It was quite interesting but only touched the tip of the iceberg. Anyway, i sent an e-mail to their general mail box & told them to look up *The Puppy Papers* on Amazon and, if they are interested, i would send them an autographed copy... hope that's okay with You. i really do think it's a book that they will find fascinating. However, if they want to do another show on "Secret Sex in the Suburbs," and include the book, i will let You make the appearance! i'll let You know if they respond.

Missing You greatly.

Love,
Your slave puppy

Sat, 20 Nov 2004
Steven wrote:

Dear puppy,

I know I'm nuts, but you're nuttier. You sent her show an email on *The Puppy Papers*? Someone on her staff just might read the book and say you're just another looney toon looking for 15 minutes of fame. But if it should happen, it's your show. I'll watch from the couch while eating my pineapple and grapes.

Are you feeling better? Why didn't the doctor have both instruments? Can he do the procedure again with the right instrument? You should not be charged. He should have known. Can he do it when he freezes those bad cells?

Rest up.

Sir

Sat, 20 Nov 2004
sharon wrote:

Dear Master,

Arthur has now admitted that he was unable to buy a copy of the book. They told him it was unavailable. So it would really save me a lot of grief if You would take it off of Amazon until we can get this worked out.

Of course he could be lying to me again. i don't know what to believe anymore. i feel like i'm being knocked around by his mood swings and i just want it to stop. So tired.

Love,
Your slave puppy

Sat, 20 Nov 2004
sharon wrote:

Dear Master,

    (moaning) i think i over-did it today, too soon after the surgery. my belly is all puffed out and hard. i can't seem to remember that i'm not a kid anymore... that the body doesn't necessarily keep up with the mind.

    The talk with my parents went better than i expected. my mother said she wasn't surprised, and then went on to preach at me... i.e., this is all happening because i quit going to church, etc. my father keeps everything inside, but i could tell he was upset... he took the dog for a long walk right after i told him. But they were generally supportive... so long as they don't know about the book. They wanted to blame everything on Arthur, but i just told them it's a mutual decision.

    On the other hand, Arthur wants to blame everything on me. He is totally oblivious to the idea that he had any part in this. We had a big discussion on the financial stuff tonight. Of course he was drinking beforehand, but i think we have agreed that i will get the house (equity) and in exchange, he will keep all of his pension. Arthur is also convinced that if we go to court, he would walk away with everything because i have committed adultery. The whole discussion is so tedious and must be even more tedious for You to read about, so i'll quit.

    Except one more thing, he wants me to sign something that he gets half the proceeds from the book. i told him he could have everything i made off the book... no problem there!

    Regarding the Oprah show... appearing on a show because of *The Puppy Papers* would amount to instant termination from my job, not to mention estrangement from my family... probably not a good idea. i'm sure You would do quite well speaking on my behalf. Besides, You always look so sexy when i watch You talking to someone else... must be that perfect profile of Yours. Brings to mind watching You with Natasha... such a nice view of Your whole anatomy!

i am reeeeealllly missing You. The doc says nothing in my pussy for at least a week, but i could be available tomorrow for any cocksucking duties You may require...

i love You & miss You.

Your slave puppy

Sat, 20 Nov 2004
Steven wrote:

Puppy,

What the hell is this fantasy about appearing on her show? I think you and Arthur have lost your marbles. Or is this a suburban thing? Or does it have to do with something in the suburban drinking water?

Sir

Sun, 21 Nov 2004
sharon wrote:

Dear Master,

i'm sorry about unloading everything on You, but You're the only one i can talk to about all this stuff. The nice thing about e-mail is that You don't have to read it if You don't want to.

On the other side of the roller coaster, Arthur talked to his parents today and his mother set him straight in no uncertain terms. In fact, i'm sure she'd whip his ass if he tried to take advantage of me. She, more than anyone, knows what i've been through all these years, and even though i never thought of her as an ally, i think she would take my side regardless of the circumstances. Anyway, he came home from there quite meek & cooperative and with a change in his overall attitude. He even made dinner for me and we were able to have a sane discussion regarding everyone's best interest.

The response from both sets of parents is kind of surprising to me. i thought they would be more upset, but they all just seem grateful that we stayed together until the kids were raised... like they knew long before we did that the marriage was dead and it's a relief to them too that it will be over. So hopefully things will be smoother from now on. i will talk to the lawyer tomorrow to see what the next step is. i just want You to know that Your listening and advice and patience have been invaluable to me. If it wasn't for You, i would have caved in and really screwed myself by now. Thank You.

Love,
Your slave puppy

Mon, 22 Nov 2004
Natasha wrote:

Dear Steven

It was wonderful last Friday. I felt that I belonged to you so completely – it was an amazing feeling. But please don't be disappointed it is hard for me to express myself and when I with you I shut down. What ever thoughts I have when I'm with you go into hiding when I leave you. I am looking forward to seeing you again.

Yours,
Natasha

Mon, 22 Nov 2004
Steven wrote:

Hello Natasha,

You were lovely Friday. I am enjoying the scenes, the playing, the places I'm taking you. You know I couldn't do that if you did not let me. Each time we have gotten together, you have gotten more and more relaxed. Thank you. As I said the other night, I enjoy spanking you. I get a wonderful reaction from you--you cry no matter what. It's funny to me that I can singletail you, but the spanking on your tush is most painful. Are you busy Friday night? If not, let's get together.

Steven

Steven writes:

When Natasha came over, I sent her upstairs to my bedroom. On my bed were handcuffs and a blindfold. I told told her to go over to the stereo, press play, go back to the bed, put the blindfold on, put the cuff on one wrist, put her hands behind her back, put the other cuff on the other wrist, then lay face down on the bed and wait for me.

Mon, 22 Nov 2004
Steven wrote:

Dear puppy,

      Your thinking is sound. You just have to get through the next 6 months. You're in the worst part of it now, the first 3 months. Your parents already know, so anyone who needs to know will know, which is good for you. It will be out in the open and everyone will be supportive. They all knew it was coming long before you and Arthur did. As for the kids, they will handle it a lot better than you think. They're starting their own lives and that is what is important to them. Their big question will be who will pay for their school and lifestyle now. They will not judge who is right or wrong; they love you both equally.

      Tell me what happened at the lawyer's office. Remember, you will be with me on Sunday.

See you tomorrow.

Sir

Mon, 22 Nov 2004
sharon wrote:

Dear Master,

      It has been a rather busy afternoon for having a day off, but i did get an appointment for Wednesday to see the lawyer. i also gave an interview for a local newspaper... that would be regarding hospice, not *The Puppy Papers*. I also hired a (male) nurse for the inpatient unit, which will help a lot. Also got a call that they saw several things on the mammogram, which is no big surprise, so i've been trying to get the films from Indiana sent over here so i can avoid having another biopsy, but i still have to go in for an ultrasound, etc. for that. That is all sooooooo annoying... the whole idea of not having breasts to start with and then having to mess with this stuff all the time... a real pain. Seems like it would be much easier to just remove them and get fake ones... might just bring up that idea to the doc... maybe a set of 34D's for Christmas !

      Anyway, i think You're right about the kids. Don will take it harder than Dale, but they are a good support system for each other and they'll be fine. Don is more dependent on us at the present time since he's just starting out in school. i will make sure his tuition, etc. is paid no matter what. It is just as big of a concern to me as it is to him. In fact, i will do without a lot of other things before i'd let him take out loans when he is a freshman/sophomore. That's really why i didn't have visions of getting a divorce at the present time, but such is life.

Last night, Arthur did agree to be here so we can tell them together... probably Wednesday night. i think they'll be the least surprised of anyone. i'm sure Dale will want to leave for school early Sunday afternoon and i'd like to be here when he leaves so i can get all my hugs, etc. What time is the book-signing scheduled for?

Also, i'm going to my mother's for dinner at noon on Thursday, but won't be going to the in-law's in the evening, so can be available to help You celebrate the holiday if You would like... although i might be too full to get down on my knees! Then again, a little exercise might be a good thing!

i am missing You lots.

Love,
Your slave puppy

Wed, 24 Nov 2004
Steven wrote:

Dear puppy,

This Sunday, be there at 10 am for the Fetish Market at the Purple Hotel, 4500 Touhy Avenue in Lincolnwood-- I think it's just off the Eden's. Yes, it will be all day until 6 pm. Check with mapquest, because if I give you directions you'll wind up in Iraq.

Also, can you get away in December to Boston for the Fetish Flea Market? The dates are Friday 12/17, Saturday 12/18, and Sunday 12/19. It will be another book signing. See you Sunday.

Sir

Mon, 29 Nov 2004
sharon wrote:

Dear Master,

i've been thinking about some of the things You said last night. In truth, You have been the center of my universe ever since i met You, and You know i would do anything in the world for You. But You are right... loving and serving someone is more than just words and/or feelings... and it's past time to get my head out of the clouds. (Sorry to digress, but You possess a magnetism that inexplicably sends my compass spinning in circles the minute i see You.)

Anyway, i will agree that i've been overly self-absorbed (and thus, inattentive) lately and i do apologize for that. You are the most important person in my life and i want more than anything for You to be pleased and happy, and i'm feeling really bad to think i've disappointed You...once again. i want to do so much better. i want to make You proud.

i love You

Your slave puppy

Wed, 1 Dec 2004
Steven wrote:

Dear puppy,

I need you to tell me about how you felt about the book signing last weekend, how you felt about talking to the people, and how they responded to you, etc. Also, tell me about the pussy play last night and how you feel today. I will be doing more of that. You were so very wet.

Sir

Wed, 1 Dec 2004
Sharon wrote:

Dear Master

Sir... i will definitely be thinking about You all day today!

The book signing was fun. People seemed interested in the book without me having to tell them all about it, which is a good thing because i don't feel comfortable trying to promote something about myself. It was a different kind of crowd than the one in North Carolina... more casually connected to the lifestyle and, like You said, more the kind of audience the book would appeal to.

As i'm writing this, i'm thinking about what You said last night about me being different than a year ago, and that i'm one of the more experienced people at these events. That seems so strange. i've been so focused on You that i haven't thought about anything like that. i still consider myself a novice in all aspects of the lifestyle, playing, serving, submissiveness, etc. But when i think back on where i was when i first met You... very different. i never could have imagined everything that has happened in the past year. You have made it the best and happiest year of my life.

When i think about what i was doing before i met You...it was so wrong, ignorant, frustrating, unsatisfying, disconnected. There hasn't been a day since i met You that anything hasn't felt right and good...like things are supposed to be. You are truly the definition of a Master. How did i ever get so lucky to find You? The gods must have been smiling on me that day! (laughing) It seems as though i've got my head in the clouds again. It's just that when i think about where i was and where i am now, i'm a bit overcome with gratitude and love for You.

So now that i've gotten way off the subject... Your question about the pussy play last night. First of all, i want to state that it was extreeeemely frustrating to be totally immobilized with such an excellent view of You standing over me playing with Your cock and i couldn't even come close to touching or tasting You. That was definitely torture!! And when You were fucking me while i couldn't move a muscle, that was also torture! And when You were spanking/whipping my most sensitive parts... well, i think You get the picture. i still don't know why the front of my thighs are so dang sensitive.

Anyway, the clamps on my pussy hurt too much and the longer they were on, the more they hurt. i couldn't relax. And while i was quite grateful for the word "red," You kept putting the damn things back on!! It was really more than i could handle and i felt totally out of control.

Now i really hate to admit this, but... You are quite right that it made my pussy very wet. When the clamps would come off, after the initial jolt, it felt... incredible... hot and gushing. And every time they went on & off, it got more intense... going from extreme pain to extreme pleasure and back and forth before i could catch my breath... more than the mind/body could comprehend. All i can say is that when You untied me and fucked me, it felt sooooooooooo good. And my pussy has been so sensitive all day that all i could/can think about was/is that i wish You were fucking me right now. So i can't say that i enjoyed the clamps at all, but the after-effects are delightful!

Love,
Your slave puppy

Steven writes:

A woman approached me at the Fetish Flea Market about presenting a class. I had first met her at IML (Hyatt House, May 27-30,

2004). She had come over to my booth and introduced herself, then asked if I would be interested in doing a demonstration or educational class at Galleria Domain 2. I thought about it for a moment and said I could do a fisting class, or a class on Porn History, or the legal side of sex. She said she liked the idea of a fisting class and would be getting back to me. I gave her my email address, but I never heard back from her.

In July, I received and filled out a presenter's form for people in the local area who feel they have something to offer in the form of a class and/or demonstration to the kinky community. I thought I wanted to do a class. Did I really want to present or teach something, or was it for my ego? My answer to myself: it was for my ego. I never did the class.

Wed, 1 Dec 2004
Beth wrote:
Hi Steven,

I think I remember your badge at the Fetish Market saying Steve, but Natalie from the CLC has you listed as Steven under presenters. Which do you prefer?

I just wanted to touch base about January 8th. It is a Saturday evening and the discussion would take place after our Newcomer's Social, from 6:00 pm until 7:45 pm. Our club opens at 8:00, and we must make sure that those who are not members or guests of members are not on the premises so that we can keep our private club status. You and yours would be the guests of my owner Jim and myself for the evening, so you are more than welcome to stay and play if you choose.

The topic you wanted to discuss is "Gangbang Fisting," and I think we would get a huge turnout. The discussions are free and open to the community as a whole. If there is anything I can do to make it easier on you (equipment you need to have, transportation to and from, etc) please let me know, and if this date doesn't work and you would like to choose another one, I have most of the year open except March.
Thanks!

Beth

Wed, 1 Dec 2004
Steven wrote:
Beth,

Puppy just told me that she is going in for a female procedure the third week of December, so I do not know how she will feel 2–3 weeks later. As far as what I will present, I would call it a fisting scene with some audience participation. I feel if it's called a fisting gangbang, people will expect to join in and might feel disappointed if I don't let them. We will be there on Saturday to hear Jack and to get a feel of the room.

Steven

Wed, 1 Dec 2004
Natasha wrote:

Dear Steven,

Thank you for your kind words. I only hope that you can enjoy our meetings as much as I do. It was wonderful last Friday. I feel that I belong to you so completely – it is an amazing feeling. I will be happy to meet tomorrow and Saturday.

I am looking forward to seeing you again.

Yours,
Natasha

Steven writes:

I asked Natasha out for dinner because I needed to talk to her. We were still playing "Kinky 101" and I wasn't getting what I needed – feedback. Sexually, she was coming along fine; she was getting more relaxed and I was reading her well, but I wanted a lot more from her. I needed her to open up to herself; I needed to know what she was learning about herself. At dinner, I asked her how she was doing and if she was enjoying this strange new world. She said she was very happy and excited to be with me, but it was very difficult for her to express herself. She was amazed at her submissive side. It wasn't something she would even think about exhibiting at work or with colleagues. Her schooling, work, culture, and position demanded that she always be in charge and, to her, submissiveness was a sign of weakness.

I told her it doesn't work that way. Everyone's personality is different in who they are and what their needs may be. I told her, "Don't judge yourself too harshly without learning the strengths of what you think is inferior within you. Knowledge of who you are is a strength, not a weakness. You have to understand the dynamics of yourself." I told her that she is allowing herself to be submissive to me, but outside of our relationship, her life doesn't change. She is who she is. It's the combining and accepting of both sides of herself that would bring satisfaction. Of course, I had no idea what other issues were within her, or if what we were doing conflicted with those issues because she didn't share them with me.

Let me state that Natasha never exhibited a dominant side with me. If she had, then I would have worked with her and taught her the art of switching. I would have brought in someone for her to play with as a Top while she bottomed for me.

She said she wanted to continue. I told her I was going to change the rules and take more control. She would need to submit, to spend time acknowledging and accepting who she is and what she wants. She would also address me as "Sir" or "Master" when we were together. I did this because I wanted her to bow to me both mentally and emotionally when she uttered these words. I wanted her to accept the feelings resulting from her acts of submission. I do not do this in casual play. We had been together two months and had played more than a few times. I wanted her with me only if she would go along with my program and take submitting seriously, if she would feel it, want it, and desire it. Understanding of the mindset would follow only if we were able to communicate. She was now at a place where our relationship should not be superficial.

After a light dinner, we went back to my house to play. I used a violet wand and permanent marker in a scene in which I wrote all over her body while I was spanking her; it ended with a long fucking.

Fri, 3 Dec 2004
Natasha wrote:

Dear Master:

It was a wonderful evening yesterday. I enjoyed immensely our conversation; I also loved the rest of the evening. My back aches; my chest has something written on it. It feels great. See you tomorrow night.

Thank you Master,
Natasha

Fri, 3 Dec 2004
sharon wrote:

Dear Master,

i am curious what You thought about last night.

Love,
Your slave puppy

Fri, 3 Dec 2004
Steven wrote:

Dear puppy,

    I was happy with the evening. Natasha is starting to express herself, but how long will she be able to continue this until she comes to another emotional crossroads? I have no idea. You, my Dear puppy, have committed. You make me proud to be your Master. Since my world is sexual, I enjoy playing and exploring with Natasha. I do enjoy her yelling, as I enjoy your wincing and yelling as I inflict pain. In fact, I love it. You have been getting very wet lately. Tuesday you were dripping, how delicious. I have been happy with you for a long time.

Sir

Fri, 3 Dec 2004
sharon wrote:

Dear Master,

    Natasha does seem to make You happy and that is good. As for me, it seems very strange/disturbing that i don't feel any kind of connection with her since we've all been together several times now. i am always able to find some sense of commonality with people the first time i meet them, and i meet people from all different backgrounds, cultures, and experiences on a daily basis. i have tried to reach out to Natasha in various ways and... nothing. The response is not good or bad; it is nothing at all, not even in body language. i don't remember having that experience before and i don't understand it. At the very least, it would seem that we would have a common interest in wanting to please You. It leaves me feeling... disoriented? confused? disconnected? i guess i am not grasping the *real* dynamics of this arrangement.

    You have asked her to be Your submissive, but all she said is that she wants to play. It is my perception that she is much more dominant than submissive, yet she said she wants to call You Master. The whole thing just seems very incongruent and confusing to me. i don't know how i'm supposed to relate to her or if i'm even supposed to relate to her at all. Am i supposed to try to make her feel comfortable & welcome, or am i supposed to pretend that she's not really there? i just felt rather lost last night. But then, what else is new? 😊

Love,
Your slave puppy

Fri, 3 Dec 2004
Steven wrote:

Dear puppy,

    Thanks for your feedback. The only reason she is there is for play. Play is what she was looking for in the first place, but she is getting much more. How she is processing all this, only time will tell. Will she grow? Will she set limits? Will she relax and have an epiphany? I don't know. From my vantage point of loving to play, she offers a change of thought and direction for the moment. As for her being a dominant personality, you're right, but her dominance does not deal with me. It deals with her other world. She's permitting herself to explore unkown regions within herself. Will she grow and stay? I do not know. If she doesn't grow, then her only place is in play and sex for as long as that might last. She is not a negative person, which is a plus. As far as you connecting with her, that would be good, but I am only interested in you connecting and serving me. Let's not forget this is all about me.

    As far as you being confused, this is the first time you have been in this situation. I did not ask you. I brought her in. Our one-on-one relationship has taken on another dimension. As far as you feeling distance, that could be because you're sharing when you didn't have to share me before. I kept it separate. You've closed yourself off in fear of being hurt – Don't. You are my slave and you have my commitment. You serve me; you are there for my pleasure; and my pleasure is you. Your focus is only on me. After we are finished playing, I expect you to lay next to me, suck on my dick, even if I am sleeping, or talking on the phone, or to Natasha. She is the opposite of you. You're quiet while she is talkative, not a bad thing – no one is fighting for airtime.

    Your divorce has a lot to do with your feelings – the roller coaster ride, the threats and fears, your family, the boys, not knowing where you are going to live. These are not stable times; they're times of change.

    You and I have grown in our relationship. You have changed your life based on what you have with me. You and I are doing good; just focus. My life is a little unconventional, as you are experiencing, and you will experience more of it as time goes on. You will be my slave, my sex slave, serving and taking care of me for years to come.

Sir

Fri, 3 Dec 2004
sharon wrote:

Dear Master,

  Thank You for Your kind words. Yes, You are probably right that there are other things clouding my perception at the present time. If it sounds like i'm feeling insecure, i don't think that's the case. i trust You. i was definitely not focused last night though... may have been better to just put me in the closet for an evening of meditation.

  If it seemed to You like i was closing myself off, then it probably seemed the same way to Natasha as well, so maybe it's me instead of her. With all of my up and down days lately, it does seem like i'm scraping myself off the bottom whenever i happen to see her... probably transferring my own issues onto her, and that's not a good thing. It would be much easier to just focus on You. According to stress theory, a person's perceptive ability narrows as their stress/anxiety level increases. You see, i'm actually conducting research to prove the validity of that theory... or am i just the guinea pig?!!

Anyway, tomorrow will be a better day.

Love,
Your slave puppy

Sun, 5 Dec 2004
sharon wrote:

Dear Master,

  Last night was unique... interesting... so many dynamics at work. i think i'm starting to understand how Natasha fits into the equation of things. She is what i am not. And You're going to love this one, but i think i was wanting her to submit and to serve You according to my concept of the words when that isn't at all what You want. Before, and even last night, i kept thinking she was being rude & selfish... and that's why i couldn't seem to connect with her (my thinking, not hers). Now, i'll be the first to admit that i am far from perfect in these matters, but it was somehow...

offensive?... to me that she was not serving You perfectly... according to my idea of how she should be doing so. And yes, i know this is ridiculous and makes no sense. i think, perhaps, it was a protective instinct... that i was somehow not connecting with her because i was protecting You... from her?

Again, this doesn't make any sense, but it's similar to the feeling i would get when my kids were little and i perceived that someone was trying to harm them. (chuckle) People used to tell me i had an over-active mother grizzly bear instinct. Anyway, i'm not at all saying that she was in any way trying to harm You, but just that she wasn't fitting into the mold that i wanted her to. Whew! Doesn't that sound egotistical! Though, actually, it sounds a bit like i was wanting to control her, doesn't it? So what i have realized (and this is probably what You've been trying to tell me all along) is that You want something different from her than from me and it's not up to me to decide what You want or how she should give it to You. (i figure if i keep writing long enough, all of this will eventually make sense!)

It brings to mind that class i went to on poly relationships where they talked about each person having a separate, defined role, so all of the Master's needs were met by the person best suited for each. For example, i am very happy to suck on Your cock or sit at Your feet while You chat with Natasha... separate things, each for Your pleasure. So, like i started to say in the beginning of all this rambling, the fact that she is what i am not makes it better in the overall picture of things... (a) + (b) = c. And beyond that thought, i have no clue where i'm going with all of this!

On a lighter note, i didn't wake up until almost 8:00 this morning! You must have worn me out last night! i could still feel the tightness around the bottom of my ribs when i got up & i had to keep telling myself to breathe normally... it kept me thinking of You. i'm not sure how to explain this, but being uncomfortable for You makes me very happy. i've also concluded that kneeling and cocksucking are the two things that keep me feeling connected to You, regardless of anything else that happens. i hope You were pleased with the evening.

i love You.

Your slave puppy

Sun, 5 Dec 2004
Steven wrote:

Dear puppy,

I was pleased with the evening, even though I initially lost my sexual feeling for the scene. Instead of the play beginning at the start of the evening, it began after conversation and socializing. I'm not used to that. I lost my focus; didn't feel comfortable. But as always – you being an excellent sexual slave – brought me back to reality. I finally became centered and comfortable because you were ready and responsive.

You have it right. I don't want her to be the same as you. I do not want anyone to replace you. She is learning about her submissiveness, which both frightens and intrigues her at the same time. How far and deep she will go with it, I don't know. If she stays, then she will become more a part of things spiritually and emotionally. My feelings are that she is intrigued and wants very much to belong, but that it really depends on how she comes to grips with her inner conflicts. You and I are pretty open and honest, which is unusual and refreshing for her. We are very real and respected in this "forbidden" lifestyle, and we have no hidden agenda.

From what I have learned about Natasha, I think this openness is important to her. Right now, everything is sexual with her. If she stays, then over time her position will change, and she will have her place with no inner conflict. Just so you know, she is not here to decide what position she will have in my family. It is what I give her and how I see her fitting in and enhancing my desires. If she stays, she will learn a lot from you – your understanding and acceptance of yourself, serving, and obedience – the things that bring you satisfaction in serving me.

I believe she wants very much to feel whole, with both parts of her working in unison. She is out of sync, dominant in her profession and worldly life, but privately she is fearful and conflicted for wanting to submit. She is struggling with this new knowledge about herself. At the same time, she is excited with the freedom of being a sexually submissive woman with a man, yet still being respected for who she is. She is having a hard time intellectualizing all this. She read your book and she knows it's an amazing story.

Things you know: I am not monogamous and never have been. I've always told you that I date and play. I have not brought anyone else in with us until now. The nice thing now is that I don't want to date. I enjoy my work immensely, and I have you and an apprentice sub. Since you are a do-me-queen, I always have to be on my toes.

I believe, like you, that she very much wants to find her inner sexual self and to be accepted for who she is by another person. She does not want to have gender wars for control over her personal life, or to have to deal with jealousies about her accomplishments, or to be judged for her submissive side, or to be fearful of having it used against her in an argument. She struggles with an internal feeling that if she submits, she is inferior. She would like to be accepted and respected for both sides of herself. What she will get from us is praise, support, and friendship.

By the way, what happened with those men who came over? Also, were you bleeding today?

Sir

Sun, 5 Dec 2004
sharon wrote:
Dear Master,

A do-me-queen!!! me??? 😊 It is all for Your pleasure Sir!!! The fact that i so thoroughly enjoy it is simply a bonus...a fringe benefit!! 😊

Regarding the three blind mice, i only know the first one's name, Peter, because he was wearing a nametag. Natasha & i were sitting on the couch talking when he came over, sat on the chair next to the couch, and eavesdropped on our conversation. Then he asked me something (i don't remember what). i gave him a "not interested" answer and then turned back to Natasha. (i do have to say here that i've spent enough time in bars to recognize a leech when i see one). Then he asked Natasha something and she responded in a friendly way by asking him a couple questions about himself. (And here i have to wonder if the poor girl has ever been in a bar before). Basically, from the conversation we found out that he is a lonely, single guy who goes to GD at least a couple times a month to proposition every woman he sees. He stays until closing time, never doing anything but watching, then lives off the fantasy until the next time. Natasha was being so friendly, telling him about her job, background, etc. and i really wanted to give her a kick in the shins. After a few minutes, he started talking about how he wanted to take us in the other room, tie us up, etc. (laughing) Natasha was so shocked, she just sat there with her eyes wide and mouth open. i just told him we were there with someone else and he backed off.

Then when i went to get something to drink, i saw Jack, so i stopped to tell him i enjoyed his presentation. As i was talking to Jack, this other guy came up and stood next to me, about an inch away, eavesdropping. Patrick was trying to hurry Jack off to dinner, so i turned to go back to the couch by Natasha. The guy took hold of my arm and asked what i was in such a hurry about. i backed away from him and he kept coming closer. He asked if i was there with anyone. i said yes, and he said it didn't matter in a place like this. He had this disgusting grin on his face and was practically drooling. i told him to please take his hand off of me, that it did matter to me, and then i turned and walked away.

 i got about half-way back to the couch when another moron stepped in front of me and asked if i was looking for someone to play with. i told him "no thank you," and about that time, Natasha came looking for me. i got the impression from the look on her face that she had had an experience similar to mine.

 Then You came over and introduced the couple You were talking to. It was all quite harmless, but of all the places we've gone, it's the first time anyone has been less than completely respectful of the fact that i just might be there with someone else.

 No bleeding today... but my pussy has been feeling rather needy...

To be continued

Love,
Your slave puppy

Sun, 5 Dec 2004
sharon wrote:

Dear Master,

 The place itself seemed very nice... comfortable... except for the fact that the play areas were freezing. The atmosphere seemed warm and friendly, like a neighborhood bar for kinky people. Being there with Natasha was good when You disappeared, but otherwise she was kind of a distraction. i was probably less focused than You when we started playing... more aware of other people being there & watching. The blindfold and bondage helped a lot. When i was on the cross, i was wishing You would keep whipping me hard so i could go straight over the edge, but every time i'd start to relax You would stop. Even when You took me off the cross and told me to get on my hands & knees, i was still self-conscious about who might be watching.

 Then when You started fisting me... well, i pretty much forgot where i was or that the rest of the world even existed. When You held me after that, i felt like i was slowly waking up from a dream... kind of like coming out of anesthesia. i'm not sure what put me so far out in space so quickly... maybe the humiliation of being fisted on my hands & knees on center stage. i don't recall humiliation doing that to me before, but then i don't exactly remember the fisting You've talked about when we were in Indy either. That was kind of like waking up from a dream too. In both cases, i was definitely in slave zone by the time You were done with me... completely focused on You...and so hungry for Your cock... and so eager to do anything in the world to please You. Did i have a goofy grin on my face?

i've also been thinking about what You said about submissiveness being a strength. i didn't see myself as a strong person when i met You, and i certainly never associated submissiveness with strength. Since i've been serving You, i have come to see that it really is a strength. In fact, i definitely feel much more inner strength and confidence now, in all aspects of my life, than before i met You. i've realized that a person has to *have* strength in order to give it away, in order to truly serve and uplift someone else with body, mind, and soul. It requires not only knowledge about oneself, but also comfort and confidence in oneself. It also requires a strength that comes from maturity, from living and experiencing life. i now understand that submission is not just obedience, and it's not just a cleansing process or a stress-relief mechanism.

i have derived strength from our relationship, from my submission to You. i think part of it is that You are non-judgmental. i think being judged makes a person fearful and it takes away from their strength. It has taken some time for me to comprehend that no matter what i do, You aren't going to become angry, critical, and lose control. By being consistent in Your responses, You have given me the freedom to grow in strength.

At the same time, if i had not successfully accomplished and experienced certain things before i met You, i wouldn't be in a place where i could gain strength from submitting because i would still be insecure and struggling to prove myself. In other words, i had to be at peace within myself before i could make someone outside of myself the center of my world, if that makes sense. i guess it amounts to the fact that You have led me to really acknowledge and assimilate the strength that was always there The inside has become congruent with the outside, and for that i am grateful. Thank You.

i wish i could explain all of this to Natasha, but i don't think it's something that can be intellectualized or taught. It has to be lived and felt and absorbed over time. When she becomes comfortable and at peace with herself, she will understand, and then she will be proud of her submissive inclinations.

Love,
Your slave puppy

Mon, 6 Dec 2004
sharon wrote:

Dear Master,

     i hope Your day has gone well. mine was very busy! i never even managed to sit down in my office all day... or anywhere else, for that matter. i decided yesterday (once again) to start running and (once again) overdid it, so between that and the busy day today, i'm thinking the Jacuzzi sounds pretty good right now.

     The thing with those guys is no big deal. More important is the fact that i've been highly impressed by the unusual politeness and respect shown by <u>everyone</u> at all the other places we've been to. Now, that is pretty amazing and worth talking about! The "vanilla" world is a much tougher place. Hell, the grocery store is a much tougher place!

i miss You.

Love,
Your greedy tart ☺

Steven writes:

     Galleria Domain 2 (GD2) is a beautifully appointed club/dungeon in Chicago. It was started around 1996-97 by Monica, a well-known personality in Chicago's BDSM community. The club became an instant success and acquired an excellent reputation throughout the U.S. Around 2002, Monica sold the club to Mistress Carol. Monica remains active in Chicago's BDSM community, owns an exclusive fetish, leather and bondage boutique, and hosts many of Chicago's best private BDSM parties and gatherings.

     GD2 is a well-run private club, and it is one of the hubs for BDSM practioners and BDSM education in Chicago. It's a place where kinky people meet, socialize, and play with other like-minded people. Galleria Domain 2 has monthly classes and demonstrations on all aspects of BDSM life, presented by knowledgeable people within the BDSM community. They also have a monthly newcomers' social, which provides an introduction to the club and into the world of BDSM.

The other Chicago Club is the LRA (Leather Rose Association), which officially opened in May of 2004. The LRA continues in the footsteps of the old Leather Rose Club. LRA is also a meeting, play, and social club. It follows the same philosophy as GD2, as far as BDSM etiquette, protocols, play, education, and classes.

Mon, 6 Dec 2004
Steven wrote:

Dear puppy,

I'm not a club person, so my perspective is a little different. Most of the people who go to the clubs are respectful. I suspect every once in a while there will be a foolish person, but overall wherever we've gone, people have been respectful.

How is everything at home? Are you finishing up the paperwork for the attorney? Tomorrow night I want to go to the movies to see *Kinsey*. I'll get the animals fed early so we can get a bite to eat before the movie. Everything is on Wells Street. Isn't life easy?

Sir

Mon, 6 Dec 2004
sharon wrote:

Dear Master,

Yes, Your world on Wells Street is lovely... like a small village hidden in the middle of the city. i was hoping we would go to see that movie sometime. It sounds very good.

Things at home are going well. Arthur went out drinking Saturday night & came home totally wasted about 5 a.m., which made him very docile and agreeable when he finally woke up. We were able to talk more than we have in a long time, with him being honest about thoughts/feelings instead of yelling & accusing. We even talked about seeing other people and i gave him advice on dating. That was kind of weird!

We will do the uncontested, no-fault divorce to be final in April, and we'll just pay off all the bills this month so they don't have to be part of the settlement. i was planning to call the lawyer today but never had a chance, so will do it in the morning.

i think the worst is over now. His only remaining request is that i don't bring You here to play while he is sitting downstairs. i don't think that will be a problem... that would just be too weird!

i always feel completely safe wherever i go with You. Part of the reason for that is because i know You won't go berserk over some moron. There are likely to be a few in every crowd and they aren't worth the effort. A disapproving look is far more powerful than returning rudeness for rudeness.

Okay, i'm off to the treadmill, the Jacuzzi, and then to bed.

See You soon!

Love,
Your slave puppy

Fri, 10 Dec 2004
sharon wrote:

Dear Master,

Your day is no doubt going better than mine. i think i'm going to just crawl under a big rock & not come out for at least a decade. i spent the whole damn morning getting bitched at by the hospital CEO over things i have no control over, which made me late getting out of there, so i didn't have time to go back to my office to get the directions to the clinic. i figured i'd be able to find it, but i got lost and was about 20 minutes late getting there, so they wouldn't take me. (Of course, last time i had to wait an hour & a half for them.) So then i had to wait a half hour to make another appointment and then still didn't have directions to get from the clinic to the other doctor's office (names, addresses, phone numbers, and directions were among the stuff that was stolen from my purse and not returned), so i again got lost trying to find the doctor's office. Then he did the cryotherapy which, as usual, was much more painful than he claimed it would be. Then after he was done, he said no sex for four weeks. If i would have known that, i would have elected to have the hysterectomy and would have been done with the whole damn thing by now & never have to go back. It's all sooooooooooooooooo depressing.

When i got up this morning, i was all ready to go for the mental cruelty divorce and be done with it in a month. Now i can't do that either because my insurance will be all fucked up and the way things are going, it's likely to be next Christmas before i'm done with all this shit. This is all getting to be too much. Maybe i'll just have a mental breakdown & go spend a year in the psych ward.

Love,
Your slave puppy

Sat, 11 Dec 2004
Steven wrote:

Dear puppy,

      How are you doing? I'm a little tired and discombobulated, but that's par for the course.

Sir

Sat, 11 Dec 2004
sharon wrote:

Dear Master,

      i'm fine. What has You so discombobulated?

puppy

Steven wrote:

      It may be that time of the month.

Sat, 11 Dec 2004
sharon wrote:

Dear Master,

      i am worried that You're not feeling well. Tired and discombobulated...are You coming down with something? Perhaps You need a nurse to take care of You? Some healing touch? A bit of TLC? i keep a nursing bag in my trunk and can make an emergency visit, if needed. Can't be having a discombobulated Master walking around...You might accidently start whipping the wrong person! Please let me know if i can be of assistance.

i miss You.

Love,

Your slave puppy

Sat, 11 Dec 2004
Steven wrote:

>Thanks for the laugh.

Sat, 11 Dec 2004
sharon wrote:

Dear Master,

>Have i said or done something wrong?

Love,
Your slave puppy

Sun, 12 Dec 2004
Steven wrote:

Dear puppy,

>Of course not. I'm sitting here writing, getting lost in my mind. I am looking forward to Boston – it can't get here soon enough. Right now my plan for Boston is to blindfold you, put you in bondage, and secure you to a chair at the booth with a stack of autographed books in front of you for your adoring, admiring fans to purchase. See you tomorrow night.

Sir

Sun, 12 Dec 2004
sharon wrote:

Dear Master,

>i'm sorry. Your messages have been a little cryptic and unusual since i last saw You and they could be taken in more than one way. i know You are busy finishing Your book & i hope You get a lot done this weekend. Perhaps i've been a little over-sensitive…because it's that time of the month! Oh no! Surely not!!

i love You.

Your slave puppy

Steven wrote:

Surelyyyyyyyyyyyyyyyyyyyyyyyyyyyyyyyy NOT, OH MY GOD!
GOD

Steven writes:

    I had met Natasha on Friday night. She wanted to get together before she left on her Christmas vacation. We went to a movie and then played afterwards.

Mon, 13 Dec 2004
Natasha wrote:
Dear Sir:

    It was a wonderful evening on Friday. The movie was great. I enjoyed so much being with you, chained to your bed, covered with hot wax and scraped with a knife! I still have bubbles running in my blood today.

    I know you work out, but if you should be interested in relieving stress, I go to 2 yoga studios. They are owned by the same people and have the same teachers. One is on North Clark Street the other is on North Milwaukee. I like the Clark studio better. They have Website if you want to check it out.

    I am leaving for Hawaii on Saturday, early in the morning. We will be back January 2. I was wondering if we could meet again this week? I am thinking about you and miss you.

Yours,
Natasha

Winter 2005

Wed, 15 Dec 2004
sharon wrote:

Dear Master,

  Why am i so slow to figure things out when i'm around You? The things You were talking about last night have slowly sunken in. When i saw You last week, You said You were *not* dating anyone and didn't want to date anyone. Then last night, You said You *are* dating someone. So, may i presume You started this relationship over the weekend? May i also presume that's what had You so "tired and discombobulated" all weekend? The question is, why didn't You just say so instead of letting me worry about You all weekend?

  i've been thinking about what You said last night and some questions/thoughts have come to mind…and there really isn't any emotion tied to these…just curious. Can You please explain to me what the difference is between dating and what You've been doing with Natasha or myself? Also, what is the difference between a "submissive partner" and a slave or submissive? This may sound elementary to You, but i'm not grasping the distinction. i don't care who You want to date/play or whatever with, but i'm not fond of the idea of being tied to a bed while You go out on a "date" with someone else. i don't want to be put on a shelf five nights a week while You're out having fun. The way i see things, if You're not around then i'm on my own and free to do as i please. Right?

  i get the feeling that You're suddenly in a big hurry to bring in all these other women because You're feeling trapped because i'm going through this divorce. Don't. You will never be trapped into anything by me. i am perfectly capable of taking care of myself. This thing may have knocked me a little off-balance, but it isn't fatal. i think it would be quite a miserable existence to live with someone who felt trapped or manipulated into it. In fact, that is the main reason i want to get a place of my own when the divorce is over…so neither of us feels trapped or pushed or that there was no other choice.

  Something else i want to state for the record is that i am just not sexually attracted to women, and as much as i want to please You, i can't manufacture any enthusiasm for it. i can live with touching or kissing, but oral sex with a woman would be a big turn-off to me. And, while i'm on the subject, i'm sure i've told You before that i do not want to serve a woman. i only want to serve You. So when You talk about dating and looking for a woman to be Your primary partner and that i will be expected to serve her

and give her oral sex…well, i don't know how You expect that to work out…just for the record.
  Okay, i think that about does it! However, i do want to add that despite the fact that my pussy was out of commission last night, You managed to send me home feeling a million times better than when i arrived. Thank You. i really think You could make a fortune if You opened a business called "Stress Relief for Women!" i hope You were pleased.

i love You.

Your slave puppy

Wed, 15 Dec 2004
Steven wrote:

Dear puppy,
  Great letter. No, I am not dating anyone. No, I wasn't out last weekend with anyone. Feeling trapped? No, I am doing what I always do. I think you know that if I do feel trapped, it would be goodbye. I talk to you. Do you want me to stop? As far as others, that's how I live. You being tied to a bed 5 nights a week? Figuratively speaking, I like one or two better.

Sir

Thu, 16 Dec 2004
sharon wrote:

Dear Master,
  Was i sounding neurotic again? i think i can still claim "that time of the month!"
  Regarding tomorrow, i don't know how long it takes to get to O'Hare from Your house, but we might want to leave a little earlier than 2:00. i'll go ahead & make a parking reservation today for 3:00. It sometimes takes longer to take the shuttle than to get to the airport itself. i'm leaving work hopefully by noon, so could potentially be there by 1:00 if no traffic.

Have a lovely day!

Love,
Your slave puppy

Fri, 18 Dec 2004
Steven wrote:

Dear puppy

    Regarding "that time of month" – In the conventional world, how a woman acts during that time of the month is a woman's prerogative. Since it happens monthly, a pattern of behavior is established with hormones running amok, until it becomes physically intolerable. That pattern is a nuisance in the Dom/sub world, and very disobedient in a Master/slave world. I will explain tomorrow, but I think you already know.

    I have to add that your situation at this moment, and in the near future, will keep you emotionally and mentally unbalanced and unsound. A padded cell may be the best thing for you.

Sir

Fri, 18 Dec 2004
sharon wrote:

Dear Master,

    i am sorry Sir. i was just kidding. You are right that "that time of the month" is no excuse for anything... for anyone. my mental status is fine... just too hyper this week... good for work, bad for corresponding with one's Master. i am sorry. A padded cell actually sounds good to me. On the other hand, if i just think about You i will be fine…

Love,
Your slave puppy

Mon, 20 Dec 2004
sharon wrote:

Dear Master,

    i want to thank You for a wonderful weekend in Boston. i had a lot of fun. You, Tammy Jo, Fox, and Patrick are fun to work with... all such different personalities! The necklace & pin are beautiful. Thank You. You are very generous.

    i have to go get that mammogram by 7:00 this morning so will write more later.

Love,

Your slave puppy

Mon, 20 Dec 2004
sharon wrote:

Dear Master,

    Are You staying warm? A good night for the dogs to wear their coats & hats! i need to look up the weather in Fort Lauderdale... i wonder if it got to 80 or 85 degrees today in the hot sun 🌐. Thinking about it makes this frigid weather tolerable, for a couple days anyway. i'm thinking we should fly to Florida, Texas, Arizona, Jamaica, Virgin Islands, etc. all winter to sell books... what a good idea!! i bet the people in those places are in desperate need of kinky reading materials.

    Did You get Your writing done today? And have that chat with Patrick? i'm guessing he would be a little relieved not to have to plan everything himself.

    i have to say that i've done superbly today. Did all my Xmas shopping, wrapping, and preparations all in one day (actually about 4 hours). It used to take me months and i would still be working on it on Xmas morning. Due to my extreme efficiency this year, i would be delighted to serve You tomorrow night, if You would like. After all, i can't have my Master being neglected for over a week while i'm off lounging in the hot sun.

i love You.

Your slave puppy

Mon, 20 Dec 2004
Steven wrote:

Dear puppy,

    It's good you had a good day. I am writing now, finishing up "Puppy Play." I spoke to Patrick; he is still on the road. He should be in tomorrow. See you tomorrow night.

Sir

Mon, 20 Dec, 2004
sharon wrote:

Dear Master,

The weekend in Boston was interesting. i didn't expect to see so many younger people there... with such nice bodies. It seemed to be more of a fashion & art show, i guess more fetish than specifically bdsm. There were a lot of curious beginners mixed in with people who were mostly interested in looking good... and i certainly don't have any complaints about people looking good! i love the mixture of people at these shows, everyone making a statement about who they are, and everyone getting along & accepting each other. i was thinking about that last night after i dropped You off.

Our group was quite a mixture too... a male slave, Mistress, gay male slave, female slave, and a Master – all with different viewpoints, sitting together having dinner while discussing things like love, poly relationships, writing, serving, history, childhoods, etc, etc. The thing i really like about everyone in the group is that you are all so straightforward about everything. People ask questions and get honest and thoughtful answers. A phenomenon! It's a level of communication far above the jokes, gossip, and criticisms most people exchange when they get together. Very refreshing. i learned more about the concept of poly relationships from that dinner conversation than from the two classes i attended in North Carolina.

i also want to say that i am very touched that You are buying all these things for me. i'm not used to receiving gifts, especially of a personal nature. In fact, i don't ever remember receiving a personal gift from anyone. (laughing) i usually got a frying pan from Arthur for Xmas every year. It had to be opened before breakfast so it could be put to use right away. How will i ever manage to survive in the future without a new frying pan every year ☺! It also means a lot to me that You would actually care what i look like when we go somewhere...another new experience that will take some getting used to. i like the idea of dressing to please You.

i'm going to have to quit here for the night as my eyes are getting droopy and i need to go fall into bed.

i've just spotted the book about knots on a shelf. i'm still not sure where or when i acquired it, but will bring it tomorrow to add to the collection – since it is highly un-useful to me.

See You soon!

Love,
Your slave puppy

Steven writes:

The Boston Flea Market was our (Kinkybooks) second long distance event so we knew it would be a tiring show. We had four authors signing their books at the booth, and two days to sell enough books to make back our expenses and hopefully a small profit. puppy was fabulous; she did whatever was asked of her.

At the end of the first day of vending, we took some time to relax before dinner. We went up to our room where I tied puppy up on the bed while I cleaned up, got myself organized, and talked out my thoughts.

Mon, 27 Dec 2004
sharon wrote:

Dear Master,

i'm back from Florida and i've missed You tremendously. i hope You're feeling better.

Love,
Your slave puppy

Wed, 29 Dec 2004
sharon wrote:

Dear Master,

It was so good to see You last night. You have improved my spirit immensely... re-energized. i was able to accomplish a lot today & am thinking much clearer. Thank You! And my backside was also very aware of Your presence all day!

Your obedient and loving slave puppy

Thu, 30 Dec 2004
sharon wrote:

Dear Master,

i hope Your day has gone well. Arthur got me so angry tonight that i ended up cleaning the entire house in an effort to work it off. Took out three bags of trash from my office and now i can actually see the desktop for the first time in months. i even found the gift card they gave me when i left the job in Indiana a year & a half ago. i think my second New Year's

resolution will be to get more organized. It used to drive me crazy to have anything setting around, but stuff just keeps piling up en masse around here lately. i think i must be turning into my mother...oh no!!! 😊
    What time do You want me to arrive at Your house tomorrow night? Is it okay to wear jeans? (i don't remember where You said we are going). And when will i be returning home? It seems i was rather distracted by Your delicious cock when You were talking about all this the other night...

Love,
Your slave puppy

Sun, 2 Jan 2005
sharon wrote:

Dear Master,

    i really enjoyed spending the weekend with You, though i will be sooooooooooo glad when my body gets back to normal because i very, very, very much miss Your presence in my pussy... there's nothing else that feels quite so good. Thank You for being so patient and understanding. i know it's at least as frustrating for You as is it for me.
    i also want to thank You for the privilege of reading and helping You with the transcript for Your book... very fascinating and thought-provoking. i'm thinking those lawyers should have paid You for the opportunity to work on such an interesting case. Those interviews provide such a unique insight into the thought processes of the people involved in BDSM, so many ethical issues that go far beyond the definition of obscenity or the morality of pornography. A person could write a hundred books and still not adequately address all the intricacies of the case.
    Despite all You had to go through, it must have been fascinating for You to watch all of this debated in court. Just reading those three interviews definitely gave me a better understanding of the importance of the case, not just for people involved in the adult industry or the practice of BDSM, but for the basic human rights of all Americans. If the case had actually been decided by the jury, and if the prosecution had won, there would be far-reaching negative effects on the entire population. Now i can hardly wait to read the Park Dietz transcript.
    There is also something else You talked about that has gotten me thinking. The idea that i like being watched, in other words, that i am somewhat of an exhibitionist and that's why i chose to be with Warren. my

first reaction to that is to say that no, i prefer to be in the background, that i don't like to be watched at all, that i definitely don't want to be center-stage. However, it's hard to deny the fact that any kind of public play makes me very wet and results in some pretty mind-blowing orgasms. The thing is that when i think of someone who likes to be watched (an exhibitionist), i think of someone who enjoys showing off their stuff, and that's not at all where i'm coming from. Despite what You've seen, i still have to say that i'm embarrassed at the thought of exposing my body to anyone. Despite what You've seen, i would have to describe myself as more modest than most women (okay, don't laugh).

i think the thing that gets me going is the utter humiliation of it all. It somehow causes a break in my mind and sends me off into another world. But the only way it could work is if i'm totally focused on the person i'm with. If someone else were to say something to me or make eye contact, i think i would go crashing straight to the ground.

You have very insightfully had me blindfolded whenever my body has been introduced to any onlookers. However, Your idea of me walking around naked serving water to people prior to a fisting demonstration... i don't know how You could possibly keep me focused on You enough to be able to do that. What would You do if i froze or started crying or ran out of the room or something? The fisting demonstration itself doesn't have me worried because i assume that You will be right there where i can see or touch You, but i really don't think the rest of it would work, not because i don't want to please You, but because i don't think it's something i'm capable of doing. It was different walking around at the Bijou because i have never once looked at anyone's face there except Yours & have never said a word to anyone. Does any of this make sense?

Love,
Your slave puppy

Steven writes:

Because of puppy's medical procedures, there has been very little pussy play lately; and she will have this problem for the next three months. However, this has not stopped our rough play or denied me a warm, wet, tight place to put my dick. I've been taking her ass, which she gives to me with great joy as she continues to orgasm.

The other thing puppy is talking about is a book I am writing called, *The Destruction of the Moral Fabric of America*. (She will later become the organizer and editor of the book). It is an intricate book with many parts woven around an S/M trial I had back in 1989. I was involved in the first wave of obscenity prosecutions (Operation Postporn) coming out of the Meese Commission's Pornography hearings in 1987. The first wave of prosecutions focused on companies selling sexual materials through the mail, while later prosecutions focused on manufacturers and distributors.

Mon, 3 Jan 2005
sharon wrote:

Dear Master,

    i hope You had a good day, despite the rain. i'm feeling really good today – energized and productive. Do You suppose that spending three days with You will cause me to feel so good for the following three days? i think i'll keep track of that in the future! It's always amazing how, after spending time with You, that all of the daily crises and irritations seem to shrink down to nothingness. How do You do that? You make me smile... and You enable me to do the things that need to be done. Thank You.

i love You... a lot

Your slave puppy

Mon, 3 Jan 2004
Natasha wrote:

Dear Sir:

    Had a wonderful vacation. Missed you. I would very much like to get together.

Yours,
Natasha

Mon, 3 Jan 2004
Steven wrote:

Dear Natasha,

    Happy New Year. Hope you had a wonderful vacation. Good to have you home. How is Tuesday at 7:00? You will join puppy and me. Do you remember what you are to do when you come over?

Sir

Mon, 3 Jan 2004
Natasha wrote:

Dear Master,

      Yes I do. I have been thinking a lot about it. I've missed you.

Natasha

Mon, 3 Jan 2005
Steven wrote:

Dear puppy,

      How was everything when you got home? I enjoyed spending the weekend with you. How are you feeling?
      I am at the final stages of putting the book together in rough form. Now I need at least 12 more revisions. I will talk to you about your thoughts on public play and exhibitionism tommorow. It also seems that tomorrow I get to relax and play with two subs. Did I say relax?

Sir

Mon, 3 Jan 2005
sharon wrote:

Dear Master,

      Arthur was upset when i got home. He said he was worried to death about me, didn't know whether i was dead or alive, and that i don't have any idea what it's like to sit home and worry about someone. It is almost incomprehensible to me that he could be in such denial about all the times when i did just that. i couldn't even respond to that statement... just sat there with my mouth open.
      Anyway, he said he was so stressed out that he had to go out for a drink, but came back about an hour or so later and was fine. After all these years, it is still hard for him to comprehend how i felt all the times i waited up for him... and it's still hard for me to comprehend where in the hell he's coming from! It's like living in a perpetual twilight zone. Can talk more about it tomorrow if You want.
      Play with two? Shall i assume Natasha is back home? No rest for the Master!
Good night!

Love,
Your slave puppy

Wed, 5 Jan 2005
sharon wrote:

Dear Master,

    Well, i don't know where my head was on the way home last night. i drove about 10 miles past my exit before i even realized i missed it. Talk about spaced out!

    i had a nice time last night. i'm smiling because i had the strangest things going through my head while we were playing... kind of like my own private movie theater. It must have been the prior discussion about exhibitionism and voyeurism... and then the blindfold. It was funny because after You finished using the vibrator on me, my clit continued to vibrate for quite awhile. It felt like it was the size of a grapefruit, which created quite a visual image while blindfolded. Then when You moved over to Natasha and the bed started to shake... well, it was quite an unusual sensation and it was all i could do to keep from laughing at the outrageous picture in my head of a gigantic clit being jiggled around like a bowl of Jell-O. Even makes me laugh now thinking about it.

    i am happy that You finally had a pussy to fuck, and i absolutely loved Your smile when i reached over to play with Your nipples. i also discovered something while You were fucking Natasha, and with all the discussion about exhibitionism and voyeurism, i'm not sure what this would be called... perhaps my own peculiar pleasure.

    Watching You play with her doesn't really do a lot for me. i like watching Your body move, Your muscles ripple, but it's kind of a detached observation, doesn't create much in the way of sexual excitement. But when i closed my eyes and touched You, ran my hands over Your body, it was wonderful. i could feel Your energy flowing like electricity. It was like i was "seeing" the scene through my fingers... more clearly than i could see with my eyes. Very strange. i don't even know how to describe what it did to me... sort of made me melt... created this beautiful, perfectly defined picture in my head and i felt like i was floating, like in a dream or something, like an out-of-body experience. Now is that weird or what! (chuckle) Perhaps that could be considered "tactile voyeurism?" Have You ever heard of such a thing?

In any case, it had me smiling all day...and also thinking i've gone a bit daffy in the head. Made it quite a challenge to follow the subsequent conversation...and, apparently, to drive home too!

i hope You enjoyed the evening. It makes me very happy that You got to have a good orgasm. i had been getting quite depressed about the uncooperativeness of my body. It is so nice that Natasha can step in and give You such pleasure!

i love You.

Your slave puppy

Wed, 5 Jan 2005
sharon wrote:

Dear Master,

Do You remember (has it been a couple months ago?) when You told me to write something for the collaring ceremony? Well, shortly after that i started writing the attached message and intended to add to it, but with everything else happening, i kind of forgot about it. So tonight i was looking for another document and came across it again. i am wondering if this is what You had in mind, so i figure i will send it to You to see what You think... because i really don't know what a collaring ceremony is supposed to consist of... though since it isn't a legal ceremony, i suppose it would consist of anything You want!

Also, do You want me to serve You tomorrow night? i need to stay in practice with sucking Your cock... feel like i'm making progress lately!

Love,
Your slave puppy

Master,
I want to be Your slave
Because I trust You and respect You
More than anyone I've ever known.

Your whips and chains,
Your knife and hands and cock
Have set my body on fire.

Your honesty and integrity,
Your consistency and Your willingness to stand up for what You believe in,

Have soothed my mind.

Your kindness and patience,
Your strength and compassion and passion for life
Have touched my soul.

You have fed me and covered me with Your scent.
I belong to You
Body, mind, and soul.

And so I kneel before You to humbly offer myself
To be Your slave, Your property
To serve You, without reservation, in any way You desire.

I will always strive to bring You honor, happiness, pleasure, and pride
And I will always love You
With all my heart, mind, body, and soul.

Thu, 6 Jan 2005
Steven wrote:

Hello Joseph,

    I am finishing up a book and would like to use six paragraphs of an article you wrote called *Old Guard? If You Say So.* I want to use the material to emphasize a point about the popular viewpoint that "my S/M is good; yours is bad," using the paragraphs that deal with the film *The Wild One*. Of course, I would state those paragraphs were written by you and permission was given. The book is centered on an S/M trial I had. Please let me know.

Thank you,
Steven

Thu, 6 Jan 2005
Joseph Bean wrote:

Steve,

    You are welcome to use the paragraphs in your book. Thanks for asking. I like it much better this way than the usual way of finding out about citations (often poorly used) when it is too late to do anything about it. I also know that you will know what you are writing about and what you are referring to. Yes, you have my permission.

Stay well,
J

Steven writes:

In *Destruction of the Moral Fabric of America*, I stated an opinion in a chapter called "The Taming of S/M." To further clarify my point of view, I wanted to use part of Joseph Bean's article, "Old Guard? If You Say So."

The book was conceived after I met Guy Baldwin, for the first time, 15 years after a trial in which Guy was instrumental in helping my attorneys form my defense. It was an obscenity trial for the *Slave and Master* films made by David Rosen and myself. The title of this book is a phrase that was directed at me in three different jury trials over a 16-year span. The book contains government documents and depositions, pre-trial interviews, and trial transcripts, along with my opinions, e-mail correspondences, and other articles I have written discussing the subject of BDSM.

The book also includes my theory on "Certifying Masters, Mistresses, slaves, and ProDommes," "A Slight Taste of Sexual History and Social Change," and my views about "BDSM and the Sexual Future." The final chapter is about Jeffery Dahmer, a serial murderer who killed Jeremy Wienberger, one of my employees. Park Dietz, from the Meese Commission, was the prosecution's expert witness at my trial, and he was also one of the prosecution's expert witnesses at the Dahmer trial. This story has nothing to do with S/M, but I wanted to put it in the book in memory of Jeremy.

Fri, 7 Jan 2005
sharon wrote:

Dear Master,

Did You notice that i got another parking ticket last night? i parked in the second space since the one in front of Your house was occupied, and got a ticket for parking in a loading zone ($50 !!!) It makes me rather angry because the time on the ticket was 6:39 and the sign right next to the car says it's a loading zone only until 6:00. Is there any way to fight that or do i just have to pay it? Seems like robbery to me. How can they get away with that?

i saw the doctor today – he said everything is healed up fine and it's okay to have sex. It was funny because he blushed when i asked him about it. i can't imagine why a person would become a gynecologist if he's embarrassed to talk about sex! Anyway, he thinks the prolonged bleeding is due to a hormone imbalance, so he gave me a prescription for progesterone (the bitchy hormone 😼). So if the bleeding isn't stopped by the middle of next week, i'm supposed to start taking it for 12 days and (theoretically) it should stop within a couple days. Then after the 12 days, i would supposedly have a regular period and then everything is supposed to be back in balance. If the bleeding is stopped by Tuesday or Wednesday, then i'm supposed to start taking it the following week with the same end result. That is plan B.

Plan C is that if the hormone doesn't work, i would have to have another procedure like the one in November except they would use a balloon-shaped instrument for better results. i am definitely not in a hurry to try plan C. In any case, if he knows anything at all, i should not be bleeding next weekend for sure, so if You want to do that thing at Galleria Domain, the next two weekends would be the best time. (chuckle) Of course, if i become a devil from this hormone stuff, it might be a good idea to bring a gag, plenty of rope, and a sturdy whip! Just kidding! You know i'll be an angel for You no matter what.

Now, i do have to mention that last night was quite the intense experience – vibrator, ass fucking, and spanking all at the same time. Do You have any idea what that does to one's nervous system! Three such different and intense sensations all at the same time... it's amazing it didn't make my hair curl... or fall out! It definitely falls in the "losing control" category... wonderful! And there i was laying in a heap, still trying to locate all my body parts and determine which way was up, and You were running around all full of energy! All i could do was lay there and smile because even if the bed was on fire, i couldn't have managed to get my feet on the floor at that point. i most certainly need to take extra special care of You the next time i see You!

Love,
Your slave puppy

Sun, 9 Jan 2005
sharon wrote:

Dear Master,

Thank You for letting me come over last night. my pussy is feeling a bit less needy today! Though i'm thinking there is an awful lot of catching up to do... hmmmm... i'm thinking that fucking about three times a day every day for an indefinite period of time ought to do it! Now wouldn't that be the fantasy life to live!! 🌐Or is that what You had in mind when You said something about tying me to the bed and...

Have You been writing all day again today? i apologize if i had a puzzled look on my face last night. After reading most of the parts in no particular order, i'm having a little trouble grasping Your vision of how it all flows together. It's hard to see the flow of things on a computer screen. i am eager to see it all on paper and read it from start to finish. Somehow i missed this whole process when You were putting *The Puppy Papers* together. That must have been a big job to get organized... and it looks so simple in the final form.

You produce an excellent product, but it's interesting that Your method of getting there is so different than mine would be. i would have to progress from start to finish, making sure each paragraph was perfect before moving on to the next while never considering the larger picture. If i worked like You do, i would end up with gibberish. (chuckle) i guess that's why i just do whatever You say and trust that You've got everything under control... and then at a later time, replay everything in my head from start to finish to try and figure out what happened! Sounds like an excessively structured thinking pattern doesn't it... must be why i need someone like You in my life... to keep my head spinning!

i love You.

Your slave puppy

Mon, 10 Jan 2005
Natasha wrote:

Dear Sir:

I did not hear from you last week. Is everything okay? I miss you.

Yours,
Natasha

Mon, 10 Jan 2005
Steven wrote:

Hello Natasha,

It has been very busy and for some reason, I lost track of reality. I have gotten very involved in the book. In going through the first draft, I'm realizing there is a lot more research that needs to be done. I am also working with people who are restoring and digitizing my films from the original 16mm prints, and I've been researching old fetish, lifestyle, and sex magazines for my website, besides working with the programmer who is building a new foundation for the various websites, as well as getting ready for the next event where we'll be vending with Kinkybooks. There's just not enough time in the day.

How was your week? How are you doing in this cold weather? Are you free Wednesday at 7:00?

Steven

Tue, 11 Jan 2005
Natasha wrote:

Dear Sir,

I am glad that your book is coming along. I was busy here too. Many things to do and write this semester. I will be teaching a lot. My course for graduate students began yesterday. I have 40 students in class and this is a lot for a graduate course. Busy is good. Hawaii is nice but real life is here, don't you think?

I will be there on Wednesday at 7:00 pm.

Yours,
Natasha

Tue, 11 Jan 2005
sharon wrote:

Dear Master,

i hope everything is okay with You. Do You want me to serve You tonight? i have to leave for a meeting in a couple minutes, then go to a doctor's appointment this afternoon, so if You want me to come over tonight, please leave a message on my cell phone. Thank You.

Love,
Your slave puppy

Fri, 14 Jan 2005
sharon wrote:

Dear Master,

i hope You are staying warm today. The sunshine was deceiving, but nice for a change. i spent the day at a conference on "Dealing with Difficult People." It was interesting & fun, but i was rather distracted by my sore pussy and over-sensitive clit...and thoughts that Your cock would do much to relieve my distress.

Not that i'm complaining because i know i deserved it, but i just want to say that those pussy clamps are evil devices. i'm wondering, Sir, if it is possible that a slave ☺can, most respectfully, persuade her Master to reserve those only for when she has been very bad? i think that if anything is going to keep a slave's responsibilities foremost in her distractible mind, it would be the prospect of pussy clamps...particularly in the spots that You seem to enjoy putting them... although i do hope You derived an enormous amount of pleasure in direct proportion to my pain. my pussy is really very distracting every time i move...

i love You

Your slave puppy

The Art of Cocksucking

Sat, 15 Jan 2005
sharon wrote:

Dear Master,

i have finally gotten around to reading the book You gave me on fellatio and feel like i must say that it is rather ridiculous. Have You actually read this book? It is apparently written for someone who has never had any kind of sexual contact with another human being and has never before laid eyes on a penis. i am half-way through the book and, so far, have been "enlightened" to such revelations as the fact that the genital area is covered with hair, something that the author finds necessary to describe in detail multiple times. The whole thing seems to be about overcoming a psychological aversion as well as an aversion to the taste and smell of the cock. All i can say is that if a person had such aversions, this book is only going to strengthen them...or scare the person to death!

Love,
Your slave puppy

Sat, 15 Jan 2005
Steven wrote:

Dear puppy,

    The world is waiting for your definitive piece on cocksucking. How many billions of people are there in the world? How many books have been written in the last 200 years? How many books have been written on "The Art of Sucking a Dick to Erotic Perfection?" The answer is: NONE. The books we saw at Barnes & Noble are as generic and sexless as you can get. The only cocksucking credentials the authors listed are the colleges they went to for unrelated courses of study.

    Does graduating from college mean a person is qualified in the art of cocksucking? They didn't list how many dicks they sucked before, during, or after college to give them the expertise to write a book on the subject. How often were they sucking dicks and whose dicks were they sucking? What were the credentials of the people whose dicks they were sucking? Do they have letters of recommendation? And if they do, by whom? Do they give classes? Do they give lectures and demonstrations to show the many techniques of sucking a dick and making it erupt? Is there any recorded film or video documenting their expertise? Lastly, I did not see a B.A., M.A. or a PhD in "Cocksucking" next to their names.

    Puppy, the world is waiting for your Pulitzer Prize essay on "The Art of Sucking the Dick."

Sir

Sun, 16 Jan 2005
sharon wrote:

Dear Master,

    Yes, the ultimate idiocy of this "ultimate guide" is rather inspiring. i just finished writing a very long e-mail to someone who is experiencing severe pain which is being totally mismanaged by a host of ignorant physicians. It is so frustrating that apparently the ONLY people who know how to manage pain effectively are hospice nurses and trying to educate the entire medical community, including so-called "pain specialists," on the very simple concepts of pain management seems to be an impossibly large task.

As with the current books about cocksucking, physicians get so caught up in irrelevant nonsense and clinical theory that the real issue and purpose (patient comfort) is forgotten. i don't understand why people have to make things so damn complicated...perhaps to cover up the lack of real knowledge or experience?

You are right that sucking a dick is an art, not a science; and it is the same with pain management. It's sad to think that in both cases, the real-life experience of the individual is overlooked while the "experts" are pontificating on the subject, as if we were talking about a concrete statue instead of a human being. It is, i think, a matter of overly "educated" people who are unable to learn from real-life experiences. Surely, someone who knows nothing at all about the detailed anatomy and physiology of a penis would ENJOY the cocksucking EXPERIENCE far more than the person who approaches it from a sterile, clinical, and theoretical perspective, or someone who requires all the "facts" before even trying it... just my opinion, for whatever it's worth.

Love,
Your slave puppy

Steven writes:

I presume that cocksucking has been practiced just as long as fucking, but I am not aware of any historical documentation, like cave drawings, to verify this presumption. So, as far as the origins of cocksucking are concerned, anyone's guess is as good as mine. My guess is that cocksucking has been around for quite a while. So why aren't there any good "how to" books on the subject? I don't know. To remedy that situation, puppy and I have put together this little "how to" story on cocksucking. Before we begin, it should be understood that good cocksucking and pussy eating should not be taken lightly, so get the snickering and embarrassment out of the way. The art of cocksucking is no laughing matter.

It is also important to note that this piece is only about cocksucking and deep throating with the mouth. It does not include the many nuances of a blow job, such as using your hands to masturbate the dick, which is usually done while sucking the dick to climax.

To practice the art of cocksucking, a person needs to be in wonderment about, or at least like, the dick. Many women are fascinated by the things a dick can do (like stand up on its own), and they may relish their power to inspire that dick to whistle Dixie. But there is more to cocksucking than making a dick hard. You have to feel it, and you have to know what effect you're having on the person attached to it.

Most of the women I've been with feel that they are good at cocksucking. They often say, "Everyone I have been with has told me how good I am and how experienced I am." In fact, I haven't played with a single woman who hasn't told me how good she is, or that she's never had a complaint. Some of these women had been with a few partners, and others had been with many partners, but the story is always the same. Of course, most men who eat pussy will say the same thing about their own skill and expertise. For a lot of men and women, just the erotic thought of another person going down on them gets them hard or wet, so the technique is not even an issue.

To be good at most things in life takes practice, and practice means you have to work at it. Most people don't equate sex with work. Working at sex doesn't mean that quick and simple sex is not satisfying, but rather that it should only be a small part of your overall sexual repertoire. Good sex is more than just spreading your legs, moving to a rhythm, moaning, talking dirty, and letting the man pump away. Good cocksucking doesn't mean putting two or three inches of his dick in your mouth, sucking on the head, and flicking your tongue while jerking on the shaft. Don't delude yourself into thinking this is all that's needed for a good blow job. And don't think that you're so hot (men as well as women) that your very presence is all that's required for good, satisfying sex.

It doesn't matter how much sex you've had or how many partners you've been with. You have to understand what you're doing, why you like the cock, what it does for you, why you get pleasure from it, and why you want to give pleasure. This understanding will open up doors for more satisfying sexual experiences for both you and your partner.

Good cocksucking skills first require practicing your style and technique. You will always learn more from a person you're having a relationship with than from a stranger, because communication, trust, and closeness will, of course, bring out your best efforts. You need to be able to see and feel your partner's body respond and be able to ask him questions while you're performing. This open communication will help you understand what you're doing, how you should do it, and what pleases both of you.

Dick size is a very important factor in cocksucking. Shorter dicks (under six inches) are, of course, easier to deep throat, but the thickness of the dick and the size and shape of the dick head will also affect your ability to deep throat.

The Basics:
Your mouth should be like your pussy and ass – a warm, wet hole that a dick loves to nestle into. The dick wants to feel wonderfully engulfed in a warm, wet place, a place where the warm, wet friction of in-and-out thrusting will bring erotic pleasure and will climax into an eruption. Who wants to be in a loose pussy? Likewise, who wants to be in a loose mouth that is afraid and doesn't want to feel the dick? The dick wants to feel tightness and suction on the shaft and up to the head (no teeth unless requested). A dick needs erotic friction with surrounding pressure.

The goal in cocksucking (deep throating) is learning to control your gag reflex. For some, it will only take four to six sexual encounters to start understanding this technique; but for others it may take a few dozen cocksucking sessions. In the beginning, learning to control your gag reflex will produce some unpleasant reactions. You will gag, of course, and you might even throw up a few times, but these reactions aren't fatal and the final rewards are sexually empowering. Other side effects when learning how to deep throat include panic, running mucus, and runny eyes. In other words, you will be snot-faced for a while, so keep a towel handy. Learning how to breathe with a hot and pulsating cock lodged in your throat takes commitment, practice, and perseverance. Don't worry about whether you look sexually or erotically beautiful because the important thing is that he feels the pleasure you're giving him.

Learning to Deep Throat:
Stage 1: Take the cock into your mouth to the point of gagging, then hold it at that position for a few seconds while you concentrate on relaxing. Once the gag reflex has passed, then come back out, breathe, and go back down again. Repeat this process for about 10 to 15 minutes and do not chicken out before the gag. Breathing is almost non-existent with a dick in your throat. Think of it like holding your breath under water, but instead of water rushing in, saliva will be running out, and you will breathe as you come up off the dick. You will learn various rhythms, but always hold the dick in at the deepest point because this position feels great for the dick.

After you've practiced this procedure for about 10 minutes, your throat will start to relax and open up. You will need to adjust your head and throat position to more comfortably take in more of the dick. Your face will look like you've had an emotional workout, with eyes tearing and thick mucus running out your mouth and nose onto your face and all over the dick. I call the mucus ejecting from the back of the throat "mouth cum." This mouth cum should be covering his balls and running into the crack of his ass if he is lying down.

Concentrate on deep throating for at least 20 minutes each time for the next few times you're giving head. Of course, you can do it as long as you like, but remember that it takes a few minutes for you to warm up and relax.

Stage 2: Once you've had three or four serious practice sessions, think about how much more of the dick you're now taking in than when you started. Your gag point should now be deeper because you know how it feels in your throat. Now, instead of stopping and then coming off the dick, you should stop at the gag point, wait, and then swallow more of the dick up to the next gag point. At this point, you may throw up, but so what! It's the price you may pay to be a great cocksucker.

The end goal is for your throat to be fully open, the gag reflex fully controlled, and your nose nuzzled in the public hair on his lower abdomen. As you improve your skills and your throat opens more easily, you will have less of the tearing and runny mucus. The length of time it takes to control your gag reflex depends on your dedication and the pleasure you derive from giving and receiving, but it will happen sooner rather than later.Most people are only able to take in 6 to 6 ½ inches of dick, while others can take in the whole enchilada. Taking in anything less than 6 inches indicates you're not interested in mastering the art of cocksucking.

Stage 3: After learning to control the gag reflex, you will need to learn how to apply suction while the dick is in your throat. Suction is accomplished by using your jaw and tongue muscles to create tightness. Practicing suction on the dick may leave your jaw a little sore for a couple days because you have never used that muscle like this before.

The final accomplishment in becoming an expert cocksucker is adjusting and getting in tune with the dick's movements and, for example, the tightening of the balls just before it explodes, so it doesn't erupt in the back of your throat and cause you to choke. In the beginning, if you can't feel the moments leading up to ejaculation, then have your partner, who is attached to the dick, give you a signal.

Overall, mastering the art of cocksucking means you have to like the dick and enjoy giving pleasure to your partner, which will, in return, give you pleasure. It's wonderful to both feel and see the sexual pleasure we are giving. Cocksucking is not rocket science, so don't consciously over-think it. Set a pace; taste the texture; enjoy your sexual power in a natural rhythm that brings forth erotic pleasure.

The following is puppy's story on how she learned to suck my dick.

Steven wrote:

How did you feel about sucking dick years ago and now?

sharon wrote:

i think i always liked it, but in the past it was a rare opportunity. i am getting much more practice these days! You're probably not going to like this, but i've concluded that there is a relationship between my enjoyment of cocksucking and my enjoyment of smoking... like an oral fixation or something. See, i am not really smoking, i'm sucking on tiny little dicks all day every day. That can't be such a bad thing!

i think i like sucking Your cock the best because You seem so comfortable with it. In the past, most guys got uptight about it. They got nervous if i spent too much time on it and pushed me away, like it was too intimate or something. Then again, maybe i was so bad at it that they couldn't stand it any longer! i really think it was an intimacy thing though. It was like they wanted it but they were embarrassed to have me do it. Such is the vanilla world! Actually, Rob was quite comfortable with it, but in that case there just wasn't much to work with. i'm sitting here thinking about the various cocks i have tasted and, at the risk of repeating myself, i have to say that Yours is superior to all the rest... must be why i keep coming back for more!

Steven wrote:

Do you connect with the person you're giving a blow job to?

sharon wrote:

Historically speaking, i don't think i could say one way or the other. It depends on the person, the circumstances, and the response. i'd have to say that my primary focus is on the cock itself. i tend to get kind of lost in what i'm doing and shut everything else out. i enjoy, maybe even prefer, communicating by touch. It just seems like the most honest, real, and expressive means of communication. When giving a blowjob, it's like a dialogue between the cock and myself, with each responding to changes in the other. Cocks are very expressive creatures, as i'm sure You already know!

Sometimes when You talk to me while i'm sucking Your cock, it seems like a distraction, almost like You're intruding on this private dialogue. It depends on what You're saying and when. Other times when You talk to me, i make a transition to become aware of the rest of You, to connect with You as a person. When You don't say anything, i eventually make that transition on my own. i think it's when my hands are moving that i'm connecting with You as a whole person.

Steven wrote:

Do you just want to give that person pleasure or is it for your own enjoyment?

sharon wrote:

In the beginning, for the first minute or so, it is about that person's (Your) pleasure. Then, as i said, my focus narrows and it becomes at least as much for my own enjoyment. It's hard to explain, but it really is a back and forth thing... give and take. Then when i come out of my "zone," it once again becomes about Your pleasure, which is my pleasure. The fact of the matter is that if we didn't both enjoy it, i wouldn't be spending so much time doing it!

Steven wrote:

What enjoyment do you get from it? Do you like cock, making a man orgasm, the cum?

sharon wrote:

Actually, this is something You taught me for Your enjoyment, but it turns out to be just as much for my own... the idea of "cum" from my own mouth. When i take You deep in my throat, Your cock becomes coated with a thick, creamy mucus. It changes the taste and texture of Your cock, magnifies it. i guess it sort of acts like a surfactant, allowing me get down to the real thing. In any case, it makes Your cock exponentially more delicious. i also simply enjoy the feel of Your cock on my tongue and the inside of my lips. It's apparently an erogenous zone for me. Massaging my mouth with Your cock makes my pussy wet. Making a man orgasm/cum with my mouth is okay, but i much prefer it in my pussy. You can justifiably consider me selfish on that matter! 😊

Steven wrote:

How did you give a blowjob before and how do you do it now? Do you feel any difference within yourself?

sharon wrote:

In my apprentice blowjob years, i rarely got beyond licking because the guys would cum too quickly. Then as the recipients of my efforts matured, i added sucking to my repertoire. Even though i couldn't get much of the cock into my mouth without gagging, i was pretty content with my performance, thinking the guy would be completely pleased with it. Then i discovered i could suck the balls into my mouth one at a time and roll them around with my tongue. This was for my own playful enjoyment. i never really knew whether or how much the recipient liked it since the cock would usually become soft during this playful excursion.

It wasn't until i got involved in D/s that guys started to tell me what they liked and what they wanted me to do. The consensus seemed to be similar to what You directed... deep throating and swirling my tongue around the head of the cock in a certain way. i could manage the tongue thing with some degree of success, depending on how fussy the Dom was about how it should be done. But no matter what method or position i tried, deep throating seemed to be impossible. i couldn't even come close. The guys would get impatient, i would get frustrated, and we would move on to something else. Eventually, they would just quit asking. Then i met You. You did a much better job of explaining the how and why, and You didn't force Your cock down my throat.

Thinking back, i have doubts whether the others had ever been deep-throated because they didn't seem to understand the process. They wanted to immediately shove their cock down my throat and if that wasn't possible, i had failed. On the other hand, You were very patient and encouraging. With You, it was a very gradual process, going a little farther each time. The poppers helped a lot. i'm not so sure they physically relaxed my throat, but You had me convinced they would do so, and i think that did a great deal to remove the mental blocks (fear of choking), which then allowed me to relax enough. Also, i really wanted to do this for You so i wasn't going to give up anything short of success. Another thing that helped a lot was that You didn't seem to mind all the gagging, choking, and snot-facing... (smile) even providing a towel for me to wipe up the slobber. With anyone else, they would get annoyed the minute i started to gag, so that would be the end of the attempt because they would indicate that i wasn't doing something right. i guess they interpreted it that i didn't really want to do it.

Anyway, to shorten this up a bit, i did eventually learn to deep-throat, some days better than others, and felt like i had accomplished the impossible. Then with some further instruction from You and a little practice, i believe i have it figured out how to create that suction with my throat to squeeze the head of Your cock as it's coming out of my throat.

Steven wrote:

What are your thoughts regarding new techniques, satisfaction, and pride?

sharon wrote:

i think cocksucking is something a lot of women want to do, but not having cocks of our own, we don't know how to do it well. We don't know what feels good. It is, of course, the same thing in reverse. So i wouldn't call it pride, but i feel like i've learned a couple well-kept secrets about cocksucking that i would be happy to share with any woman who is interested. For me, doing something well and producing the desired effect (pleasing You) always brings more satisfaction.

Steven wrote:

How do you feel when I fuck your face and hold my dick deep in your throat and when your face and my cock are dripping wet from your mouth cum?

sharon wrote:

i like it. i wish i could receive it better...wish i could figure out how to breathe through my ears!! It feels like a loss of control; it feels like You are taking what You want, which is what i want You to do. i can't breathe or swallow so everything (saliva) that is produced by my mouth just goes everywhere and i'm sure i look like a mess but, and maybe i'm wrong about this, but my perception is that i must have done something to get You aroused to that point. Then again, maybe i'm not doing such a good job so You find it necessary to take over the situation...hmmm. In either case, i presume it feels good to You and it makes me feel very... submissive.

Note: i wrote most of this before i saw You last night and as it turned out, You brought up several of the same points... so i guess that must mean i'm not too far off?

Steven wrote:

Do you have a current technique?

sharon wrote:

There is not a lot of thinking involved in cocksucking... not a certain procedure that i follow. It's more like just responding to the moment. Let's see... usually when i start, my mouth isn't wet enough, so i use my tongue more. i take Your cock into my mouth and move my tongue in circles on the underside of the shaft and around the head, which seems to stimulate the saliva. Then i might lick it all over so my lips will slide over it more easily. At this point, You're not usually fully erect so it's easier to suck. i might take You all the way in my mouth and move my tongue in waves, like if you were moving food to the back of your throat and swallowing or drinking something quickly. i like doing that. It feels like i'm swallowing (consuming) Your cock and i can feel it growing and filling my throat. Then when Your cock becomes too large and hard, i would probably return to the tongue action since i've just swallowed all the saliva.

Then i might start sucking only on the head, move the tip of my tongue in circles around the ridge a few times, and then take You in a comfortable distance to the back of my mouth. i would stay there and maybe suck for a bit, or just stay there and move my tongue around on the shaft. i would probably go slowly back and forth from the head to the shaft a few times, maybe going up and down the shaft a few times, sucking on the way out, and not swallowing during any of this so my mouth becomes sloppy wet. i frequently have the urge to chew on Your cock, but try to refrain from doing so, although You may have felt the molars a few times.

At some point, i would take You in and start working on relaxing my throat. i guess to do that, i would keep my lips snug around the shaft of Your cock and flatten out my tongue...from the back to the front...kind of like when a doctor is looking in your throat with a tongue depressor and tells you to say "ahhhh." It's a matter of being able to consciously control the movement of that very back part of your tongue where the gag reflex usually takes over. For me, it seems to happen in stages. So i open up my throat like that and take You in slowly until it feels like i'm going to gag, and then i just stay there until my throat relaxes. i have to go slowly to be able to do that. Then depending on the angle i'm at, depending on whether i can breathe, i might take You in a little deeper or i might back off enough to breathe and swallow, swallowing only with my throat. i would probably keep doing that until my jaw got tired, which also depends on the angle.

    i do want to say though, that the gagging actually helps the process because it brings forward the thick saliva from my throat, which makes everything easier. Of course, it also brings forth the snot from my nose, which can make things like breathing rather difficult. i think the biggest thing to overcome was the automatic panic when i would start to gag. i had to develop (with lots & lots of practice) an automatic relaxation response to the gagging sensation. Do You have any idea how hard i worked on that? i couldn't have done it without endless patience on Your part. What in the world was going through Your mind while i was crouched between Your legs those many hours, gagging and blowing my nose and being generally snot-faced? i can't imagine that would be anything even close to a turn-on!

    There are a variety of other things i might do like sucking on Your balls or occasionally rimming, but i seem to stick mostly to Your cock for some reason...i guess the ease of accessibility... being the somewhat lazy slave that i am.

* * *

Sun, 16 Jan 2005
sharon wrote:

Dear Master,

    i went out for dinner with Arthur last night and we had a long talk. He's come a long way in the past few weeks and is really okay with everything now. We agreed that the marriage was over 20+ years ago and that it isn't anyone's fault, but rather we were never right for each other in the first place. We only stayed together out of a sense of responsibility, doing "the right thing." He has become very interested in astrology and has been on several dates in the past few weeks. He also told me he got a tattoo on his arm last summer, which i never even noticed. i guess i was more distracted than i thought. We were leading totally separate lives to a greater extent than i even realized.

    It was, i suppose, kind of weird, but he was telling me about his dates and i was giving him advice on improving his sexual encounters. i also told him about my relationship with You, and he said he wanted me to tell You that You are welcome to come to the house any time, that he has no bad feelings toward You, that he would be pleased to meet You, that he is happy for me that i found You, and he hopes that You and him can become friends some day. As i said, it was kind of a weird evening. It was like there was a huge weight lifted off both of our shoulders, so we could relax and talk to each other as friends without the tension of pretending to be something we're not.

At the end of the evening, he took me to the home of a woman he's been conversing with and wanting to date. She hasn't wanted to become romantic with him because of the fact that he is still living in the same house as me. i explained the situation to her and told her that it's all okay. (laughing) i think she was a little dumbfounded by the visit... might be just a little too weird for her.

Anyway, it seems like the divorce is already done and the actual legal paperwork will only be a minor, hardly noticeable thing. We have agreed that as soon as i get this breast thing taken care of, we'll go ahead with the legal part asap... and we are both happy with that plan. So if all goes well, it should be done within a month. It seemed like a real turning point last night, like things have evolved to the point that everything will be okay, without anyone being angry or hurt. i feel good about it.

Love,
Your slave puppy

Mon, 17 Jan 2005
sharon wrote:

Dear Master,

How is everything? Staying warm? i just want to let You know that i won't be able to serve You on Thursday night this week because i have to do a board presentation. There is big time financial stress within the hospital system, so all directors have been mandated to appear. A lot of departments will be closing and people losing their jobs, so i will have to justify the existence of hospice. We are one of the less valued departments and we don't have a lot of system support, but we have financially carried several of the "glory" departments like cardiac & neuro. i fail to grasp why hospice isn't enthusiastically embraced here like it is everywhere else. It's getting wearisome having to spend all my time fighting about budget & not being able to reinvest our profit to grow the program. Sometimes it feels like i'm talking to a bunch of blockheads.

Anyway, i can be available to serve You any other night this week... in fact, all other nights would be good! i started taking that hormone this morning & feel like i'm ready to strangle the entire world population... slooowly and painfully... one by one... all except You, of course 😊. By administering a daily dose of heavy flogging, You may actually save the rest of the population from unexpected demise! 😀

i miss You.

Love,
Your slave puppy

Wed, 19 Jan 2005
sharon wrote:

Dear Master,

Well, did we wear You out last night? i very carefully avoided washing "Property of S.T." off my chest this morning. It's rather smeared & faded, but still there... i like it 😀. Thank You! Are You taking some time to relax now that Your writing is momentarily finished?

Also, i am wondering if it was just my imagination, or did i sense some resistance from Natasha last night... just little things, like she is trying to reconcile the contradictions in her mind... teetering on a fence. Does she ever talk to You about her thoughts/feelings or only about silly stuff? It seems like there is a potential of her being hurt (emotionally) by all of this... like she doesn't really understand. Of course, i don't know her well enough to say anything... it's just a vague impression. Am i way off-base on this? It just seems like something was different.

Although i can't serve You tomorrow night, i can be available Friday, Saturday, or Sunday... next Tuesday is sooooooo far away. Don't know if i can survive that long without tasting You! 😊

Love,
Your slave puppy

Wed, 19 Jan 2005
Steven wrote:

Dear puppy,

I don't think you're off base. I think she is getting in a little over her head and is trying to figure out this relationship and her feelings. She is not very talkative, so I will need to sit down with her and have a chat. The things she was saying at the end of the evening about not knowing how to explain me, herself, and you to her friends is something she never thought about before. This is a situation that she never dreamed of.

I understand her difficulty in dealing with her private moments (with us) and not being able to talk about them, not wanting the exposure. The possibility of having others judge her in a negative way is very difficult for her. Our world is not like the world she comes from or the world she is in now. I think this unconventional world she is experiencing with us will cause her a great deal of anguish in the future unless she starts to feel comfortable inside herself, which I do not think is going to happen. I could be wrong.

How did your meeting go today?

Sir

Thu, 20 Jan 2005
sharon wrote:

Dear Master,

Yes, that is what i sensed too, although not only at the end of the night. You're just better at describing it. i think she has fallen in love with You and no longer appreciates my presence. i also think she would like to transform You into a more "acceptable boyfriend."

It is difficult to comprehend Your lifestyle and the progression of this kind of relationship with nothing remotely similar to compare it to. i have also struggled with it at times... though i must say that i've never had the slightest desire to change You. i feel like it would be helpful to her if she & i got together to chat sometime. She did seem to be saying she needed a "girlfriend" to talk to. That is what some of the other submissives i have met also craved. However, You are much more experienced at these things than i am, so unless You think it would be a good idea, i'll leave it alone.

These goofy hormones have got me so wired up i'm ready to climb the walls... can't sleep & would really like to break something. It is in this frame of mind that i went to talk to a room full of board members. Not a good plan. i wasn't very nice... but i do think i got my point across without being too offensive, so we'll see what happens. I think i need to start taking these pills at a different time of the day so i don't get so uptight in the late afternoon & early evening. Four down, eight to go. Stay tuned for the next episode when we'll find out whether or not the world population will really survive. (That would be soap opera music You hear playing in the background).

i am really missing You tonight.

Love,
Your slave puppy

Steven writes:

I've said this before: Natasha is talkative, smart, intelligent, informative, but still says nothing of a personal nature. She is very closed, except to say "I have never experienced anything like this before." Last night was the first time she expressed her confusion about our relationship. In the beginning, we were all strangers with no connections, very mysterious, no emotional involvement, and no investment.

It's different now that she has connected; but our relationship is still that of a basic sexual Top and bottom. Now she wants more. She's happy when she is with me, but is finding it difficult because she cannot tell her friends who I am, what I do for a living, what the relationship is about, or that there is a third person who is the primary woman. This relationship is so unconventional for her. It opens itself up for judgment from all of the people she knows. She has nothing to compare it to or to learn from, let alone understand its structure. I have always told her it was going be different. The relationship is of a sexual nature; and it will be my way, in my world. No one ever believes me. There always comes a point in time when they want to change it into a conventional relationship.

Sat, 22 Jan 2005
sharon wrote:

Dear Master,

Thank You for the wonderful evening. Do You suppose that venturing out into that blizzard last night demonstrates my undying devotion to serving You, or simply demonstrates that i've totally lost my mind? i must say that the trip home was a creative adventure in driving for the unbelievable number of us idiots on the road – at least i think we were on the road!

i'm looking at the writing on my body today and trying to figure out what it is that i like about it. i was on the verge of orgasm when You were doing it last night and i don't know why...seems very strange. Maybe it's something like when You cover me with Your scent or feed me...a gift. i continue to be amazed at the strange things that give me pleasure.

i am also thinking about what You said about me knowing You and about Natasha trying to comprehend and come to terms with things in her mind. Even though You are very open about everything right from the beginning, i think that knowing and comprehending You is a process, a journey, a gradual absorption over time...not something that can happen in a couple months...or even a couple years. You don't fit into any known category. i can't even put You in the same category as other Masters/Dominants i've known... and Natasha doesn't even have that much to draw from. You are more like a treasure chest in which i am continuously discovering wonderful new things.

From the outside, You appear to be a bundle of contradictions. From the outside, You appear to be shallow and capricious. But over time, You have proven to be a core of unwavering strength wrapped in a cloak of genteel kindness and consistent integrity. It is these latter things that make You so unique. It is these things that i have mentioned to Natasha (rather effusively) when You are out of the room. If you did, in fact, have the former characteristics, it would be much easier to understand, to manage, to come to terms with... to explain. If it was "just" sex or "just" playing, that is a comfortable, safe (shallow) place... and i think Natasha is reasonably comfortable with it and would probably agree to anything You wanted.

i'm curious, of all the women You've known, how many of them have fallen in love with Your irresistible charm, but have remained sitting on the fence, not willing to take the risk of being hurt and thus, never really understanding who You are. Do You remember when i was sitting on that fence? i think some of those letters are in *The Puppy Papers*.

The thing that got me off the fence is that You never moved, never changed, never compromised... so i was able to trust You and take a leap of faith. If You had wavered at all from what You had previously laid out, this would have deteriorated into a shallow and unsatisfying relationship... You would have appeared weak, no different than anyone else. You have proven over and over that no matter how freaked out i get about anything, You are not going to deviate from Your chosen path. That, probably more than anything, is why i can say "i love You."

In thinking about all this, i've decided i don't want to interfere in whatever Natasha is trying to understand about her relationship with You, or with us. As uncomfortable as it might be, i think she needs to struggle with her feelings on her own... without hearing my (biased 😊) opinions. Otherwise, she will never truly understand You for herself.

As far as her relationship with the two of us, there would be no relationship between her and me without You. i just sort of come along with the package like the many other things that make up Your life. i think she needs to remain focused on You to see whether she is willing to risk crossing over the line. If she does, there will be plenty of time for "girl talk" later. If not, it will be her loss.

i love You.

Your slave puppy

Sun, 23 Jan 2005
Steven wrote:

Dear puppy,

This snowstorm is something else. How is it where you are?
Please explain to me how you viewed me as being "shallow and capricious" and why. What did it mean to you? Was I being lumped in with all others with the same conventional motive, under the same criteria (from the outside)? How long did it take you to understand me?

Sir

Sun, 23 Jan 2005
sharon wrote:

Dear Master,

It must be a full moon! Everyone is going berserk this weekend!
The snow is deep and the snowplows are scarce, but we can still get out & about. i actually enjoy the challenge of navigating in this kind of weather. They do a much, much better job of keeping on top of things in Indiana though.

i did not mean "shallow and capricious" to be offensive. my perception of You in the very beginning was, of course, based on what i knew of other people in the past. i knew that Your business revolved around sex and i didn't perceive that "type" of person to have a whole lot

233

of depth, which You also have stated about others in the same business. i also knew that You had been on Alt.com for at least as long as i had been because i had received several polite soliciting letters from You prior to that when i was seeing other people. my perception of the hundreds of people on Alt who sent form letters to "everyone" on the list was that they desperately wanted sex with anyone and everyone they could find and they were not interested in anything else. (chuckle) i guess i had been on the site too long myself so i had developed a rather tarnished impression of everyone else doing the same thing.

However, You reinforced that idea by saying that You had no intention of limiting Yourself to one person and that you would continue to see others. There is nothing wrong with that and i appreciated Your honesty, but it made You sound rather shallow and impulsive. Of course, i was no different, and i wasn't looking for, or expecting to find, anyone with depth or character on that site. The difference was that You had been doing it for 30+ years and had seemingly not gone beyond the superficial.

On my part, i sensed there was something different about You the first time i met You, and it would be very hard to describe what that was, but i was strongly attracted to it. i very much wanted to see You again. However, i figured we would play a few times, then You would lose interest and move on to someone else... and i was okay with that. i would have been happy with whatever happened. my experience with Doms up to that point was exactly that. They told me they wanted an in-depth relationship with one submissive, but as i have said before, after a couple sessions they would find something wrong or inadequate about me and have me looking for someone else to add to their "harem." i guess it could be called the "always looking, never finding syndrome." You said You weren't going to have me soliciting other women for You, but the rest of them had all said the same thing.

Do You understand that no matter what You said, i had heard it all before & it had all proven to be just a lot of hot air? Do You understand that i couldn't just wholeheartedly believe everything You said until i experienced it for myself? What i discovered over time was that You are for real, more than a casual encounter, more than a "player"... and that i love You. However, the "L-word" sent up a million red flags... DANGER ZONE AHEAD!! i do not say i love someone unless i mean it, but again, in my experience, other people will say they love me and it means nothing to them, but because they said it, i believed it. Does that make sense?

In my experience, it was when i said i loved someone, that was when all the lies started... or got worse. i think that love must mean something different to me than to other people because i don't see it as a smothering or possessive or demanding or clinging or dependent thing, but that is apparently what other people have experienced in their past.

Anyway, the fact that i had these unbidden feelings was a critical point in our relationship. i was sitting squarely on the fence. i could either play it safe and not say anything, or tell You what was on my mind and risk messing everything up. It required a tremendous amount of trust for me to say anything to You and, even then, i was prepared for You to run for the hills.

What i was not prepared for was how You responded when i told You. You said You didn't love me... hallelujah!... AND You didn't run away! It didn't seem to change anything. You were still there and You were still the same person i had grown to love. This is very important: You didn't try to become someone that You thought i wanted You to be. Your knowledge of who You are and what You want in a relationship is an admirable strength. Your honesty and openness in dealing with my little revelation was something i had never, ever experienced before. If You had responded in any other way, it would have ruined everything...i wouldn't have trusted You. As time went on, i continued to tell You that i loved You and, while You acknowledged it, it didn't seem to change anything. It was wonderful.

Then last fall, before i went to Washington, due to whatever personal/emotional/ hormonal crises i was going through, i was feeling very emotionally needy & clingy. i wanted You to tell me that You loved me... but again, You said that You did not. If You had said anything different, i would't have believed You because i would have felt like i coerced it from You. Once again, You proved Yourself trustworthy and that You were not going to compromise for the sake of my nonsense.

All of this is just one aspect of who You are, but there are many other areas of Your life where i've seen You function with the same consistency and honesty. It isn't how You deal with one thing; it is who You are. What i was trying to say yesterday is that if i had never taken that uncomfortable risk of telling You what was on my mind, i never would have really understood the depth of character that You possess. For me to tell Natasha these things about You is not the same as her experiencing them for herself. Words and actions are not the same thing... actions always reveal the truth.

Okay, now that i've written another book, i need to get some of the dreaded housework done!

Stay warm & dry.

i love You.

Your slave puppy

Sun, 23 Jan 2005
Steven wrote:

Dear puppy,

I did not take offense (I was flattered). It was a well-thought-out letter. I was curious and wanted to hear those thoughts. You had never told them to me. I was fascinated. I'm still fascinated by your response (in a good way). But there is something you are forgetting – you were married; I am not.

I went back through my mail to see if I had written to you. I didn't find anything, and I do not remember if I wrote to you or not. I looked through another list to see whom I sent emails to and again I didn't find you. I remember that you contacted me and we discussed why you emailed me when we first met. Is this all a female thing? Are you trying to see if the male remembers? Women, women, women. I do not care if you're a slave or not, your purpose in life is to make a man (me/Your Master) nuts.

Sir

Steven writes:

In my response to puppy's email, I avoided the issues and feelings that puppy expressed. Why? I needed time to think things out. It is easier for me to discuss emotional issues face-to-face (which I did with her) where I have a broader range in which to express myself than in a letter.

We had already discussed the issue of love in our D/s relationship. The first time was in December 2003. (Those letters are in *The Puppy Papers.*) The last time we discussed it was in September, 2004, when I felt I was being put into a position that I had to say what she wanted to hear.

This is the point where I get a little nutty at times. Her thoughts were putting me in an uncomfortable position and I didn't want to hurt her. For me not to hurt her at that moment, I had to placate her, which would make her happy, but I would not be entirely truthful. So I didn't answer her right away. I wanted to think about what she said, the situation, our relationship, and my feelings. I didn't want to be put into a situation where I would later regret what I had said. I did not want to be untruthful in expressing my feelings to puppy and then later try to find a way of backing out of what I had said to her. Retracting my words would disappoint and hurt her; and it would cause difficulties in trust and communication, which is the foundation our relationship.

I have a responsibility to puppy to not violate her trust, to be as honest as possible, and to support her in her life. She has given herself to me to guide her in fully understanding herself, as well as in understanding her place with me and her service to me. For this, I respect and appreciate her submission. For puppy to serve me, she has to respect and love me. I do not take that lightly; I admire and love her for that.

Sun, 23 Jan 2005
sharon wrote:

Dear Master,

     i did not explain clearly. i had various other profiles on Alt long before the one i was using when i winked at You. You had written to those, but i had never responded because i wasn't looking for someone like You at the time. You were *way* out of my league! Yes, i was the one that first contacted You just prior to our first meeting. Sorrrrrry ☺!

     my profiles all said i lived in Chicago. i certainly couldn't put that i lived in small town Indiana and give any kind of accurate description of myself. You see, i was playing the game too. The fact that i put any profiles on there at all or corresponded with anyone was out of boredom. i'm sure it was the same for many other people... nothing wrong with that. But every once in awhile, a jewel can be found among the baubles... lucky surprise for me!

Love,
Your slave puppy

Sun, 23 Jan 2005
Steven wrote:

Dear puppy,

     Aliases? That's not fair. How many did you have? Is this what people do?

Sir

Sun, 23 Jan 2005
sharon wrote:

Dear Master,

  Now, i don't have an answer for that question. i don't even remember what handle i was using when i met You! One thing i can say though is that many people would send the same form letter 20 or 30 times to the same profile and You were not one of them. i don't recall getting more than one letter from You to any single profile... and You were always such a gentleman, unusual for that site. It just sounded like You were light years beyond where i was at the time. Actually, discretion was my biggest concern at the time, so i preferred married men who were as concerned about that as i was.

Love,
Your slave puppy

Mon, 24 Jan 2005
sharon wrote:

Dear Master,

  i hope Your day has gone better than mine. Photography is sounding like a better career every day. i've been trying to talk Arthur into paying to send me to photography school, but he says he doesn't know how he would explain that to any of his girlfriends. i don't think it sounds so unreasonable. He just needs to find more open-minded girlfriends!

  i am having some difficulty removing Your artistic graffiti from my body, and i have an appointment with the surgeon tomorrow. How do You suppose i should explain the reason i have writing in my armpit? ☺

  my appointment is for 3:45, so if You want me to serve You tomorrow night, chances are that i will be later than usual.

i miss You.

Love,
Your slave puppy

Wed, 26 Jan 2005
sharon wrote:

Dear Master

It is interesting sitting here thinking about You spending the evening with Natasha. i don't think i've known about those things before until after-the-fact. Hmmmm....do You have her tied up in the next room or is she sitting by your side as You're reading this? Guess I better keep it short.

Have fun.

Love,
Your slave puppy

Fri, 28 Jan 2005
Natasha wrote:

Dear Sir:

It was wonderful on Wednesday. I enjoyed the dinner and our time together. I do understand what you want of me. It is all so new to me. I never knew it was in me. I'm scared by it, but I can't stop thinking about it and you. I hope that I will be able to please you.

Yours,
Natasha

PS. I still have your writing on my chest

Steven writes:

I took Natasha out for dinner because I needed to talk to her. I told her that if she was uncomfortable, if what I wanted from her was too difficult, then she should not be with me. We discussed how different my world is from hers, and that I understood how hard it was for her not to be able to say anything to her friends. She told me how everyone at the lab has noticed how happy she's been over the last few months. She didn't want me to send her away.

I told her I needed her to communicate with me. She said she could not communicate like puppy, that it was "very difficult" for her, but she would try. I told her I was going add some protocols and push limits in our relationship and play, to make her more submissive to me, and that she might find it too humiliating at first. She understood; she knew from watching puppy, and she admired puppy for her strength. That evening we did some puppy training and I secured her in a stock.

Sat, 29 Jan 2005
sharon wrote:

Dear Master,

i've decided i've been working too hard, so i'm taking a break to think about You 😊! i am thinking about Your delicious cock... and also how much i enjoy sleeping next to You in Your bed, of all things! i really do have to laugh at myself sometimes for the silly things that come to mind. i'm also thinking about the show we're going to in February. i really enjoy going to those things with You... (chuckle) though i'm not sure if it's the book-selling or the people-watching or spending the day watching You... or all of the above. Anyway, i'm looking forward to it. Maybe i could wear the leather skirt You bought for me?

i was talking to a woman at the hair salon this morning who was telling me about a "huge" swinger's convention held every spring at the Rosemont. She said there are thousands of people who go there and lots of vendors, demonstrations, etc., with much of it related to bdsm... nothing too serious, but lots of people curious about it. It sounded like a good place to sell how-to books... as well as *The Puppy Papers*. Are You familiar with what she was talking about? She couldn't remember the name of it. It was actually a rather interesting conversation. She has attended quite a few swinger events but, of course, denied participating in anything. i always figured swingers' events would be a very relaxed & open atmosphere with everyone walking around nude and just having sex with anyone who caught their eye... well, i guess i never really thought that much about it 😊.

From what she said, however, they have all these rooms that people can go into, and there are guards posted at all the doors so no one else can go in or out, and people usually go in a room with the person they arrived with. Now, perhaps i'm missing something, but what is the point of going to a place like that so you can go behind closed doors and have sex with your spouse/partner? She also said there is a lot of drinking that goes on, so by the end of the night there are always a couple of drunk women out on the dance floor with their tops off. Again, i fail to see the excitement of this. From what she described, it sounded like a bunch of children pretending to be "naughty" and giggling at the mention of the word "sex."

She also described a "dungeon scene" where everyone was given a script in an envelope and had to act out whatever part was given to them. Although a little strange, it sounded like a real scene except it all blew up when someone's spouse got jealous and ruined it. It was a fascinating conversation that lasted about an hour. The things that one can learn at the hair salon never cease to amaze me!

i am still thinking about You & wishing i was there serving You. Are You busy tomorrow? If i don't get out of here, i'll end up working the whole day... not good... not good...

i miss You.

Love,
Your slave puppy

Sat, 29 Jan 2005
sharon wrote:

Dear Master,

i hope things have settled down a little for You & that You're enjoying the weekend. i have a favor to ask of You. One day this week when i was at Your house, i was reading an article on the front page of the paper about a court case where they were arguing about stopping the tube feedings on a woman in Florida. i'm wondering if, by chance, You still have that paper and if You do, would it be possible to scan the article and send it to me? Or if that can't be done, if You could find the names of the people involved so maybe i can find something about the case on Google. i have an issue going on at work with some similarities to that case and i have to meet with lawyers, ethicists, and a state guardian about it next week. The info would be very helpful. Thank You.

Love,
Your slave puppy

Sun, 30 Jan 2005
Steven wrote:

Dear puppy,

The case you are referring to is a tragic situation in Florida that has turned into a politically charged, nationally reported court case with many issues and points of view. It is a case in which the state tried to pass a law dealing with a comatose woman (It is called "Terri's Law"). The husband wants to take her off of life support and her parents have been fighting against it. It is a right-to-die case. Her name is Terri Schiavo. According to the paper, she was 26 years old when she suffered brain damage in 1990 after her heart temporarily stopped beating because of an eating disorder.

Sir

Sun, 30 Jan 2005
sharon wrote:

Dear Master,

Thank You for the info. There are about 20,000 articles on-line about "Terri's Law!" It is very relevant to the case i'm dealing with about a 67-year-old Down's Syndrome woman. It is also outrageous that Terri's case has been taken to this extreme considering this was all decided in federal court about 25 years ago. What's really outrageous, however, is that Jeb Bush intervened out of ignorance, emotion, and misguided morality to overturn the decision of the courts.

Furthermore, the general public is riding on a wave of ignorance and emotion that could result in the loss of the right for each of us to make decisions regarding our own medical care. This is the kind of case that infuriates me because Terri's well-being has been forgotten amidst all the radical right-wing misguided moralist imposition, so the woman continues to suffer daily while the lawyers collect millions.

The most ironic thing of all is that Terri ended up in this condition because she herself chose not to eat enough to sustain life. Young women end up with eating disorders due to over-controlling parents who refuse to allow their daughters the right to independent thought. Starving themselves is a desperate attempt to gain control over at least one aspect of their own lives. It is a battle that Terri lost 14 years ago and yet her parents continue to desperately fight for control.

Okay, You are probably not interested in any of this, so i will get off my soapbox. Again, thank You for the info.

Love,
Your slave puppy

Sun, 30 Jan 2005
Steven writes
Dear puppy

Sir
        Stand on your soapbox anytime for as long as you want.

Steven writes:

I don't really know how Terri's parents brought her up or how they treated her. From what I've read and seen on TV, they come off as controlling, self-righteous people, saying this is all for the love of God and their daughter. I believe money was an issue at one point and that it caused animosity between the husband and parents. I feel there is no question that the parents love their daughter, but they have discovered celebrity status because of their daughter's tragedy. They found huge support in the religious right and in right wing politics. Both of these groups, as well as President Bush, used Terri and her parents for their own agendas. At the same time, the parents used religious groups and politicans to become long-term celebrities. Also by using the name of God, Terri's parents entered the argument as good and caring people. I feel her parents' other agenda, which gave their life meaning, was in taking care of their brain-dead daughter for 15 years. This caregiving role gave them a purpose while elevating them into sainthood in the eyes of others.

Realistically, Terri's welfare was not important; she became lost in other people's causes. I believe in the right to die, and that we should have a choice. I feel if you believe in the sanctity of life, you should believe in the cycle of life, not just what works for you at the moment. I have come to this conclusion after listening to countless interviews of the parents, reading many editorals and articles, and watching many discussion shows on this situation. So I agree with puppy, but from a different perspective.

If you don't know who Terri Schiavo was, she was a woman who had been kept alive by tube feedings while living in a comatose state for about 15 years. This was a national right-to-die situation played out in Florida, then later in Washington, DC. It pitted Terri's parents and right wing religious groups against her husband and the right-to-choose groups. It involved the court system, a lot of people with agendas, local politicians, conservative religious leaders, congressmen, and finally President Bush who rushed in at the last minute for political gain. Eventually Terri's tube feeding was stopped and she died.

An autopsy was later performed, revealing that the damage to her brain "was irreversible, and no amount of therapy or treatment would have regenerated the massive loss of neurons." Dr. Jon Thogmartin, the Pinellas-Pasco County Medical Examiner who led the autopsy team, also reported that, "Her brain was profoundly atrophied" and, as far as her eyesight was concerned, the vision centers of her brain were dead, which meant she was blind. He also said his examination turned up no signs of abuse or trauma – allegations leveled by Terri Schiavo's parents, Bob and Mary Schindler, against Terri's husband and legal guardian, Michael Schiavo.

Wed, 2 Feb 2005
sharon wrote:

Dear Master,

Thank You for letting me serve You last night. i know it isn't any fun for You with me bleeding all the time and i appreciate Your patience. It's gone on way too long. If You would rather not have me come over tomorrow night, that is perfectly understandable. i don't want to take away from what You could be doing with Natasha and besides that, i have a lot of work to do. i hope You're feeling better.

Love,
Your slave puppy

Wed, 2 Feb 2005
Steven wrote:

Dear puppy,

She is also bleeding, so we'll get a little dinner and go to the movies.

Sir

Wed, 2 Feb 2005
sharon wrote:

Dear Master,

(laughing) You are really having bad luck this week! One of the benefits of having more than one woman in Your life ought to be that *someone* is available for Your pleasure. Perhaps You need a couple more subs/slaves to increase Your odds! Though, in one way or another, i fully intend to have this problem permanently resolved within the next month... and then there will be no more rest for my poor Master! i will see You tomorrow.

Happy Groundhog's Day!!

Love,
Your slave puppy

Fri, 4 Feb 2005
sharon wrote:

Dear Master,

     i had a nice time last night. i didn't think we'd get back to that restaurant until springtime, but the weather was rather nice for a walk last night... and the food delicious!

     My niece was over in Rwanda during the time portrayed in the movie and, as i was watching the movie, i had visions of my niece running across a field in Rwanda and being shot at. i clearly remember when she first got back and she was telling us about the experience and how she was "protected by God." At the time, all i could think of was how stupid it was to let a naive 18-year-old girl go to a place like that! i was definitely one of those apathetic Americans who didn't care what the African natives did so long as i was sitting comfortably in my own home and my own family wasn't involved. The movie makes me feel guilty, which is the purpose of it, I think. However, if each of us were to bear the burdens of the entire world on our shoulders, none of us would be able to do any good. i think we have to focus on what we can do whenever and wherever we have the opportunity, without feeling guilty that we can't help everyone or solve every problem in the world. There is so much to be done, so many needy people right here in our own country, in our own backyards. Okay, now i will quietly step off my soapbox... seems i'm doing that a lot lately 😊.

     Anyway, You seemed kind of concerned about me at the end of the night and i want to apologize if i seemed kind of distant even before the movie. It has been a really rough week at work. i was so preoccupied thinking about it when i was waiting in Your office that i probably would have sat there all night if You didn't come through that way. i wish i could be one of those people who can do these kinds of things without losing a wink of sleep.

So anyway, physically i'm fine. The bleeding is just a tremendous annoyance because it interferes with things i want to do... like serving You. i did get to talk to the doctor today. Now he wants me to go on birth control pills for a month to stop the bleeding, then schedule the surgery for 4 weeks from now, which is also very aggravating because i just want to get done with all this so i can get this divorce over with and get on with my life.

What i really, really need is for You to make the world stop for just a moment... and make me fly.

Love,
Your slave puppy

Steven writes:

The movie was *Hotel Rwanda*.

Fri, 4 Feb 2005
Steven wrote:

Dear puppy,

I knew something was a little off last night but I didn't know what it was, so I kept on talking at dinner. I think I was stupidly trying to talk through the distraction of silence. I should have asked you what the problem was, or better yet, if anything was troubling you. Natasha was happy to be there, and I should have been more attentive, knowing that something was not right. That is my place, my responsibility. I hope all is better today. What is going on at work? What surgery will the Doctor be doing?

Sir

Sun, 6 Feb 2005
sharon wrote:

Dear Master,

Good evening Sir....You certainly know how to get my attention. i promise i will be a more obedient slave.

First the ball gag, which is too big to fit comfortably in my mouth, then the handcuffs, which are always too tight to find a comfortable position, then the blindfold and those damn clothes pins. i knew i was in for a lecture. i don't know how i'm supposed to pay attention when i'm sitting there struggling with my jaw aching, wrists hurting, spit running down my chin, and my nipples being crushed to smithereens.

However, that was not Your problem. You were not pleased with my service and my lack of attention to Your needs. i presume You didn't want to hear any of my excuses... except perhaps a muffled "Yes Sir." i guess i need that every so often to keep me from getting so wrapped up in my own issues. i don't know how i would have made it through the last few months without You to help me keep things in perspective.

You know i love You and want to serve You. Thank You for reminding me why i'm there. i will do better.

Love,
Your slave puppy

Sun, 6 Feb 2005
sharon wrote:

Dear Master,

my experience last night has gotten me thinking. You asked me a while back how i have changed since i met You and i doubt that i gave You much of a response... then again, maybe i did. Anyway, i think the change has been so gradual that i haven't fully comprehended it. i think i have really and truly developed a slave mindset, not something i can turn on or off depending on whether i'm actually in Your presence. i'm wondering if You really comprehend how much control You have over me... and how lost i am without You. It's almost like i've opened myself to You to the point that i've lost the instinct to protect myself from anyone or anything else... vulnerable... like i need You to protect me because i've lost the ability to say no…

Love,
Your slave puppy

Sun, 6 Feb 2005
Steven wrote:

Dear puppy,

This doesn't sound like you; the world seems to have landed on you feet first. With all the changes in your life, the physical problems and stress, it's starting to take its toll on you mentally and emotionally. I know

it's wearing you down to where you can't see the forest through the trees right now.
My dear puppy, look how you have opened yourself up to me in your letters. I have always appreciated your trust in me; I need that trust from you. Puppy, you have always been truthful and obedient. You're a good slave; I have trained you well. Yes, I have noticed the change; I wanted that change. I will hold you up, support you, protect and guide you. We will get through all this garbage in your life.

Sir

Tue, 8 Feb 2005
sharon wrote:
Dear Master,

How is everything? What is Bill doing with the manuscript all this time if he hasn't even decided whether he will work on it? He must come from the same school as Your computer guys! You must be getting frustrated. It would be hard to work on anything else with that being unfinished. i bet i could put the book together as well as anyone, and fill in the missing pieces from what You've told me... and be much more efficient at it... and i'm even free labor!

What time will You be setting up on Friday? i won't be able to get there real early... maybe 4 or 4:30 at the earliest. Does the show start Friday or Saturday? End Sunday?

See You soon! i miss You.

Love,
Your slave puppy

Tue, 8 Feb 2005
Steven wrote:
Dear puppy,

We will set up Friday afternoon; vending ends on Sunday. It's at the Purple Hotel, 4500 West Touhy. If you can get there around 4-4:30, that would be good.

I'm still waiting for Bill to get back to me to see if he will work on the book. I don't know if he's capable of understanding the complexities of it, but at this point, I don't think I want him. I will wait until Thursday. If I don't hear from him by then, you and I will talk. See you tomorrow.

Sir

Steven writes:

      Bill was recommended to me by a friend to edit my book. I sent him the manuscript, and he was going to let me know if he wanted to take on the project. Three to four weeks had gone by and I had not heard from him, so I sent an e-mail thanking him for taking the time to look at the manuscript.

      Actually, the perfect person to help me put the book project together is puppy. She is an excellent writer, takes direction well, understands how I want the book to be, and understands the direction that the book should go in. She is thorough, detailed, organized, and communicates exceptionally well.

Thu, 10 Feb 2005
sharon wrote:

Dear Master,

      i had a wonderful time serving You last night, and i appreciate You showing me what You want me to do. However, i must confess that being in a table position creates a hunger in my pussy for Your cock... not sure how long i can hold still with that going on... might be best not to use me to set a hot cup of coffee on! ☺

      i also want to thank You for letting me work on Your book, and i apologize for not being able to do it sooner. i have about 400 policies to write before the Joint Commission gets here to survey us. If we don't pass the survey, we'll be out of business. Now i have even more reason to get them done ASAP – so i can focus on Your book!

      Also, my son Dale called me last night. He was very excited to say he was hired full-time at an investment bank in Chicago. They are going to pay him over $100K per year + perks until he graduates a year from now, but he will actually only be working for them this summer. Not a bad deal! Then after he graduates, he can transfer to their main office on Wall Street. He says i was right that all the hard work would pay off in the end. So nice to hear one of my kids say that his mother was right about something! i think i will mark that one on the calendar!

i hope You have a wonderful day! It was soooooooo good to feel You inside of me last night.

i love You.

Your slave puppy

Sun, 13 Feb 2005
Joanne G. wrote:

Hi, Steven,

Just wanted to say what a pleasure it was last night joining you and puppy in a scene. It was a nice surprise to see you, and I enjoyed meeting Sharon (quiet girl that she is). I really, really appreciated your asking me to join you in fisting her. It was definitely grand fun.

Take care,
Joanne

Steven writes:

Joanne is referring to the weekend of February 12-13 when puppy and I were vending at "Sinsations in Leather" and the Leather Rose was also having a fundraising event for a member's sister who had brain cancer. The Leather Rose had classes and demonstrations, as did Sinsations. We went over to the Rose for a few hours after we finished vending. I think there were about 150 people at the Rose that night. As I looked around the room, it looked better than I remembered. They had redecorated the place and had added new equipment.

The Rose held two fundraising auctions. One was a silent auction, and the other was a live auction in which slaves and Dominants were auctioned off to the highest bidder who wanted to do a scene with them. When the last person was auctioned off, the Rose was transformed back into a dungeon. The equipment was put in place, lights turned down, and the music turned up.

Barring anything unforeseen, I knew I was going to play that night. I brought lube and towels with me; I can use my belt to bind puppy; and I can create all the pain and pleasure I desire with my hands. I found an unoccupied padded bench in a corner of the large room. There wasn't any privacy because people were talking and laughing and standing or sitting everywhere.

Since I planned to do a fisting scene, I didn't need much space. I asked Joanne, a friend who had given a class on fisting that afternoon, to join us. Joanne was most gracious and said "I would love to." To keep it simple, I told Joanne I wanted her to follow me when I came out of puppy, so puppy would have two different sensations in her. One fist after another would be the rhythm.

puppy had been wearing a corset all day and I left it on her when I started fisting her, knowing it would be restrictive and uncomfortable for her to orgasm in. puppy was great. I was surprised how well she kept her concentration and balance lying on her back on the narrow bench with her legs spread wide. After a while, I had her change position and get on all fours, which made fisting a little more difficult since she had to be somewhat close-legged so as not to fall off the bench. Then I finally took off the corset.

Puppy couldn't have been any tighter; she had wave after wave of orgasms. I told puppy how proud I was to own her. When I play/scene, I normally do not socialize; I want nothing to distract me away from puppy. I only care about being connected with her and being in control of the scene at all times. In the middle of this carnival atmosphere, I was connected with puppy and I was in total control.

As for Joanne, she seemed to be in her own world, lost in puppy's pussy. Perhaps 10 minutes went by before I gave puppy a reprieve and had her stand up so I could hug her, talk to her, tell her how proud I was of her. Then I had Joanne fist her standing up. We switched back and forth, holding and fisting puppy for about 15 minutes and several more orgasms. I stopped at the last big eruption and held on to puppy when we finished. She rested her head on my shoulder and had this big dream-like smile on her face.

Joanne thanked me for letting her participate in our scene. We cleaned up, got dressed, and as we were making our way to the door, people moved aside and nodded their approval. puppy drove us back to my home. I don't think she knows how she got there.

Mon, 14 Feb 2005
sharon wrote:

Dear Master,

i think there is a "god" somewhere with a sadistic sense of humor who is having a grand time orchestrating stress in my life. i've had so many "top priority" projects dumped in my lap that i will have to work 48 hours a day for a year to even scratch the surface. i'm thinking of developing multiple personalities and then assigning each of them a few dozen things to do... or maybe i'll just work on growing more arms & heads because it is apparently my job to do everyone else's job because they are so busy talking about being so busy that they don't have time to do anything else.

Okay, now that i've gotten that out of my system, i will try to calm down enough to remember the weekend.

Saturday night at the Leather Rose... it was a different experience. The biggest thing on my mind Saturday was that the corset was verrrry uncomfortable. Either it was tight in the wrong places or i don't think there is enough padding over my lower ribs. i really thought i was going to have bruises all around the bottom of my ribs from breathing. By the time we got to the Rose, all I wanted to do was take that thing off.

As far as the place itself, it was a different type of atmosphere than when we were at Tina's or GD. With the event going on, there were a lot more people there and it was more like a social or party atmosphere. i guess i wasn't mentally prepared for a fisting scene in such a loud, crowded place. With everyone talking so loud, i couldn't hear anything You were saying and couldn't make a connection with You at the beginning. For a while, i wasn't sure where You were. i was feeling nervous, out of sorts, and not relaxed enough to be fisted. In the beginning, i felt like my body was being used for the scene but the rest of me was not there.

The blindfold helped, but when You finally took the corset off, i was a whole lot more relaxed. I was on my hands & knees on that bench and You were fisting me, and all i could hear were loud voices right next to me. It felt like i was on exhibit at some carnival show... quite a humbling experience i guess. i guess that goes back to what we were talking about before about different kinds of exhibitionism. It's different having some level of awareness that other people might be watching... or being on display in the middle of a party where someone could potentially spill a drink on you or trip over you. i guess it's like being an object...like a piece of furniture or a toy...a very different experience than anything we've done up to this point.

i don't know how i ended up standing up and holding on to You, but by that point, i'd had so many orgasms the crowd had faded into the background. Joanne was fisting me and i had my face buried in Your neck, while You somehow managed to provide extra stimulation from the rear.

Joanne does fisting very different than You. Her fist feels much smaller, she's much more gentle, and she moves very different than You. With the two of you switching back & forth, i was all over the place. At the same time, i was completely connected to You. i don't know how You do it, but i always end up being exactly where You want me to be... and loving it.

For some reason, i feel different than all the other people i see at these places. i'm not sure why... maybe it's an ego thing... will have to think about that some more. Anyway, i have to say the evening was a very different experience, something i would have to get used to... like i'm about three steps behind the program again. It's been a while since i've had to play catch-up with You. You must think it's time to expand my boundaries... and just when i thought i had seen and done everything!!

Something else i want to comment on is the humiliation class we went to... along with the stuff You said that Steve & Karen do. i would like to have stayed to watch the scene that Steve & Karen were starting. That kind of play isn't something i've really conceived of before. The scene they (Wilson & Laura) did in that class created all kinds of unidentified emotions...like it was so repulsive as to make you sick or angry, but there was something about it that was strangely intriguing, fascinating. It was somehow a more sophisticated, higher level of play, if that makes any sense... very memorable. It seems the whole weekend is something to remember... and ponder for a while.

Love,
Your slave puppy

Steven writes:

Some months later puppy wrote to me about her memories of the fisting scene that we had with Joanne at the Rose.

Sat, 16 July 2005
sharon wrote:

Dear Master,

It's interesting that this really isn't the memories i retained from that night or weekend. my long-term memory must filter out the negatives and hold on to the positives. i just remember that it was a very energized atmosphere and i remember when i was holding on to You and being fisted by Joanne, that i was totally consumed by what the two of you were doing, unaware of anything else, and felt very...safe...cared for, i guess...like i was in a cocoon. It must be the "sub space" that I remember... nothing else.

Love,
Your slave puppy

Steven writes:

At the Sinsation event, I took puppy to a class on humiliation presented by Wilson and Laura. It was a 101 class that consisted of consensual physical assault, verbal insults, and name-calling. They talked about the submissive bringing the Dominant along as the submissive learns about herself and what areas she wants to explore. They also talked about the need for open communication and the release that humiliation scenes provide for them. This type of humiliation play is not an area that many people play in. Even on their basic level, it would be devastating to most people, and uncomfortable for many people to watch.

Steve and Karen (PhantomMaster and Femcar) are well known for their style of humiliation play. It is far more sophisticated in the area of total breakdown of the self, and encompasses all forms of physical, mental, and emotional humiliation. Steve and Karen have presented at numerous events around the country; and Steve is on the board of directors for the LRA.

Mon, 14 Feb 2005
Steven wrote:

Dear puppy,

I didn't take the corset off of you to make it easier for you to play.

I wanted you to see that class on humiliation. I wanted you to hear about the submissive's mindset, her needs, desires, and headspace. I am glad it perked up some interest in you. We already do a variety of humiliation scenes; but their scenes are more physical and aggressive. We will talk tomorrow about the variations of humiliation scenes and what intrigues you about them. Communication is everything. Wilson and Laura's scenes are aggressive, which means you cannot be passive. I believe you will like it and have some gushing orgasms. I will find out when Steve and Karen are giving a class. I think you will find it very interesting.

Sir

Mon, 14 Feb 2005
sharon wrote:

Dear Master,

    Yes, i know Saturday went exactly as You intended, and that's why i tried not to complain about the corset... i certainly didn't want to provoke any further discomfort! Though i will now admit there was a point around the time we were driving to dinner and during dinner when i was on the verge of screaming or crying or saying something not very nice, and it took a tremendous amount of effort to remain civilized... so i do hope You derived immense pleasure from my trials and tribulations! ☺ They certainly wore me out... i slept very well, thank You.

    i don't know how i would respond to that kind of humiliation play, but it isn't the aggressiveness of it that intrigued me. It was more like the... degradation?... or like Laura said, something about the confronting of emotions... in the same way that physical pain (whipping) takes you beyond what you think you can handle to a place of release. It seems like if you did the same thing with humiliation, it would also take you beyond the emotions to a similar place of release... kind of like confronting your weaknesses and making them disappear. But like You (or someone) were talking about emotional land mines... it could be dangerous. The thing about land mines is that you don't know they're there until you step on one. i suppose a person would have to get angry with that kind of thing to keep from becoming a sobbing mess... interesting. i don't know if i would be brave enough to try it in the extreme, especially in a public place. It might be interesting though to do some gradual experimenting to see where it goes...

    i hope You do realize that with all of this pondering, i'm not getting any work done and therefore, not getting any closer to working on Your book!

See You soon!

Love,
Your slave puppy

Wed, 16 Feb 2005
sharon wrote:

Subject: The Good, the Bad, and the Ugly

Dear Master,

i'm not sure where to start this letter because right now the ugly has really rocked my boat and i'm kind of in shock. i think Arthur has cancer, and i think it has already seriously metastasized. In the past couple months, he has lost about 40-50 lbs, which i thought was just a combination of stress, nerves, self-pity, alcohol, and not eating right. When i got home Sunday, he was really worried and said his hair was falling out and that he has been having seizures. He went to see a doctor yesterday and when i asked him about it tonight, he said something about this lump, which he then showed me. It looks like a tumor in the back of his throat. He showed me where large patches of hair had fallen out, and said he had a seizure on Sunday that lasted about an hour, and he's also having severe bone pain. i haven't really paid attention to what he looks like lately, but can now see that he looks horrible... something is definitely seriously wrong with his health.

Now he says he's not going to do anything about it... which IS his typical martyrdom. He says he wants me to finalize the divorce as soon as possible so he can have a life of his own. The thing is, if he keeps going like he is, he looks like he could be dead in a couple months for godsakes. Damn... talk about a guilt trip. i am going to be so pissed off if this is some kind of neurotic manipulative ploy to get me back. That's not going to happen, but i've at least got to get him back to the doctor's tomorrow, have them run some tests, and find out what this is.

The interview i went to this evening was good. I'm really excited about it. i interviewed with the president/founder of the company who has a very refreshing business philosophy, very attuned to my own. We talked and laughed for a couple hours. He is very innovative, open-minded and, of all things, he is Jewish. i am trying to figure out why i seem to repeatedly be attracted to the philosophies of Jewish men!

Anyway, since starting the business 12 years ago, he has opened multiple branches throughout the surrounding states. Although he has no specific position open right now, he wants to create a position specifically tailored to my interests, skills, and experience. We talked about something in which i would do education and QA, traveling among the other branches and working sort of like an independent consultant. Sounds interesting, fun, and stress-free... and he seemed to be agreeable to my suggested salary, which is about $7K more than i'm getting now. i always screw myself by not asking for enough, but in reality, i would be willing to take less salary than i'm getting now for an opportunity like this.

Which brings me to the bad... things are getting worse by the day where I am now. It took super-human self-control, both yesterday and today, to not walk out the door and never look back... which brings me to last night and Your request for my "analysis" of the humiliation scene.

i was really stressed when i got to Your house last night because i had been "ambushed" by a hospital administrator as i left work, who accused me of all sorts of things, and did it in front of the clinical supervisor i just hired. That was humiliation. So, i wasn't too sure i was in a good frame of mind to proceed with the humiliation scene with You... i was feeling a bit fragile.

But when You started saying things to me, i almost had to laugh because everything You said was exactly true. All my life, people have treated me like i'm some kind of super-intelligent genius, when in fact, i know i'm no smarter than anyone else and have done some pretty darn stupid things, often repeatedly. When You made the statement about how stupid i was when i met You, it was like... ahhh, finalllly someone is being truthful! It may sound dumb, but that simple statement was liberating... it was positive, not negative.

All the things You said were true and so they all, to some extent, produced the same reaction. It was kind of like being taken down from some artificial pedestal where i never should have been or wanted to be in the first place... like being released from some phony mold other people have insisted on putting me in.

Although i had said the night before that it wasn't the aggressiveness of it that attracted me to the scene we watched, when You pulled my hair and later pushed me on the bed, i wanted You to keep going... i don't know…maybe until i fought back? Then in the bathroom, i really starting to get into it and got very turned on when You shoved my head in the toilet. Again, i was wishing that You wouldn't stop.

Something else about last night, when You had me tied in the chair, the music You had on... *Out of Africa?*... that music is so beautiful. It does something to me every time You play it... puts me in a sunny, warm, happy, peaceful, submissive place.

i love You.

Your slave puppy

Thu, 17 Feb 2005
Steven wrote:

Dear puppy,

Sorry about Arthur. What does the doctor have to say? When is he going to get his test results back? How are you doing? When will you hear back from this man about this new job offer?

Sir

Thu, 17 Feb 2005
sharon wrote:

Dear Master,

Arthur is doing okay. There's plenty of beer for him to keep himself numb. He's supposed to get lab results back on Monday, so we'll see what happens after that.

The bleeding is still relatively light but getting heavier each day... will probably be a full-fledged period by tomorrow... which is still relatively light compared to what it used to be. How's that for talking in circles!

If i don't hear about the new job by tomorrow afternoon, i will call him. i want to give him a little time to think about the possibilities. He may come up with something even better!

See You tonight!

Love,
Your slave puppy

Sun, 20 Feb 2005
sharon wrote:

Dear Master

i want to say that despite the unusually stressful week, i was unbelievably relaxed both Thursday and Friday night... kind of off in my own little world, i guess. i really enjoyed serving You both nights. i'm trying to figure out if it was the humiliation/ degradation play that made me feel so peaceful, with not a care in the world... almost like it got me centered, focused, and stopped the world from spinning... a phenomenon.

Whenever i've thought of "subspace," it was always in relation to being whipped or something similar. i never really thought of it from a humiliation/degradation aspect, but if that was the source of the peacefulness, it is actually a much smoother way of getting there... interesting... more like slipping into it... much to explore.

i think i will make some hot chocolate and start reading Your manuscript... so i'll be ready to start writing by next weekend.

i miss You.

Love,
Your slave puppy

Humiliation

Steven writes:

I want to explain a little about humiliation play. First let me say that I enjoy humiliation scenes. The psychological control that is given to me and the reactions I can create in my partner are very exhilarating to me. I enjoy making a submissive do things she may not want to do, taking her to areas she doesn't want to go, yet areas that pull her in and absolutely excite her in a humiliating or demeaning way. The psychological control that is given to me is empowering. I feed off of the subtleties and dramatics of humiliation play; it feeds my sadistic needs, but not in the way most people might think. It is the bottom's masochistic needs that fuel and ignite these scenes.

Humiliation play covers a very broad range of emotional, psychological, and physical play. It creates different thoughts and feelings in each person. It takes a strong person to allow him/herself to be put into a psychologically or emotionally uncomfortable situation, and to allow another person to control that situation.

Of course, something that is humiliating to one person may be sexy to another. The people I play with want to humble themselves to me. They get excited by doing something embarrassing, by being forced, or being made to submit to humiliating acts or situations they perceive to be uncomfortable, humiliating, degrading, and demeaning to them. This type of play takes them into a forbidden emotional place within their mind. I love the connection that humiliation play produces. The energy that accelerates between us is very exciting and intense. Their masochism feeds my sadism

Before I go any further, I have to mention the golden rule of humiliation and BDSM play. Nothing that is said in confidence or used in a scene is ever thrown back at, or ever used to hurt either person outside of the scene. I want to be very clear on this point.

I'm going to discuss a little bit about humiliation play (it must be consensual), give a few examples and some simple explanations of what kind of scenes they are, but not necessarily what I do. People in the conventional world and many in the world of BDSM would never consciously think of playing anything that makes them feel psychologically or emotionally uncomfortable. They would never put themselves into such a vulnerable position, a position that would give another person such power over them, a position that would give one person the ability to psychologically, emotionally, and in some circumstances, physically abuse the other person in sexual and rough play. For BDSMers, I am not talking about a bondage, flogging or spanking scene.

Humiliation, for the most part, is the bottom's scene. If the bottom doesn't want to do humiliation play, it doesn't happen because humiliation play is cause and effect. It involves responses that feed off of each other. If the recipient (bottom) is too passive, then the Top could escalate the scene into unhealthy waters without knowing it. NOT GOOD. A Top must be aware of and read the bottom's emotional state at all times. The bottom has the right to get out of control, but the Top cannot and does not have the right to be out of control.

Heavy humiliation play should not be done by people who are sensitive to criticism, people who do not want to explore their emotional and psychological depths, people who have self-esteem issues which have not been openly discussed, or couples whose relationship is not built on a solid foundation of communication and trust. Any bad play scene can bring both of you back to the drawing board, but a bad humiliation scene can have long-lasting effects within the trust department, meaning your relationship could be history within minutes.

Most people play some sort of humiliation in various degrees without being aware of it because they don't perceive what they're doing as being humiliating. Uncomfortable, yes; humiliating, no. Some examples of humilation include having the lights on during sex, being on their back with their legs spread wide open as their partner takes his/her time inspecting their privates at his/her leisure, or being put into the mental position of submitting to a situation or sexual act they're uncomfortable with, such as licking, rimming, or tongue fucking the other person's asshole. Depending on the Top and bottom's sensibilities, moral conventions, conservative or liberal attitudes, fears, guilts, egos, and degree of exhibitionism, humiliation scenes can be very gratifying, rewarding, and erotic.

For many people, simple humiliation scenes may include having sex in the "doggy" position; being asked to do something you're not comfortable with during sex; getting naked in the bright light and being told to stand in the middle of the room while the other person is fully clothed; being tied down, fully exposed, while the other person examines you very closely and makes comments on your body; being made to wear clothing that embarrasses you; or having your partner watch you while you're using the toilet.

Some intense humiliation scenes may include the Top forcibly holding the bottom down; masturbating and ejaculating on the bottom while yelling obscenities; golden shower scenes; or forced feeding to the point where the person gags, vomits, and is made to eat it again, etc.

Simple verbal humiliation may include calling your partner a whore, slut, pig, cocksucker, or faggot; saying they are terrible in bed, saying they can't satisfy you, saying their cunt stinks or their cock tastes like shit; or bondage interrogation scenes such as extracting a credit card pin number or their parents' telephone number or playing on a personal situation that they feel guilty about, etc.

Humiliation scenes can produce a huge emotional release that ends in exhaustion, or they may produce the need for intense make-up sex after the scene is over. It can be a path of conquering fears and hang-ups, or it can be someone's worst nightmare. If both people really enjoy and want to experience and explore the edgier side of humiliation play, it must be with increased knowledge about yourselves and each other. To be successful and benefit from its rewards, both partners must have an excellent, open line of communication built on a solid foundation of trust. Aftercare is important with this type of play, and after-care differs for each person as well as the type of scene that was played. Some bottoms need to be left alone so they can gather themselves back together after a humiliation scene.

I usually don't do physically aggressive humiliation play or heavy verbal abuse, except when my partner desires it. Puppy and I do many variations of humiliation. We have gotten so used to what we do that it has become second nature to us. The form of humiliation I do is centered on control, on having her do anything I want, any time and any place I desire.

Wed, 23 Feb 2005
sharon wrote:

Dear Master,

  Arthur has an appointment at 7:45 Sat morning with an ENT, so i think it would be best if i come home Friday night. The thing has grown to twice the size in the past week and the doc says it's urgent to find out for sure what it is. i want to hear for myself what the specialist has to say.

See You tomorrow!

Love,
Your slave puppy

Fri, 25 Feb 2005
sharon wrote:

Dear Master,

  Well, once again, i don't know where my head was on the way home last night! i drove several miles past my exit before i even realized i missed it! This is the third time i've done that....talk about spaced out! Thank you for letting me serve You last night.
  Sitting in Your kitchen, naked, blindfolded, hands cuffed behind my back...i was nervous about what You were going to do next. i was nervous about whether i had done something wrong. Either way, i figured You had something important to talk about since being blindfolded always gets my attention. It immediately takes me away from everything else and focuses my attention completely on You. It makes whatever You're saying seem twice as important. Of course, i never know whether You're using the blindfold to get my attention or whether it's part of a larger scene.
  Last night You were quiet. i could hear You taking care of the dogs. Every so often You came over and played with my nipples or my pussy. It felt like You were teasing me, but maybe You were thinking about something else and absentmindedly playing with me because i was sitting there...sort of available! i kept spreading my legs wider, hoping You would pursue the pussy play a little further, but each time i did that, You walked away. It was so frustrating not being able to touch You. i

could feel the bar stool getting wet where i was sitting and my poor, poor pussy was getting no relief.

You started talking about Your day, while ignoring my distress. i don't know if You're aware how every little touch seems so magnified when i'm blindfolded and tied. When You were finished taking care of the animals, You came over and removed the handcuffs and blindfold and told me to get dressed because we were going out for dinner.

Then You made me wait all through what seemed like a very long dinner until we finally got back to Your house. Have i told You lately how much i love it when You fuck me?

Love,
Your slave puppy

Sat, 26 Feb 2005
sharon wrote:

Dear Master,

Arthur refused to let me go with him to see the doctor this morning, but he said the doctor told him it's not cancer, apparently nothing to worry about, so i'm not going to. Then he spent the rest of the day "celebrating" and wouldn't leave me alone, spilled stuff all over, etc., etc. Now that he's so drunk he can barely stand up, he just left to go out on a date. Good riddance... let her clean up after him.

On the brighter side, Dale called this morning. He's all excited that he has been chosen to do an internship in London, apparently the ultimate opportunity in the world according to him. I guess the company is the most prestigious accounting firm in the world, but he will be assigned to the investment banking branch, so it is the perfect opportunity for him. He will fly in to Rome and spend 10 days sightseeing before going to London. He's hoping the timing will be right for him to be in Rome for the installation of a new pope, which means he's counting on the fact that the current one will die soon. He's also planning to be in Amsterdam for the Tulip Festival, which he says is the biggest party in Europe. At the end of the internship, he'll spend 7 days in Paris where he plans to buy his wardrobe for the next year. While in London, he'll be staying in a five-star hotel, with his own limo service, and all other expenses paid. Damn, i sure picked the wrong profession to go into! i'm really proud of him; it is quite an honor to be chosen for that particular internship... i guess they usually go only to Harvard students.

Despite all the interruptions, i managed to read more of Your manuscript. i will write more about that in a separate e-mail.

Love,
Your slave puppy

Sun, 27 Feb 2005
sharon wrote:

Dear Master,

i have finished reading everything and, as i suspected, should have reserved my comments until done. Your introduction to the e-mails with Guy Baldwin (as well as the e-mails themselves) is what i was looking for to establish the tone for the book. i had only seen one of those e-mails before. Together they are a powerful piece. i think that excerpts from David Rosen's testimony are important to include since so much reference is made to him. Also, did You testify in the trial? If so, Your testimony probably wouldn't need to be included, but i would like to read it.

As far as dividing the book into sections, i think the important distinctions are 1) preparing the defense strategy and the events leading up to the trial; 2) the trial itself; and 3) what has happened since then...the ongoing battle...which may also be a good place for the "Certifying Masters" piece and "BDSM: The Sexual Future." i want to put things (interviews, testimonies) in chronological order so the reader can see the evolution of thought that took place... again, interspersed with Your writings directly responding to points/comments made by the others.

i don't think You need to be at all concerned about the book sounding too egotistical. It doesn't come across that way at all. The book is about opposing definitions and philosophies, strongly felt by individuals on both sides, with both sides seeking to be understood and determined to fight for what they believe in... very powerful and moving stuff.

i think the book is going to be very good, very important, and very powerful.

Love,
Your slave puppy

Sun, 27 Feb 2005
sharon wrote:

Dear Master,

Good grief! i've nearly burned the house down... have all the windows open and the smell is still enough to make me dizzy/nauseous. i really need to stay out of the kitchen. Looks like it will be bread and water for supper tonight!

i am trying to put myself in Your shoes, immerse myself in Your story, to get a feel for how it flows, to see things as You saw and experienced them. i am the ignorant one; Your experience is foreign to me.

my questions are not in any way meant to be judgmental, and Your answers probably don't need to be in the book, unless You recall something quite significant or to clarify something You've already written. But Your answers are very helpful to me in knowing how the book should go together. i want it to be Your story, not my interpretation of Your story. So i hope You will understand that i'm just trying to get as accurate of an understanding as possible and may ask seemingly unimportant questions over & over... seems to me like You did the same thing with me in the last book! ☺

Back to work!

Love,
Your slave puppy

Sun, 27 Feb 2005
Steven wrote:

Dear puppy,

There is no one better than you to put this book together. You're smart and you care. The more questions you ask, the better it will be, and I want it to be the best of its kind.

I don't think I testified at the trial; it's funny, but I don't remember.

The day of the raid, the government took what they could find, including the keys to 40 safe deposit boxes, which they turned over to the IRS, hoping to find tons of money, gold, jewelry stocks, bonds, etc. What they found were all of my masters for the *Slave and Master* films. I felt a bank was the best place to store them. It was safe and climate-controlled. Boy, were they surprised. When they hauled off the masters, they told the people at the bank that they had confiscated the largest cache of child pornography in their history. Let me tell you, I was not welcomed back at that bank again.

Sir   You're doing good my puppy. Thanks.

Wed, 2 Mar 2005
sharon wrote:

Dear Master,

So i guess the ringing in Your ears last night wasn't due to mind-blowing sex? Did You end up with a head cold? So many people at work have been soooo sick... have been out all week and not expecting to be back until next week. i hope You don't have what they have. They all sound awful on the phone. i'm thinking You may need a nurse to come and take care of You...bring some chicken soup, hot tea, vitamin C... massage... keep You warm & comfy... take care of the animals. i will be happy to do all of the above... just let me know. You shouldn't have to take the dogs out in this cold weather if You're sick or You'll end up with pneumonia. i could come over tomorrow for a little while after i get done at the dentist and at least take care of the animals for You. Let me know if that would help.

Hugs & kisses,
Your slave puppy

Fri, 4 Mar 2005
sharon wrote:

Dear Master,

i am missing You. i hope You're feeling better by now.
This dentist i went to certainly has all the bells and whistles. While he was working on my teeth tonight, he had me wearing an IMAX headset with a Cirque Du Soleil video playing. i had to keep resisting the urge to ask him to start whipping me. See what You've done to me! i think i could have just zoned out to the music and wouldn't have needed the Novocaine, except he kept pulling the headset aside to chatter in my ear.
He also gave me the thing that's supposed to relieve all my stress. It's just a little piece of wax that you put between your front teeth while you're sleeping... for $600!!!!! But he guarantees i'll wake up tomorrow feeling refreshed and tension free. (laughing) i don't think he grasps just how much stress i have in my life lately.

Love,
Your slave puppy

Fri, 4 Mar 2005
sharon wrote:

Dear Master,

When i am finished with this @#$%^&*!&%# hospice policy project, if i ever have to write another policy i think i'll just shoot myself... would be far less painful. my head is numb and pounding at the same time, vision is fading, suffering from malnourishment, nicotine overdose, muscle spasms, sleep deprivation... just plain pathetic! How's that for whining!

i need someone to take care of me, but no one is lining up to volunteer for the job. It could be weeks before anyone finds me here at my desk, dead from overwork, gnarled fingers still on the keyboard, bloodied eyeballs hanging from their sockets, brains draining from my ears... then they will write on my tombstone... "Here lies an example of what happens when you procrastinate too long"... and then i will end up in that place called hell where i'll be doomed to spend eternity writing endless moronic policies forever and ever... oh, wait a minute, i think i'm already there... it does seem to be excessively hot in here... and while i am suffering in the netherworld, the surveyor will be poring through the unfinished book, citing the omission of Policy # 968,421,399 and hospice will be shut down forevermore, forcing all the terminally ill people into the streets, desperately lamenting to the heavens about the lack of proper policies and procedures denying them the comfort they so deserve, and the sun will be hidden from view and there will be earthquakes around the world, and fire and brimstone will rain down from the heavens and devour the entire world population and the earth will explode into a cloud of dust, and that will be the end of all forms of life as we know it... all because i became delusional before getting the job done... okay back to work...

Love,
Your slave puppy

Sun, 6 Mar 2005
sharon wrote:

Dear Master,

It is 4:30 a.m. and i still can't seem to fall asleep...i think my internal clock is broken! i've been lying in bed thinking about Your book and one thing leading to another, i was thinking about Your business catering to gay men and how in the past, i've never had any interest in the idea of men having sex together, never thought it would be appealing. Then i was thinking about You, how You're obviously not gay, but how You've kind of avoided or didn't fully answer the question when i have asked You if You ever had sex with a guy. It seems to me that being around it all the time, You would have at least tried it.

Then i was thinking about watching You with Natasha and how that doesn't do anything in the way of turning me on... i think maybe because i don't find her particularly attractive... or whatever. So anyway, i started thinking about the idea of watching You with another guy, not just having sex, but someone You really cared about, and i am finding the idea much more appealing than watching You with another woman. In fact, i seem to have gotten myself rather excited by the thought. So my question from left field is whether You have ever considered or would ever consider such an arrangement... for the benefit of Your slave puppy's well-rounded experience?

i am missing You... wishing i was laying next to You in Your bed so i could move over and start sucking on Your cock... my pussy is feeling very empty

Love,
Your slave puppy

Sun, 6 Mar 2005
Steven wrote:

Dear puppy,

I'm resting, reading, and putting the "History of Obscenity" chapter together.

Do you know how many times I've been asked that question by women I've played with? I've also been asked by gay men who felt comfortable enough to ask me – besides people in the adult film industry, the dancers who worked for me at the Bijou, the kids who were in my films (hustlers looking for an easy sugar daddy). Most people were surprised to learn I was straight. Their question was, "How could you be straight when you're involved in all these gay sex businesses?"

I replied with a short answer. I wasn't interested in a long discussion to satisfy their curiosity. After the third or fourth time the question was asked, it wasn't important for me to discuss it. The same goes for being asked about why I like rough sex. I'm not here to entertain people's curiosity, which then leads to hearing about their sex lives. So I would just say, "No I haven't tried it. My preference is women." End of discussion.

I have already told you that I didn't have any desire to have sex with a man. Has the opportunity been there? What do you think? Thirty-five years owning the Bijou, plus bathhouses, gay sex clubs, making gay films, creating the bible on gay adult films, having thousands of gay men work for me in all my businesses, etc.

Yes, the opportunity has been there. I have never been shy about what I want. I like a strong, lean body on a man, a pole-vaulter's body, and a fit, lean body on a woman. I keep myself fit, have been working out all my life except for a few interruptions. I want to be physically attractive to the woman I'm with. I have no phobias that I'm aware of. My life has been sexual, so I have been in most sexual situations. If I found them to be exciting, I participated. If I didn't, I didn't get involved.

I do not get aroused by gay sex, but I have learned to appreciate good sex of all kinds. There are gay men who are good sexually, and there are gay men who are not. It's no different than the straight world. What I enjoy is providing the fantasy and a place for people to have the sexual thrills they want. Have I played with a man in a scene? Yes, a few gay men and a few straight couples. With the gay men, it was non-sexual. They were bondage or pain sluts. The couples were just learning about themselves. I directed the woman to sexually take what she wanted from her man and for him to service her. I also had him watch her being submissive to me in a bondage/pain/sex scene; I enjoyed that.

Sir

Sun, 6 Mar 2005
sharon wrote:

Dear Master,

Oops! i guess You did say that. i'm not trying to be difficult here... but how do You know You wouldn't like something if You never tried it? There are plenty of things i never had a "desire" to do, but when i tried them i found that i liked them... and even if i didn't like them, it wasn't a bad experience, and i certainly never regretted trying them. Hmmm... does that mean i am more open-minded than You are? 😊 What a novel concept!

It just seems like curiosity would have somehow gotten the better of You at some point over the years... but i suppose that would have caused You to lose Your objectivity for the business... which is, perhaps, the secret of Your success and longevity.

Oh well, i guess that is one fantasy i'll have to put on the shelf...although i am now thinking that possibility # 2 might be if we were to play with two (good-looking) gay men, since i now have this picture in my head of two sweat-shined male bodies together...with muscles rippling... hmmmm... do You know of any exhibitionist couples who would like to put on a private show? (chuckle) This is certainly not something i ever thought i had a desire for either.

Putting all that aside...What are You working on regarding the history of obscenity? More legal cases? i think it would be interesting to go back through history to find out how obscenity was defined at different times... like 100 and 200 years ago. i was very amused yesterday when i went to see my mother and she was telling me about recently going to see a high school play (*Grease*) in which my cousin's 16-year-old daughter (Alice) starred as the "bad girl." my mother and my aunt were horrified at what she called the "obscene" display on the stage... Alice actually kissed some boy on the stage 😊 and he had his hands all over her 😳 and then the story line was that she thought she was pregnant 😳!!!! my mother couldn't believe they actually allowed them to use "the PG word" in a high school play 😊😊!!!

She and my aunt (Alice's grandmother) have decided that none of the children ought to be allowed in to see such an explicit play and that it's totally inappropriate to have high school kids performing it. i pointed out to my mother that Alice has been dating this same boy for two years and i would have to assume that she has kissed him during that time. Apparently that is a possibility that neither she nor my aunt wishes to contemplate. Very funny. Welcome to the dark ages, alive and well in small town Indiana!

i am still missing You... thinking how i'd like to be serving You in so many "obscene" ways... 😊

Now back to Your book...

Love,

Your slave puppy

Sun, 6 Mar 2005
Steven wrote:

Dear puppy,

You're a funny lady. How do you know whether you like it if you haven't tried it? That is good for you and most of the world dealing with sex, fantasies, and guilt. Sex is not most people's everyday business, nor is it a subject that is openly discussed at the office lunch table. It has been my entire world, not part-time, but full-time since I was 22 years old. I've had the opportunity to explore what excites me in mind and body, what quickens my breath, what I fantasize about, what excites my dick, without worrying about what others might think. I have been at gay sex clubs, bathhouses, theaters, all-male pig-out parties, etc. I owned massage parlors [houses of prostitution (women)], produced 150-200 gay and straight adult films, as well as fetish and BDSM films. I have always had the opportunity to do what I want to do.

At this point, unless life changes, I'm still doing what I want to do, and what I'm doing is exploring you. Puppy, you are coming out of your 6-month all-consuming drama. You're starting to see some daylight, and you have a lot to finish up so you can move on. Now I've got to laugh, on top of all you've been going through, you may be starting a new job – DRAMA. Another thing, I am enjoying your BDSM sexual imagination; it is exciting to have you express new areas you would like to explore.

Yes my dick is hard. I need to do something wonderfully nasty with you and to you. My toilet needs cleaning; and my fist needs to be in your warm wet cunt. I need to see and feel your body respond when I take my punishing pleasures of you, with clips on your cunt, strokes on your back and ass, my scent on your breath, my dear obedient slave. What a wonderful world this is. With that thought and a smile, I'm going to bed. Good night.

Sir

Sun, 6 Mar 2005
sharon wrote:

Dear Master,

i guess it's just hard to comprehend how You could be so comfortable with it and yet have no interest in it at all... so different than the rest of the men in the world. i think, generally speaking, that women have a different perspective on same-sex relationships than men generally do... more of a gray area... more accepting of various degrees of hetero/bi/homosexuality within their own gender. Most men i know either hate, despise (fear) gay men or they are gay themselves... i guess they feel it somehow threatens their own masculinity.

i was reading an interesting article in *Time* magazine yesterday about the differences between the male and female brain. They have discovered that in men, there is almost no connection between the amygdala (the part of brain where emotions are formed) and the rest of the brain. In other words, men are not very capable of processing raw emotions beyond the primal "fight or flight" response... anger and fear... so other emotions become anger and fear because the brain doesn't know what else to do with them. In the caveman days, this would have been beneficial for the survival of the species... no time to be processing complex emotions when you're being attacked by an angry lion. However, today it would be the source of hate crimes, bigotry, fights, wars, etc. It kind of provides concrete evidence that different people's brains (both men's and women's) have evolved to different degrees. So the next time someone acts like an idiot, we can just nod our heads and say, "Ahh, they must have an unconnected amygdala!"

Then again, there's me who keeps wandering waaaay off of what i'm supposed to be doing... perhaps too many connections in the brain? Perhaps involution instead of evolution? And now that i have the windows open and the warm breeze coming in, i've lost all inclination to get any work done. In fact, i'm having another thought... have You ever played on the roof of Your building, in the warm sunshine and fresh air? i do enjoy sex in the out-of-doors...although i suspect there are no toilets to be cleaned on Your rooftop ☺.

Love,
Your slave puppy

Tue, 8 Mar 2005
Natasha wrote:
Dear Sir:

It was so wonderful to be with you yesterday. I truly enjoy our time together.

Yours,
Natasha

Steven writes:

Natasha needed to relax, but she was sexually on edge and had no idea what I was going to do. I wanted her fully chained, totally immobile in the center of my bed. When I was satisfied, I put a canvas hood over her head and got off the bed. I didn't want her to see or hear my movements. About every 3-4 minutes, I did something to her that surprised her. I played with her nipples, put the vibrator to her clit, ran my knife across her neck, put the sweet scent of flowers under her nose, and then I interrogated her by demanding answers to my questions. I wouldn't say this was relaxing, but she was relaxed when the night was over. The scene lasted about an hour. She spent the next 15-20 minutes kissing and licking my feet and sucking on my toes. We finished with climaxes.

Wed, 9 Mar 2005
sharon wrote:

Dear Master,

i have just finished the last of the policies & procedures. Yippity skippity, i think i will do a happy dance. 😊😊😊😊😊😊😊😊😊😊😊😊😊😊😊😊😊😊😊😊So now i can devote alllllll of my time to Your book.

Also...by the way... You did wonders for me last night... i felt 100% more relaxed on the way home... funny how that works.😊

i love You.

Your slave puppy

Fri, 11 Mar 2005
sharon wrote:

Dear Master,

i finally got through to the doctor & lawyer today. Saw the doc this afternoon and he scheduled the surgery for 3/25. That date sounds familiar...but i can't think of what is going on that weekend. Also, i have an appointment to see the lawyer Monday evening. We should be able to finalize everything then and set a court date. So hopefully these two things will alleviate a couple burdens.

okay..i'm off to work on Your book.

Love,
Your slave puppy

Sat, 12 Mar 2005
sharon wrote:
Dear Master,

    i have been trying to talk Arthur's girlfriend into coming over here to do the cooking & cleaning and think i've got her almost convinced... although i will have to starve tonight. She says she can come over tomorrow. i'm thinking it could be a good arrangement after the divorce to have her move in and take care of the domestic stuff, so i wouldn't have to worry about taking care of it. It would be like having a mother living here without having to follow her rules. Why didn't i think of this years ago!

Love,
Your slave puppy

Sun, 13 Mar 2005
sharon wrote:
Dear Master,

    In Your letters to Hans, You said You went to prison for a few years for Your first trial. Are You talking about the tax trial, which was later overturned? How many years did You serve for that? (i'm sure You've told me this, but i don't remember for sure). Also, what is Hans last name?

    You mention that You were indicted in three states and when they busted You, they had warrants from UT, TN and NE. i know You said that Nebraska was only a threat of indictment, so i want to clarify that in the text. Okay?

    The big question is, did the government approach you (your attorneys) or did you approach the government for a deal? What was the deal?

    Back to reading...

Love,
Your slave puppy

Sun, 13 Mar 2005
Steven wrote:

Dear puppy,

    I served 18 months before I won my appeal for the tax trial and was released from prison. I don't know Hans' last name. I hadn't spoken to him in 20 years until I got his email address and wrote to him.

    My trial went to jury deliberation, at which point the government approached my attorneys for settlement. I felt we had a hung jury, which would be a loss for the government. How does the government explain not getting an outright conviction on such vile films? What an embarrassment. A hung jury would be a defeat for them.

    This was my deal: No prosecution in Utah or Nebraska, my businesses stay open, and Judge Nixon does the sentencing. It was a good deal for me. I would have lost in Utah, would have been given a long prison sentence, and would have been financially bankrupt. Utah did not want the deal, but Washington didn't want to lose Tennessee. Washington finalized the deal in two hours. No Utah, no Nebraska, and the sentencing was to stay with Judge Nixon.

Sir

Sun, 13 Mar 2005
sharon wrote:

Dear Master,

    Excellent! This explains a lot about Your experience. But is this all You've gotten done today? Perhaps You would be more productive with a slave kneeling at Your feet and sucking on Your cock... or perhaps You need to stimulate Your thoughts by applying a singletail to Your slave's backside... 🙂

Love,
Your slave puppy

Spring 2005

Mon, 14 Mar 2005
sharon wrote:

Dear Master,

    i hope Your day has gone as well as mine. i met with the lawyer today & everything is going well. He will draw up the papers this week. i'll meet with him again next Monday, then Arthur will have to sign the papers and get them notarized, so the divorce should be final the week of 4/25... all for a mere $999... are You jealous? Hmmmm... if i'm not mistaken, i'll be done with mine before either You or Natasha. Do i win a prize?

    The owner from the new company made me an offer today. (He was out of the country last week.) My recruiter friend told him i'll need a contract, and if he wants me to open any branch offices, it will be an additional consulting fee in addition to the regular salary... which she said should be an additional sixty thousand or so, depending on the location. Sooooooo... i feel like i've had a huge weight lifted off my shoulders... feel like i could fly tonight without any assistance at all! The timing of everything is coming together perfectly... and in the springtime too! Things are looking good!!

Love,
Your happy slave puppy

Steven writes:

    I was married twice. I filed for divorce in my second marriage in October of 1997, shortly after I had gotten out of prison for the second time (July 1997), as a result of my Tennessee case in 1989.

    My divorce covered a lot of territory. We went through four judges and had two other judges enter the case to make rulings on the sitting judges in the divorce. My ex-wife had three different legal firms represent her at various stages of the divorce, and we had two full trials. During the first trial, her attorneys threatened to go to the federal government with certain "incriminating" documents if I didn't agree to their outrageous terms. I did not agree to their terms. Instead, I told them I would give them the cab fare to go over to the federal building. My divorce was about greed. As of this writing, I am still not completely finished with the property settlement in my divorce.

Mon, 14 Mar 2005
Steven wrote:

Dear puppy

    I am green with envy. Congratulations, you dirty rotten so and so. Also, congratulations on the job offer.

Sir

Wed, 16 Mar 2005
sharon wrote:

Dear Master,

    i just want to say that on my way to Your house last night, the thought crossed my mind that i was way too wound up to relax enough to play. i was thinking there was no way You would ever get my mind to slow down enough to even get my body to participate. Well, i don't know what kind of magic You performed, but i was certainly way out there. It never ceases to amaze me how different i feel when i leave Your house than when i arrive... refreshed, relaxed, invigorated... like all the junk has been cleaned out of my system. Thank You. How did i ever get along without You?

    i've been thinking about something we were talking about last night... about people separating their sexuality from all other aspects of themselves. That is exactly what religion does to people. It detaches them from their sexuality... breaks them into pieces and then comes between the pieces so people don't even know who they are. Religion is the complete opposite of spirituality. No wonder there are so many unhappy and dysfunctional people in this world... religion creates multiple personality disorders... fragmented, guilt-ridden people. Maybe that's why i always feel so good when i'm around You...You put my pieces back together and make me a whole person.

    Okay, enough rambling or i'll never be able to get up in the morning. Pleasant dreams!

i love You.

Your slave puppy

Sat, 19 Mar 2005
sharon wrote:

Dear Master,

Thank You for inviting me to the concert. i had a lot of fun. Her music is very different & the band was good... and the side show in front of us was quite entertaining too! You have good taste in music.

Love,
Your slave puppy

Steven writes:

I took puppy to see Marianne Faithfull. We played a little before we went; then after the concert, we came back to my home and made love to finish off the evening.

Fri, 25 Mar 2005

Natasha wrote:

Dear Sir:

You informed me yesterday that I was not writing to you enough. I am sorry. In your house, I am in different universe and when I back at my computer at work it is hard to restore the atmosphere in my mind.

This probably may explain why I am such a lousy writer. Another possibility is that I've never written about my personal/sexual life.

I felt that yesterday the reading of Pushkin went very well. I can't believe what we/you did; amazing.

Yours,
Natasha

Fri, 25 Mar 2005
Steven wrote:

Dear Ms. Pushkin,

The reading was lovely and very enlightening. You look so lovely being all tied up reading Pushkin, but you will have to refrain from the sudden outbursts of nervous laughter.

Sir

Steven writes:

Natasha had bought me a book of Pushkin's erotic poetry written in Russian, which I had her read while she was bound tightly in a chair, first reading in Russian, then translating it into English. I had puppy bound to the bed alternating between the violet wand and fisting. To be continued...

Fri, 25 Mar 2005
sharon wrote:

Dear Master,

    i want to thank You for the wonderful evening. i really needed that & i hope You were pleased. my backside was still feeling tenderized this morning...all my nerves standing on end... too bad the surgery overpowered that or i'd still be dripping.

    It was interesting/amusing watching You whip Natasha... or i should say, watching her response to it. There doesn't seem to be any connection between the rest of her body and her pussy. When i was watching her, i was trying to figure out (remember) how that connection was made in me. It was there the first time, but i think mostly because he kept going way beyond what i thought i could handle... and beyond all resistance. i had no idea where it was going or what the result was supposed to be. It was like breaking through a wall... i had no choice in the matter. In fact, it was like that the whole time i was with Rob... like being run over by a train.

    It's so different with You. You make every cell in my body wake up, come to life, and send intense messages directly to my pussy... so all You have to do is touch me and i'm cumming all over the place. Do You think that connection is something that would develop in anyone over time? Even a year ago, it used to hurt more than it does now... like there was a certain threshold of pain that had to be crossed. Now it is smoother, easier... like i can just get to a certain point, stay there, back off, get right back to the edge, back off, and keep going like that forever, for as long as You want, and when You're done, i am sooooo ready to be fucked rather than being totally exhausted and useless. It's like a dance (where have i heard that before), but it's very true. i kept wanting to tell Natasha to just relax and let it happen... to pay attention to the sensations and go with them instead of resisting them... to trust You and follow Your lead. i could almost see her blocking the sensations at the point of contact... they weren't traveling through her body. She doesn't know what she's missing.

    Do You think that connection between pain and pleasure is something that can be taught/learned, or do You think it has to be forced in the beginning so the person knows where they're going and wants to go back to that place? Or do some people never make that wonderful connection? Do they only have orgasms in their pussy without input from the rest of their body? Or people who like being whipped, but say it's not a sexual thing, do they not have that connection either? Oh well, i guess all that matters is that You know how to play me like a violin... the rest of the world will just have to fend for themselves.

i am suddenly getting very sleepy... will write more later.

Love,
Your slave puppy

Steven writes:

I enjoyed myself. I have a slave and submissive to play with any way I want. I played, as I have in the past, with puppy naked and tied spread-eagle on the bed. I then brought Natasha up to the bedroom where she saw puppy. She greeted me, got herself undressed, and I had her sit in a chair that was positioned in front of puppy's open legs. Then I bound Natasha's legs and feet to the chair so her cunt was spread open. I wrapped rope around her chest and upper arms to bind her to the chair, but left her free from her elbows down so she could hold a book. I then gave her the Pushkin book to read while I played with puppy. This opening scene lasted for about 40 minutes.

The more I was playing with Natasha, the more fearful she was becoming of our connection. This had nothing to do with the play or the pain, but rather, it was her own internal conflict.

Mon, 28 Mar 2005
Steven wrote:

Hello Natasha,

I found this article on-line and found it interesting. Since I'm biased in my opinion, I am asking you – Is the source of this article (Pravda on-line) reliable or is this a farce? I have to say that some of the other articles are wacky. How about dinner and a movie Friday at 7:00?

Sir

Here is the lead in to the above-mentioned article:

A recent report of some scientific research in Russia describes how clinical depression, addiction, etc. have been alleviated, if not cured, by whipping therapy. They hypothesize that endorphins released by painful flagellation turned mental attitudes around so that they became positive and healthy. It was also observed that the effect worked far better when the patient was whipped by one of the opposite sex. (Positive effects felt by the wielder of the whip were not mentioned.) There was no conjecture ventured whether similar benefits can be obtained by subjects who are not clinically depressed.

Mon, 28 Mar 2005
Natasha wrote:

Dear Sir:

This is an interesting article. I have not read Pravda on-line before. The newspaper *Pravda* used to be the main newspaper during Soviet times. On-line version has stories about aliens and Russians that conquered Mars 30 years ago. Well, that does not sound like a respectful source of information.

On the other hand, as you know in Russia, it is very popular *parit'sia v bane*, which means whipping people with wet branches of birch or oak tree in sauna. I tried it; it is not painful at all and extremely pleasurable. Of course, the person who does it should know what he is doing; as with everything else.

Dinner and movie sounds good.

Yours,
Natasha

Mon, 28 Mar 2005
sharon wrote:

Dear Master,

i spent three hours at the lawyer's office tonight & got all the paperwork done. Now it's up to Arthur to sign it, have it notarized, and then they can set the actual court date. She doesn't think there will be any problem getting a date for the week of the 25th as long as Arthur takes care of his part in a timely manner.

Love,
Your slave puppy

Thu, 31 Mar 2005
sharon wrote:

Dear Master,

      i have really got to get my act together. i showed up at the dentist's office tonight only to find out that my appointment is next week... duh... i think i must have stumbled into a time warp... have got to get organized...

      Since i will be spending the weekend at Your house, i'm thinking it might be best if i stay home tonight. That way i can get the rest of the pieces pasted into the book, so we will have something better to work with this weekend... and i can also get some laundry, etc. done, which are usually Saturday chores... unless there is something in particular You had in mind for tonight. Please let me know.

Love,
Your slave puppy

Mon, 4 Apr 2005
Natasha wrote:

Dear Sir

      It is good that we did not watch *Sin City* – it is made wonderfully but too violent! They killed about 100 people in the movie. Of course, it is supposed to be movie based on comics, not real but still...The actors are wonderful though.

      I realize that I cannot be fascinated by multiple ways to kill a person. What is that with American cinema? Why so much violence? How was your weekend? Did you finish your book?

Yours,
Natasha

Mon, 4 Apr 2005
Steven wrote:

Hello Natasha,

      America is a nation of mixed cultures and I feel that our frustrations reflect our cultural, religious, and moral tug-of-war. Combined with polarizing politics, the politics of fear, talking heads, and the information media, it makes for frustration and anger. We prefer violence to romance and violence to sexuality (not just porn) in its many forms and fantasies. People want to break away from the sameness in their lives, to be larger than life, to have power over their lives (for example, power and control are taken away when a person sits in the car for three hours while commuting back and forth to work). For many people, the routines at work or at home are structured routines with very little deviation, so the fantasy of violence, conquering evil, being a non-conformist, a cowboy, an adventurer, performing heroic feats in sports, and generally being the hero is great for a person's self-esteem. Americans like to fantasize about themselves as being daring, a little out of the mainstream of society. We like to see ourselves as rugged individuals. We are also a society of extremes. Remember, we fight and tear ourselves apart every 4 years to elect a president. This is just a minute's thought on what you have asked.

This weekend went great. I can now see the forest through the trees. Puppy did a wonderful job of organizing the book into a cohesive piece. She did a lot of research and creative thinking on how the book will be formed. I feel it will be done in about 3-4 months.

In the next 3-5 weeks, I will be starting *Puppy 2*, so put on your erotic Pushkin thinking cap. You will have to be creative and explicit in your thoughts. I will be asking you for a few pieces of writing and I will not accept outdated scientific papers in Russian. Do you understand?

How is Friday at 7:00? I need to try out the whipping research from your fellow Russian scientist, to see if he is accurate. Of course, as you have told me, you have a tremendous fondness for birch branches across your body when taking a steam sauna. This makes you my perfect subject.

Sir

Mon, 4 Apr 2005
sharon wrote:

Dear Master,

Are You still celebrating? A beautiful day to go for a cruise on Your scooter! And it's supposed to be even nicer tomorrow.

i dropped off the divorce papers at the lawyer's office today. They said to call back in a week or 10 days to find out the court date & time. So now it's just a matter of sitting & waiting. This almost seems too easy!

i am working on the piece about "How the Bijou Chronicles got started." i need to know what magazines the column was published in. Also, which of Your websites can the readers be directed to if they want to read more of them?

Love,

Your slave puppy

The Bijou Chronicles can be found at: www.bijouchronicles.com

Steven writes:

These next letters came about when I was cruising an alternative lifestyle website and a profile from "The Couple Next Door" caught my attention. I contacted them and they responded back with a well-written and well-thought out fantasy, spelled out in a set of rules. We corresponded for about a week, and by that point I was hooked. I gave them my phone number so we could start getting familiar with each other.

My introduction email to the "The Couple Next Door":

Mon, 4 Apr 2005
Steven wrote:

Hello,

I read your profile and have some questions: 1) Are you both servants or submissive to the Master of the house? 2) Is this domestic service, such as cleaning, making dinner, serving at dinner parties? Is it non sexual? 3) Is this domestic service such as assisting in a sexual scene without participating sexually? Or does it include participating sexually in the scene with another couple? 4) Or does it involve participating in arranging and helping out during the scene with a Master and his slave while you participate in your own sexual scene without others? 5) Is there any bondage or discipline involved?

Let me tell you some things about myself. I have a slave and a submissive. One is an administrator for hospice programs, and the other is a doctor/professor/scientist. We play together weekly and what you are offering would be interesting for us to explore.

I am an older, attractive man who is very fit. I do not want to sound skeptical, but so many people put in things that are just fantasy, or they just want cyber play without telling you this. Or they are men pretending to be women, or people who simply love the Internet fantasy exchange.

I am not a weekend or pretend cyber Dom. My life and businesses are sexual. I have been outwardly involved in the alternative lifestyle for many years, but I do not wear my lifestyle on my back like a neon sign. I am very experienced and well-known in my community. My life revolves around sexuality, rough sex, and BDSM, which does not have to involve you as long as I understand your needs.

My life is VERY unconventional. I own the Bijou Theater, the oldest gay theater and sex club in the U.S. (I am not gay or bi) and I have written a book. It is non-fiction book about a submissive woman's life and journey into BDSM. It is about her search for her Master. It's called *The Puppy Papers*. The book is about my slave, puppy. It is her story. The book has gotten some wonderful reviews. If you want to know more about the book, go to wellsstreetpublishing.com or amazon.com. I live and work in Old Town in Chicago. If you want to know more about me go to www.steventoushin.com.

What I am laying out to you are some of my credentials and experience. Yes, I am who I am, so I will be honest and up front with you from the beginning. I also have to tell you that I am very inquisitive and will ask you many questions, as I expect for you to do with me. If answering questions bothers you, then this will not work out. My home is easy to get to, and I have a wonderful place to play in. Please read my profile; it will tell you more about me, and then if you're interested, let's communicate. If you do respond, please tell me about yourself, your experience, things you like, and please send pics. My pics are on my profile.

Yours,
Steven

Mon, 5 Apr 2005
The Couple Next Door wrote:

Thanks for your note/inquiry. You certainly have an interesting profile. We are Sharon and Mark, a happily married couple of (nearly) 20 years. We live in the Northwest Suburbs where we appear to most of our friends and family as a "vanilla" couple. We have been in and out of the "lifestyle" for about ten years now. We have young kids, which limits our time for fun and frolic, and causes us to make discretion a paramount consideration in any relationship we pursue.

We are not active in the Chicago BDSM community, but in the past we have served a couple who is. So we may have some friends in common. We more or less stumbled into the serving role-play after discovering that we both enjoy relinquishing control. We love the eroticism, but have found very few people who "get it." Many of the people who contact us see domination as simply a little bit of verbal abuse followed by a three-way. Others like to send descriptions of all of the different positions and toys they want to use on us.

What we seek is an ongoing, part time friendship where we could serve on an occasional basis (once a month or so) in a safe environment. He should be creative and master of his environment. Most importantly, while he should be kind to his servants, he should possess the confidence to treat us matter-of-factly as we perform our assigned duties. Also he knows there is no need to apologize or ask permission for using us in any manner he sees fit within the scope of the rules we agree to.

Rather than try to explain what we seek, we are forwarding a set of "House Rules" which we have modified from the last couple we served. It is by no means cast in stone, but will hopefully give you some idea of what we offer. We welcome your comments. If you think you could use a couple like us around on occasion, perhaps you will allow us to formally interview with you. We look forward to your reply,

Sharon and Mark

HOUSE RULES

A slave servant in my home (you) shall be referred to as a "domestic." You acknowledge that you are applying for this role of your own free will, with no expectation of compensation. You agree that you have a clear understanding that a "domestic" is required to abide by these rules at all times.

1) Be Smart

You will never be expected to do anything to risk your health, mine, or that of my guests. I understand that discretion is of paramount importance to you. In exchange for your gift of servitude, I shall protect your privacy, and exercise judgment that protects you from any potential harm or embarrassment. I understand and appreciate that we all have busy, productive lives with families and other responsibilities. That will always be in the forefront of consideration.

2) You are a domestic slave

When you are in my home, you are to be "In Character" at all times. You are not my equals or my lovers. You are my slaves. Obedience and respect are expected at all times. You do not have a right to privacy or modesty.

3) Forms of address.

You are to address me as "Sir" or "Master." My guests are to be addressed as "Sir" or "Ma'am."

4) Punctuality.

You are expected to report for duty on time and to call me if you are going to be late. You will be given 10 minutes to prepare for duty upon your arrival, after which you will present yourselves for inspection.

5) Uniform.

You are responsible for providing your own uniforms, and required to wear them at all times in my home. Unless I have specifically directed you otherwise, the following rules shall ALWAYS apply.

- Your uniforms should match or complement one another to whatever degree practical.
- Your uniforms may never, at any time, cover, conceal, or restrict access to your genitals

6) Personal Hygiene

You shall report for duty clean and freshly showered. Any perfume or cologne must be mild and inoffensive. Fingernails and toenails should be clean and trimmed, and the female's nails should be painted a flattering color. Her legs, armpits, and pussy should be completely and freshly shaven, and free of stubble. The male's face should be freshly shaven. His cock and balls must be shaven smooth, and the pubic hair above his cock shall be shaven or very neatly trimmed. Rectal areas should be clean and reflect impeccable personal hygiene.

7) Inspection

Domestics are subject to inspection upon arrival, and at any time while serving. Domestics must pose willingly and openly for the duration of the inspection. When any domestic fails inspection, all domestics are subject to discipline and intensive re-inspection.

8) Domestic Service

Cleaning – Domestics will be required to perform the usual household cleaning duties including, but not limited to: dusting, vacuuming, mopping, dishwashing, etc. I will expect a thorough and complete job of all cleaning tasks such that they pass a white glove test.

Serving- Domestics will, from time to time, be required to prepare and serve food and drink. Domestics are expected to keep their work area clean and tidy at all times. Proactive service is expected - I should never have to ask for a refill, and neither should my guests.

Personal Attendant –Domestics may be required to assist me with my daily bathing, hygiene, and dressing activities. The servants will be required to draw a bath, and assist with washing, drying, and dressing.

General – Domestics will be required to perform duties such as, but not limited to, preparing for a party, greeting guests at the door, maintaining clean bathrooms and toilets, serving food and drink, taking coats from guests, etc.

9) Furniture

Domestics may not use my furniture, and must stand, or kneel on the floor when permitted to be "at ease." Domestics may be used as furniture as needed. For example, a domestic might be ordered to be a footstool, or coaster.

10) Bathroom privileges

The bathrooms in my home are for the use of my guests and me. A domestic may enter the bathroom for the following reasons ONLY:
1) To assist me or a guest in the bathroom (only if invited – which shall not be refused)
2) Domestics are expected to ensure cleanliness of the bathroom after each use by me, or a guest.

For the domestics, a container or chamber pot will be placed in a conspicuous area of my home. It shall be used only with my permission, and only when I and my guests are present to observe. It is the responsibility of the domestics to immediately clean the container after each use and return it to its original location.

11) Sexual service.

The Male and Female Domestic will service me orally as a regular part of their duties. The respectful way to serve me with your mouth is to remember your ABC's: Asshole, Balls, and Cock. Domestics shall swallow my cum as I direct.

The female domestic will submit to vaginal intercourse with me on demand, without question or hesitation, no matter who is present. The female domestic will never be expected to engage in intercourse with any guest unless arrangements have been made in advance.

The male and female domestic are expected to provide non gender-specific oral service to any guest in my home. Any guest in my home is entitled to request this of you directly, and enthusiastic compliance is expected, unless it will interfere with other tasks I have assigned to you.

I will make it clear to my guests that, within their reasonable judgment, they are permitted to touch, feel, and fondle you. You are expected to respond warmly and "openly."

You are not permitted to cum without my explicit permission. You are expected to do your job, therefore, outstanding performance will be rewarded with the opportunity to serve me again in the future, and does not guarantee you will be permitted to cum. If I do permit it, it will be as I direct, in a manner that entertains me (and my guests.)

12) A final word on guests:

Any and all guests in my home are special, and should be treated accordingly. I have the sole privilege of inviting guests to my home. You agree to trust my judgment in this regard, and understand you have no right to screen them. The presence, quantity, gender, or attire of my invited guests in no way changes the way any of the above rules apply to you. Modesty or privacy is not permitted for any act, sexual or otherwise. However, I accept full responsibility for, and assure you that everything that happens in my home, stays in my home.

13) On matters of discipline

Domestics will NOT be expected to endure pain for pleasure or for discipline. Furthermore, domestics should be obedient and require very little discipline. However, when discipline is required, it will be creatively administered. Domestics understand that I may invite others to administer or participate in your discipline, and that all domestics may be disciplined for the misdeeds of one.

Tue, 6 Apr 2005
Steven wrote:

Hello Mark and Sharon,

Thank you for getting back to me. I was surprised to get such a well thought out email with such an understanding of your kink. I was also very impressed with the communication skills you have between yourselves. You are both able to discuss and accept each other for who you are and what you both like, which is not easy for most people. Most people I've met through the years, and especially now on the alternative web sites, have put very little thought into themselves, except for their own immediate fantasy, and they have never connected with another person.

I do have some questions on discipline. I have been involved with domestics that wanted spanking or bondage as discipline. At times, I use a stock for discipline. As far as spanking, I will give five smacks to emphasize that orders must be followed explicitly. I use bondage for disciplining incompetent form or a lack of thoroughness, where freedom is taken away for a half-hour to correct unacceptable performance. This bondage is done in the presence of the other servant while he or she is performing their duties. I am asking you this so I will know your parameters. I do not yell or berate; I correct. I am interested in knowing what services you have performed with others and for what period of time.

I live at Schiller and Wells in Old Town in Chicago. My offices are on the first 2 floors and I live on the top 2 floors. If interested, let's discuss this further. Here is my phone #____. If you would like to talk during the day, I'm in my office from 12 noon to 6 pm and at night after 9:30. My email address is_____.

Yours,
Steven

Wed, 6 Apr 2005
The Couple Next Door wrote:

Thank you for your kind words. In the past we have experimented with several couples. Our favorite and by far most competent couple was in Evanston. We served them for a few months before a family issue prevented them from further play in their home. We also served a couple in Schaumburg for several months until he won custody of his young children and they moved in with them, and getting together became too difficult. I (Mark) travel extensively on business, so we need to schedule our playtime in advance. The other challenge we have is that our children are too old for a sitter, but too young for us to wander too far from home when we are out. All of that said, we would find a way to serve the right person/couple.

As for our thoughts on discipline, neither of us seek or like pain. Bondage is something we are more comfortable with as the level of trust increases and, in a general sense, the butler is more comfortable with this then the maid. Our Master can expect us to conduct ourselves in accordance with his desires at all times. Neither of us are bratty. We also recognize that decisions surrounding discipline belong to our Master, and they are designed to ultimately make us better servants.

Ideally, we seek maid/butler role-play with a Master who can create an occasional scene in which we are serving a small group or party.

Domestic servitude taken a step further. As you have inferred from the rules we provided, deprivation of modesty is something we desire.

On sexuality - Both of us are passively bi within the context of this role play. The way we see it, when a male servant kneels before his master, it is not an expression of his sexuality. Instead, it is a demonstration of humility and respect.

All of that being said, our biggest challenge these days is finding play time. Attached is a G-rated picture of us.

M&S

Thu, 7 Apr 2005
Steven wrote:

Hello Mark and Sharon,

Let me tell you a little something about myself and my experience with this kind of play. From 1970 to 1974, I had a manservant who took care of all my household needs. It was non-sexual service. Jim was wonderful. At night he would prepare and serve dinner for my wife and I, and then play Chopin on the piano while we ate. My disciplining of him was more on the punishment side. Jim had special needs. Through the years, I have played with three or four couples that served as maid and butler, houseboy/housegirl (not as formal) and single women who wanted to serve as personal valets performing body care. However, I have not been in this mindset for about seven years.

My businesses are open 24/7, so I am very well-versed on detail and correctness, but I am not anal. I smile when I think about playing this role again. Yes, I do like to have dinner and then to play afterwards. I would also need both of you to assist with the preparation and care of my guests.

Let me explain how a simple evening may go. At dinner, one of my guests might be tied up, so she would have to be fed by one of you. I may need one of you to perform oral sex on puppy for a few minutes while she is eating. When I am playing with puppy (either after dinner or during dinner), one of you will be attentive with my equipment, towels, etc, and the cleanup afterwards. At one point, the other will assist Natasha (who might be in bondage) to hold a Pushkin book while she reads poetry to us in Russian and then translates it into English. Your function is to make sure her reading stays in rhythm. One of you will hold a light over the book and turn the pages as she reads. This is just a short summary of what we already do without assistance, although Natasha does observe and assist me with puppy at times. Natasha is a voyeur. If we should play, you will have many responsibilities in serving throughout the evening.

Of course, clean up, tidiness, manners, professionalism, and your proper presentation will be performed and observed at all times. Discipline for the maid may be in the form of lying on her back with her legs spread and held open by her hands for full inspection by all, usually in the center of the room. If more correction is needed, then a large dildo may be placed in her for her to hold in, or a vibrator attached to a harness to hold it in place may be inserted into the maid for a few minutes.

For you, the butler, correction may involve tying a leather string with a large bell around your cock and balls and having you stand with legs spread far apart. Your hands would be placed at the back of you neck with elbows parallel to your head. If the bell should ring, one of the women will put a hood over your head and I will put weights on the leather cord that is tied around your cock and balls. This would not last for longer than a few minutes. These examples give you an idea of how I would plan our first evening together. I would keep it simple, but keep in mind that sexuality is very important in my life and in how I play.

If this is what you are looking for in employment (service), then let's continue communicating, but I would like for us to hear each other's voices. If all goes well and we feel comfortable with each after speaking, and we are in agreement, then we will plan the next step.

Yours,
Steven

Fri, 8 Apr 2005
The Couple Next Door wrote:

Steven,

It is refreshing to talk with somebody who understands the role of eroticism in this type of play and it's something we want to strongly consider. It is so difficult for us to find somebody who "gets it." We will be taking a family vacation this weekend, and then I (Mark) will be in San Diego for ten days on business. Access to email will be limited, so if you don't hear from us for a short while, please don't think of it as a lack of interest.

The scene you describe sounds wonderful. We enjoy the ritual of serving in a formal atmosphere, and appreciate a man who is a Master of

his environment. We have created many uniforms in recent years. The attached pictures show us last Summer in our most formal attire... Dressy enough to be worn when serving at even the most "upscale" of gatherings, but revealing enough not to be considered disrespectful to our Master or his guests.
    Please let us know if you like this.

Respectfully,
M&S

Fri, 8 Apr 2005
Steven wrote:
Hello Mark and Sharon,
    When you get back, please contact me so we can talk. I have forwarded your email to puppy and I will be with Natasha tonight and puppy on Sunday. Since this is role-play, I want them to know what to expect, so they will be prepared to be in character. If we do play and both you and I are comfortable and enjoy our scene together, then the next time, I will no longer prepare them, but rather let the spontaneity of the evening (what I have planned) unfold. Enjoy your family weekend and have a safe trip to San Diego.

Yours,
Steven

Fri, 8 Apr 2005
The Couple Next Door wrote:
Steven

Thanks. We will touch base the week of the 25th.

M&S

Steven writes:
    Two weeks went by with neither an email nor a phone call, so I was starting to think this was all a cyber game. I sent an email to Mark and Sharon, or whoever it was that I had been corresponding with, and I receieved no response. I then knew I had been duped by a cyber fantasy player. I also realized that this person may be playing his/her game under numerous profiles. Did I feel foolish! I had been taken in by a cyber

player's fantasy game. I do have to say that it was well thought out. The responding emails were enticing; the list of rules was excellent; and I fell for it hook, line, and sinker. Even with all of my experience in the lifestyle, I never saw it coming. I had unwittingly fulfilled that person's fantasy. For me, it was a disappointment. I had planned out a wonderful evening with a phoney who was pretending to be real. I got snookered!!

I did not see "The Couple Next Door" profile again for quite a while. Then eight months later, I saw The Couple Next Door's picture appearing on another profile under the name of "ChicagoCpl4play (in search of an owner)."

Mon, 11 Apr 2005
Steven wrote:

Dear Natasha,

It is time for you to write. I need to know how you felt erotically the night you were tied up and reading Pushkin. You have to describe your thoughts and feelings to me, and not in one word answers or with one or two sentences.

1) How did you like being tied up? 2) Does being bound and watching puppy excite you? 3) What was it like watching puppy being fisted and having orgasms? 4) What are your thoughts about reading and watching puppy as I was playing with her? 5) Was it erotic to you when you were reading and watching my dick being sucked? 6) Did you like having your nipples pinched and your pussy played with while you were reading?

Later in the other room: A) Did you like the flogging, spanking and singletail? B) What are the feelings that come over you to make you cry? C) What kind of cry is it? A pleasure or painful cry? or a releasing cry? D) What effect does the spanking and crying have on you erotically, if that is the case? E) What effect does our play have on you later in the same evening and the next day? F) How did you feel about being told to get on your back and spread your legs for me to enter you? G) How do you feel when I take you whenever I desire? H) How do you feel about giving yourself to me whenever I desire? I) What are your thoughts when I enter puppy and then you? J) What are your thoughts when I need you to feel my balls and cock when I am in puppy?

Also, do you remember the first time we all got together? I want your description of that first night – what happened, what you saw, and how you felt. What were your thoughts during the following days about this strange new world you were entering? Please take your time; I am looking for, as you know, not just a description but also the insightfulness of your thoughts, impressions, and inner feelings.

Sir

Mon, 11 Apr 2005
Natasha wrote:

Dear Sir:

I received your letter. I will be working on the answers. Apparently, it is going to be a very difficult piece of writing since I have never done this kind of story before.

Yours,
Natasha

Mon, 11 Apr 2005
sharon wrote:

Dear Master,

You have not sent me the piece You showed me last night on BDSM and the sexual future. Also, I need the introduction to the obscenity chapter. Are You still re-writing it?

i will just be going to Milwaukee for one day this week (Thurs) and will be home that evening, though at this point i don't know what time we'll get back. The new job already seems like a better fit than either of the jobs i've had since i moved here. A completely different philosophy than the others. They actually care about staff and patients. Imagine that! The nice thing about the owner is that he doesn't think he has to micromanage everything. He actually trusts the judgment of his management team. What a concept!

Okay, back to work.

Love,
Your slave puppy

Wed, 13 Apr 2005
Steven wrote:

Dear puppy,

Yes, I'm still rewriting the introduction. Here is my first draft on BDSM and the sexual future. I have revised it at least 20 times, but it's still a long, rambling piece. Please organize it for me. I seem to be lost within the quagmire of my mind. Once again, I can't see the forest through the trees. Look at it and give me some suggestions.

Sir

Fri, 15 Apr 2005
sharon wrote:

Dear Master,

    i finally got the obscenity piece downloaded and put into the text. You were right, it leads perfectly into the obscenity chapter. i had moved things around a few times since the weekend we had talked about it because the story wasn't flowing right. Now i'm back to where i started and it looks good with the introduction piece You added. i will re-visit the Meese Commission, then i think that will be everything except the piece You're still working on.

    i should be able to give it a final read-through by Monday or Tuesday, and then it will be ready to go... that is, unless there is something else You want to add!

    i also want to say that i am thoroughly enjoying this new job to the point that i almost feel guilty getting paid for it! i have an early morning flight tomorrow so i'm going to call it a night.

Love,
Your slave puppy

Sun, 17 Apr 2005
sharon wrote:

Dear Master,

    It's been an interesting evening around here. One of the things Arthur apparently remembers from reading *The Puppy Papers* was something about me and another woman... which he told his girlfriend. So she was here all evening, very drunk, and trying very hard to entice me into providing her with her first experience with a woman. She says i am the most beeeauuutifullll woman she's ever seen ☺. Thank God she finally passed out. (laughing) i guess if there's anything in life that i can count on,

it's that i will always look beautiful through the eyes of a drunk right before they pass out... must be that double vision...two heads et al.
i am trying to figure out why my legs are so tired today. It feels like i ran a marathon or something...except it's the sides of my thighs. i also have a rather sore pussy, but that i know is because Steve's fist was really too big. Aside from all these minor complaints ☺, i really did have fun last night. It was definitely a unique experience. It felt like i was being tossed around on waves in the ocean. The two of you were amazingly in sync with what You were doing. (chuckle) i must have looked like some crazed and rabid animal... definitely a loss of control.
One time when You were standing in front of me talking... when You were asking me questions... it was very strange... it was like i was standing next to myself and answering Your questions from a long distance away...like through a tunnel...like some special effects in a movie.
Another thing that was strange was that i was so aware of both Your and Steve's scent... very different from each other...but both of You have a very unusual and magnetic scent. i just somehow had a very heightened awareness of that.
You also both have a very different touch...but You complement each other well...like You've been doing this together for many years. Like i said, it was like being tossed from one wave to another...or like a pendulum swinging back and forth.
Being fisted and whipped at the same time...i don't even know how to describe it... perhaps a taste of heaven? Now wouldn't it be cool if that's what heaven was like! It was like it was so intense that it completely short-circuited my brain and became pure, raw sensation... though that doesn't seem to describe it adequately. It's a wonder i didn't just dissolve into a puddle on the floor.
Something else though... despite being repeatedly taken over the edge, i didn't know Steve, so it was it was hard to trust him. i didn't *not* trust him, except i trusted You to be looking out for me... if that makes any sense. Whenever he would get close to me and start talking to me, i could feel myself mentally tightening up, resisting, and wondering where You were, even while my body was going off in its own direction. i hope this makes sense to You because if anyone else were to read it, they'd probably take me away in a strait-jacket.
i have never been with two men at the same time... it messed with my mind... incomprehensible... but much more enjoyable than being with a

man & a woman. If You ever decide to do that again, maybe i would be more relaxed. It was actually quite an incredible experience.

i love You.

Your slave puppy

Mon, 18 Apr 2005
Steven wrote:

Dear puppy,

  As always, You were a pleasure Saturday night. As far as being nervous, I told you I was going to give you to Steve or see if he would join us, but you had no idea what was going to happen to you. (I suspect he was also a little surprised since he knew nothing of what I had in mind.) You had no idea what kind of a scene it would be: humiliation, bondage, group. Of course you were nervous. I kept it simple and not too long, about an hour and a half. I wanted a flogging, spanking, singletail, and fisting scene. I enjoyed myself very much. As you know, there are very few people who I trust and who I feel have any knowledge about what BDSM and rough sex is all about.

  Steve is a nice man. I only know him through the events and clubs. I have not gone out with him or his wife, but in a scene situation, he is one of the few that I respect. I respect his skills and his understanding of the scenes he is in, and I also admire his ability to connect with the bottom. (That ability to connect is because his wife has trained him very well.)

  Young woman, you did give your legs a workout (isometrics). You were standing on tiptoes, trying to adjust your body to accommodate the fisting, and having multiple orgasms for almost an hour.

  As far as another scene, a double humiliation scene with you and Karen, with Steve directing, has great possibilities. Of course, I don't know if they would even consider this. If it should be arranged, I will make sure you hear about it a week before it takes place. I want your anxiety level to be sky high, to blind you, and to make you delightfully stressed, so when we play you will be wet and cumming to the touch, on command.

Sir

Steven writes:

  Steve knew nothing about the scene I had in mind. We had gone over to the Leather Rose that Saturday night because I knew he was giving an introduction class for newcomers. It was during that class when I made him the offer to join us in our scene. Steve is known in the BDSM world as PhantomMaster and Karen is known as Femcar.

Mon, 18 Apr 2005
sharon wrote:

Dear Master,

  Ahhhh... such a perfect day for sunbathing... except for the bumblebee who has claimed ownership of my upstairs deck. Fortunately, he allowed me the use of his space, though he felt the need to hover close by.

  It seems like i have so much to do this week that i've been putting off for too long, but i will work on the book this evening. It will be done by the end of the week. i work best under the pressure of a deadline... put things off until the last minute, then become very energized and productive. i am thoroughly enjoying the relaxed atmosphere of being home during the daytime during the week. i could get very used to this.

  Regarding what You said about nervousness and anxiety, i was thinking this morning about how my body deceives me (traitor that it is). When we were at that class listening to Steve, and afterwards when we all went out for dinner, i put the whole thing completely out of my mind, but by the time we got back to the club, my pussy was dripping wet. i can't believe we were playing for an hour & a half...it seemed like about 10 minutes! i am happy You were pleased. A double humiliation scene could be interesting...

Love,
Your slave puppy

Tue, 19 Apr 2005
sharon wrote:

Dear Master,

  i hope You're having a better day today. Personally, i'm having one of those days when nothing is working the way it should be. i've concluded my lawyer is not making enough money off of me to put any effort into anything. It took three phone calls and getting angry with them to get a court date, which now isn't going to be until May 5 since they screwed around & didn't get the job done...but at least i have a real date now. i also had a doctor's appointment today to follow up on that surgery and the normally 15-minute drive over there took an hour & a half. Then when i got there, they had forgotten to put my name on the list (even though they had the appointment in the computer), so i had to get angry again just to see the damn doctor.

i was also going to open my own checking account today, but the stupid bank has come up with some new rule that you can't take out more than $300 from an existing account in any one day, so i guess i'll have to go back 4 days in a row to get enough money to open another account. So then i decided to stop off at a store where i have a gift card (from Christmas) but haven't been able to find anything there. So today i found several things, but now i seem to have lost the damn gift card. i also showed up for my dentist appointment today except they had written today's date on the card and yesterday's date in their appointment book. So now i get to go back there again tomorrow. i feel like i've been busy all day and have accomplished nothing.

   Soooo...how was Your day?

Love,
Your slave

Tue, 19 Apr 2005
Steven wrote:

Puppy,

  My day wasn't as exciting as yours, but I did have a drink tonight. What you need is some electricity followed by hot wax, and then removal of the wax with my knife. It will relax you and rid you of all that anxiety. You'll sleep like a baby

Sir

Wed, 20 Apr 2005
sharon wrote:

Dear Master,

  What happened? It must have been bad if it drove You to drink. Do You need a slave to take care of You?

  When i have days like this, all i can do is sit back and laugh about how ridiculous life can get! Do You remember the cartoon with the little invisible imps going around and fucking up peoples' day? i can't remember their names, but they must have been busy having a lot of fun today! Except now it's going to drive me crazy trying to think of their names. Electricity and hot wax are going to relax me? i guess i'll just have to trust You on that one. i can be there in 20 minutes.

i love You.

Your slave puppy

Steven writes:

    Puppy arrived at my home 45 minutes later. I punished her for being 25 minutes late. Then I bound her and zapped her with some electricity (violet wand), followed by the hot wax. Two hours later she was sound asleep.

Wed, 20 Apr 2005
Steven wrote:

Natasha,

    Are you still there? Has the writing assignment frightened you away? Was I asking you to reveal too much of yourself? Have you taken up with another band of perverts? Or are you now going celibate since there is a new Pope? If I don't hear from you, then I will suspect that you have taken a journey to contemplate what the fuck you have gotten yourself into. While you are deep in thought, think about how you have submitted and given yourself to me and all those delicious orgasms you had.

Sir

Thu, 21 Apr 2005
Natasha wrote:

Dear Sir:

    I apologize for the long silence. I actually wrote you yesterday but apparently the letter did not get through. I did not go on a journey or take up celibacy as of yet.

    There were more simple reasons. There were meetings all of last week with several people from out of town, then it was my birthday.

I was hoping to see you later today, is that right?

Yours,
Natasha

Thu, 21 Apr 2005
Natasha wrote:

Dear Sir:

Here is what I've written so far.

Do you remember the first time we all got together? I do remember the first time we were together. My eyes were closed, but I knew what was going on. When I saw puppy sucking on your dick that night, I broke into sweat. I felt so excited and scared that I became so sweaty and smelly in just a second – it was embarrassing. *What did I feel?* I really do not know. Like being in a movie or in a play, like I am just a participant there, an actress. This whole "parallel" existence is so unusual to me and very unreal.

The next day I thought, "What am I doing?" I also thought, "I want to explore this further." The relationship is unlike anything else that I've known before. I am curious to be there.

What did you feel reading Pushkin? You see, Pushkin is a difficult subject. He is such an integral part of Russian culture that what I felt was frustration that I could not translate what I read properly. These were not even the best examples of his poetry. Still, some of them were rather good, but I knew I couldn't convey this at all. Not that you cared, but still. Also, when I was reading and trying to translate, it was very frustrating. My brain works too much and was blocking my erotic feelings☺. So I struggled.

When I am with you and Puppy, I think what I like the most is the flow of events and the energy between people, not specific occurrences. When Puppy is tied up, she looks so relaxed and happy; it makes me happy for her to watch this. You remember that this is my first experience with three people together, so I am mostly lost in emotions that I do not have words for.

Watching puppy being fisted, I cannot believe that this can be an enjoyable experience – it looks painful, but she loves it. I guess everybody is different.

Another thing – *What am I doing in BDSM with my fear of pain and low tolerance for it?* I like being bound and watching. It is

surreal and takes me out of "regular" existence to some different place. What is this place? I still do not know. Why do I need this? I do not know.
Later in the other room. I like flogging and single-tail. Spanking is really painful. I cannot say that I like it too much. There was no particular feeling that made me cry. Again, it was just a wave of an emotion for which I do not have the definition. I just cried – not because I was upset with you. I guess it was a release of some sort. Also, the tears in such a situation come and go as they please. It does not require my participation.
How did you feel about being told to get on your back and to spread your legs for me to enter you? This actually feels great. It gives me a sense of belonging and it is also extremely pleasurable.
What are your thoughts when I enter puppy and then you, and when I need you to feel my balls and cock when I am in puppy? I do not think I have any thoughts at this time. I guess I am raw sexuality at such a moment.
Your thoughts the following days about this strange new world you were entering? I feel great, relaxed, complete, and loved. It is so separate from the rest of the world that I feel like I am exploring secret pathways that are not accessible to anybody else. I do not know how you do it, but I am completely comfortable with you and I enjoy immensely the participation in your plays.

Fri, 22 Apr 2005
sharon wrote:

Dear Master,

Good evening Sir! Thank You for a lovely evening last night. i was thinking today that i have sampled more different kinds of food since i met You than i have in my entire life... not to mention all the other new experiences i've had. You have definitely expanded my horizons!

Natasha seemed more quiet ("sub-dued") than usual last night. Do You suppose her venture into writing has made her more contemplative?

The attached message is from a discussion group that i joined a long time ago. For the life of me, i can't remember what "TPE" stands for, but the reason i'm sending it to You is because i looked at the bookstore they're advertising and noticed they have Jack & Guy's books on there, but not *The Puppy Papers*! How can this be! i'm thinking they would surely be eager to include the P.P. in their offerings too. What do You think?

Love,
Your slave puppy

Steven writes:

TPE stands for "Total Power Exchange." Puppy has given me total power over her when we are together, in and out of the bedroom. Natasha has given me EPE, "Erotic Power Exchange," over her. That is the power given by a submissive to a Dominant only in the bedroom. Does TPE or EPE happen with every Top and bottom or Dominant and submissive? I don't know. I only know this is what happens with me.

I have never thought about these terms and have never discussed them. Women who are with me know about me. I tell them what I do, and if we mutually feel good about each other, then we start to play/scene. When we start to play/scene, power is automatically given to me; it is never questioned. I take total control without hesitation. My partners are given a safe word, "red," and when the safe word is spoken, everything stops. As we get to know each other, I use my knowledge, experience, instincts, and then at times, I disregard "red." Disregarding the safe word doesn't mean that I don't listen. Rather, it means that I don't pay much attention to useless fear. Lastly, all of my partners are given the choice to leave at any time.

Sat, 23 Apr 2005
sharon wrote:

Dear Master,

i am reading a book called *Built to Last* that starts out by saying "Winston Churchill once said that writing a book goes through five phases. In phase one, it is a novelty or a toy. But by phase five, it becomes a tyrant ruling your life. And just when you are about to be reconciled to your servitude, you kill the monster and fling it to the public." Just thought You might appreciate that! ☺

Love,
Your slave puppy

Sun, 24 Apr 2005
Steven wrote:

Dear puppy,

You have no excuse not to finish the book this weekend. It's too cold to sunbathe, your laundry is done, and don't worry about cleaning the house, you're selling it. You are at the end of your deadline, says the slave-driving Master.

Sir

Sun, 24 Apr 2005
sharon wrote:

Dear Master,

Good morning Sir! i promise i will be working on the book all day today and i will do absolutely nothing else until it is finished... unless You would like me to come and serve You since i have been unusually horny the last couple days. However, i will stifle the strong urge to go shopping on this beautiful sunny day. You can rest assured that my part will be done before Yours is or i should be punished severely and without mercy... hmmm... now that's something to think about... ☺... or maybe i should be punished severely and without mercy if i do get it done today... 😀

i love You.

Your slave puppy

Tue, 3 May 2005
Natasha wrote:

Dear Sir:

It was wonderful yesterday. Have a good weekend.

Yours,
Natasha

Steven writes:

I had Natasha crawl up the first flight of stairs to greet me and play with my cock for a few minutes before we went up three more flights of stairs to my home where she got undressed, laid on her back on the bed, and spread her legs wide. As she laid in this ready position, I did things around the room while talking to her.

She was relaxed now. The anxieties of her day were far away, and it was time to play. I took her into the other room and spent about 15 minutes doing puppy play because I needed to get into my headspace. After the puppy play, I told her sit in a chair next to my billiard table and I bound her to to the chair with rope. I then blindfolded her and put on the sound track from *Out of Africa*. I picked out a billiard cue, put the balls on the table, and started playing. Natasha looked peaceful, and after a few minutes I started talking to her. The rules were that when I asked her a question, she was to answer me by barking. I keep things simple. She was to howl if things were not good, bark twice if everything was good, and bark repeatedly if everything was super good.

    I talked; she barked. If she spoke instead, I twisted her nipples until she jumped slightly. When I finished my billiard game, I untied her and told her to go into the bedroom and get into position. She went in, got into position, and waited. I came into the room five minutes later and entered her. All through our fucking, I kept asking her the same few questions: How are you doing? Are you okay? Are you happy? and she had to bark her answers to me. If she spoke, I spanked her. At times, I told her that I needed her to bark louder so I could hear it. I always told her that the barking brings me such pleasure.

Wed, 4 May 2005
sharon wrote:

Dear Master,

    You asked me to write about the weekend and i should have done that on Monday because now it seems like ages ago. i know i was feeling really drained when i got to Your house, and feeling a whole lot better when i left. i don't remember the order of things. It seemed odd to be strung up in front of the mirror in the daytime. i don't know why, but i feel uncomfortable looking at myself in the mirror like that. When You had me licking off the floor, that was different too...a most unusual taste... very sweet, like sugar water...not at all what i expected.

    i could feel stripes on my ass...like lines of welts...but nothing visible. (laughing) It doesn't hardly seem fair to be whipped and have nothing to show for it! Something i've noticed in the last few months is that it used to be that when i was whipped, it would get to a point when i felt like i couldn't take any more, but lately it seems like You could go on forever and it would be good. i don't know if You're not whipping me as hard or if i'm reacting differently. According to medical research, people don't build up a tolerance for pain, so that can't be it. It does feel different though...more raw and tingly, less sharp and stinging. Good grief! Nothing like "contemplating the navel of a flea" as You would say!

    i like wearing the ankle & wrist cuffs, though i always feel like i'm marking up Your wood floor with the clips banging when i walk around in them. i like wearing a collar too...but You hardly ever put one on me. Why is that? i also like the idea of getting undressed as soon as i get upstairs and... OMG i've had a brain attack...i can't remember what else i'm supposed to do...there were two other things...

    i liked going in the bathroom with You at the restaurant (even though it was kind of skuzzy). It seemed kind of adventurous...like someone was going to come in and say "you can't be in here"... and i would, of course, just smile, point to You, and say "talk to Him." The poor old guy in there taking a piss could hardly get out of there fast enough. He gave me a wide-eyed look worth a thousand words...like DOES YOUR MOTHER KNOW YOU'RE DOING THIS!!!!!! ARE YOU SO STUPID THAT YOU DON'T YOU KNOW THIS BATHROOM IS FOR MEN ONLY!!!!!!!!! Very funny!

    And then the guy sitting next to me at the theater was a case too. He kept rubbing his leg against mine and i kept moving away, but i was soooo tempted to reach over and run my hand up & down his thigh...just to see his reaction. i'm sure it would have been entertaining. i kept thinking that this guy is getting off thinking he's doing this to some poor, innocent woman in a movie theater, but he has no idea where i've been or what i've done in the past few weeks! He reminded me of the guy, who i think i wrote about in *The Puppy Papers*, the college student that Diane harassed and he ended up getting himself fucked...blew his mind, poor guy.

    i also want to say that BB Gun was a gentleman this weekend...He did everything just right without getting greedy!

    Okay...You'd think i was writing a book here...God forbid! i hope Your day was less stressful today than yesterday. Hopefully i didn't screw up the book too bad. i was just trying to make it perfect for You...the way i thought You wanted it. i'm sorry.

i love You.

Your slave puppy

Wed, 4 May 2005
Natasha wrote:
Dear Sir:

I will be in Italy next week. I will be back on Sunday, May 15.

Yours,
Natasha

Thu, 5 May 2005
sharon wrote:

Dear Master,

    my divorce is final. It only took 15 minutes in the court room and that was only because i had to wait for two other couples to go first.

Love,

Your slave puppy

Sat, 7 May 2005
sharon wrote:

Dear Master,

Are You home tonight?

Ysp

Steven wrote:

I just came home.

Sir

sharon wrote:

Dear Master,

i miss You. Would You like some company?

Ysp

Steven wrote:

    If you want to come over, that's fine. I'm going to sleep after I write this piece. I'll clear off the bed.

Sir

sharon wrote:

Dear Master,

Ysp   i will sneak in quietly and not disturb You toooo much...

Sun, 8 May 2005
sharon wrote:

Dear Master,

  Here is the piece i had written before. Now that i look at it though, it isn't really a "ceremony" and i'm not sure what a collaring ceremony consists of. Perhaps a little more direction on this could produce something more useful?
  i've also attached an article i saved sometime in the past. i thought You might be interested in reading it... if i haven't already sent it to You before.
  i had a nice visit with my parents today. We went to Tiebel's for dinner. It's supposed to be the best restaurant in NW Indiana, but the food was quite tasteless compared to the restaurants in Your neighborhood. You have gotten me spoiled.
  Thank You for letting me spend the night last night. i guess it was just one of those nights when i was feeling lonely. It felt good just to lay next to You in bed...and of course, it always does wonders for my day to wake up in the morning to a spanking and ass-fucking. Thank You.

Love,
Your slave puppy

Steven writes:

The ceremomy piece that puppy mentions is in the email from Wed, 5 Jan 2005.

Wed, 11 May 2005
sharon wrote:

Dear Master,

  Okay, here are some more thoughts....am i going in the right direction now? Please guide me.

i offer myself, without reservation, for You to own as Your property, for You to have complete ownership of my body, mind and soul. i will serve only You and no one else, unless You tell me to do otherwise, and i will serve You in any way that You desire, at all times, in all places, with the understanding that i also have work and family responsibilities.

Love,
Your slave puppy

Sun, 15 May 2005
sharon wrote:

Dear Master,

      How is Your weekend going? Are You finished with *Puppy's Tales* yet?

      i have been recommending to everyone that they should go see that movie *Crash*. It is a requirement in health care that we do a yearly education inservice on cultural diversity, and i'm thinking when *Crash* comes out on video, it would be a great idea to show for discussion.

      i have accomplished a lot this weekend. Even finished reading two books that have been sitting under my nose for a couple months. They are both very good. i think You would like them. Both are written by Jim Collins - *Good to Great* and *Built to Last*. Your business philosophy very much parallels the companies in the books. Maybe Your book # 5 ought to be on business management.

      The wedding was nice. i saw a lot of old friends that i only get to see once every few years. (laughing) It seems like everyone (except for me, of course) has gotten old, gray, fat, and/or bald since the last time i saw them. These were all the big-time party people 25+ years ago who are now highly conservative, cynical, upper middle-class, boring people with nothing better to talk about than their big houses, big cars, big TV sets and big vacations. It was kind of depressing to think that's probably all the bride and groom have to look forward to as well. i am so glad my kids were determined to get out of the small town and take advantage of what else life has to offer.

      i don't know what else You want me to write for the upcoming ceremony. What else can i offer You besides all of me? Do You want me to list specific things that i will do or will not do? i need some guidance on this. Perhaps it would help if You could send me a copy of the contract. Is it supposed to be something like wedding vows... i.e., "i will love, honor, obey, serve, etc.?" Or should i talk about why i want to be Your slave? Or something else? In all honesty, i feel like i am offering You myself and You are the one to determine what You want from me and what it is that being Your slave does or does not entail. i will serve You in any way that You want. i don't know what else to say. Please help!

Love,
Your slave puppy

Mon, 16 May 2005
sharon wrote:

Dear Master,

    i hope Your day has gone well. i miss You. From Thursday to Tuesday always seems like such a long time... especially when Thursday doesn't include playing... such a poor slave puppy i am.

    i've been working on the ceremony and think i'm getting closer (despite the fact that Word insists on changing all my i's into I's). Please let me know what You think. i know You think it's foolish to offer oneself unconditionally or without limitations, but that's honestly the way i feel. i don't know how to do it any other way. It's just the way i've always functioned... all or nothing. It isn't meant to burden You. It's more like...a purity of commitment... trust. i tend to trust someone until they give me reason not to trust them – perhaps a personality flaw that we both have in common? i suppose it does create the risk of being hurt, but it seems to me that life would be quite miserable if i didn't trust people. i would rather risk being hurt. i don't think it makes me a mindless zombie, nor does it remove all self-preservation instincts. It's simply a decision i've chosen to make.

    i will be there tomorrow night with pen & paper to await Your words of wisdom. i'm getting all nervous about this event... will be lucky to remember my name when the time comes!

i love You.

Ysp

Wed, 18 May 2005
Steven wrote:

Dear puppy,

    What you have written is good. Remember the foundation is honesty, trust, respect, and love. Nothing in your offering is to be implied. Be direct and explicit. You're offering yourself to me unconditionally, with no reservations. There is no equality in this relationship. Look at it as being a good submissive born-again Christian woman saying the old marriage vows, but it is a one-sided offering in its structure. You will love, honor, and obey without question. I will love you as my slave and protect you as my property. It is not "til death do you part." This is a one-year contract. The formality of the collaring and contract is based on our needs, wants, desires, our understanding of the dynamics of our personalities and the relationship, and in wanting to be in this kind of relationship.

Sir

Wed, 18 May 2005
sharon wrote:

Dear Master,

    Well, i am happy that You approve. Thank You for pointing me in the right direction 😳. Maybe i should add that to the list... "slave needs Master to point her in the right direction when she appears slow or dense."

Love,
Your slave puppy

Fri, 20 May 2005
sharon wrote:

Dear Master,

    i hope Your day has gone well. i just got home from seeing my mother. The doctor has no idea what is wrong with her and can't do any more tests until Monday at the earliest. She looks and sounds good though, and the pain she was having has subsided for the present time.

    i have discovered it is definitely not a good idea to attempt driving to Indiana during rush hour...it took almost four hours to make a one-hour trip. i have driven 425.2 miles since leaving home yesterday morning. About 420 of those miles were through road construction. i'm sure i will still be seeing flashing yellow lights in my sleep tonight. 😊

    i hear it's supposed to be a beautiful, sunny and warm day tomorrow... a good day for a scooter ride! Also a perfect day for officially becoming Your slave! i am sooooooo excited... You may have to fuck me for several hours before the actual ceremony just to calm me down enough

so i can speak! i am going to be a good slave for You... much better than i have been. i want You to be pleased and happy and proud.
> Do You want me to spend the night tomorrow night?

i love You.

Your slave puppy

Sat, 21 May 2005

Collaring Ceremony:
puppy's offering of herself in body, mind, and soul
to be Steven's slave and property

- Because I love You, respect You, and trust You, I want to offer myself as Your slave, for You to own as Your property.
- Because I trust You, I do not want to set any limits or conditions to Your ownership.
- I want You to have complete control over me and to use me in any way that You desire to bring You pleasure and happiness.
- I want You to make all decisions regarding any aspect of my life that You choose, and I will take full responsibility for anything You do not wish to control.
- I want to please and serve You in all ways, not only sexually, but in any way that You desire.
- I will make You and Your wants, needs, and desires the center of my world.
- I will make Your needs, wants, desires, pleasure and happiness the first priority in my life to the greatest extent possible.
- Under all circumstances, I will give You the highest degree of respect and honor as my Lord and Master.
- I will always be open and honest with You to the best of my ability. I will not hide anything from You or do anything to cause You not to trust me.
- I will always be loyal to You and will not participate in any sexual activity or relationships without Your permission. I do not wish to serve anyone but You, but I will do so with respect, honor, and obedience if it will give You pleasure and happiness.
- Because I trust You, I will always obey You without question and without hesitation.

- If at any time, You feel that I have failed to please or obey You in any way, I hope that You will firmly and consistently punish and discipline me and teach me how to be a better slave.
- It gives me tremendous pleasure and satisfaction (and makes my pussy wet) when You are pleased and happy with my service to You, and I will always strive to make Your life easier, better, and happier.
- To that end, I offer myself to You, with full rights of ownership, to be Your humble, loyal, and devoted slave.

Contract: Recognition and Acceptance of Voluntary Servitude

Dated: *May 21, 2005*

We the undersigned parties, recognize and accept the submission of *puppy sharon,* hereafter called the "slave," to *Steven Toushin,* hereafter referred to as the "Master," in a relationship of Voluntary Servitude, hereafter called "slavery."

By this instrument, Master agrees to direct, train, and discipline slave in a manner to guide her towards perfection of obedience and submission that she would never achieve without Master's guidance. Slave desires to be dominated and owned by Master for His pleasure and profit. The slave's tenure will continue for a period of one year, beginning on *May 21, 2005* and ending on *May 21, 2006*.

It is agreed that this period of slavery will be under the Master's direction and control and will be subject to the following conditions:

Virtue will be a significant part of our relationship. Therefore, we agree that fundamental to the slavery will be the practice of the virtues of trust, honesty, openness, loyalty, and obedience. Without the practice of these virtues, there can be no true slavery. Their practice, therefore, is expected and required at all times.

The slave wishes to be an integral part of her Master's leather family and will treat each person in that relationship with the respect, honor, and obedience due their position.

The slave wishes to bring the Master physical, sexual, intellectual, emotional, and spiritual pleasure by the submission and service of herself to the Master's will, wants, and desires. She will do this through her practice of obedience to the Master's will and through compliance to the Master's rules.

1. As slave, my body is now my Master's property. It is no longer my right to protest any use He chooses to make of it. Rather, it is an honor that

He uses my body, and it is my duty to always keep my body in a healthy condition and in a state of cleanliness for my Master's use and pleasure.

2. As slave, I will restrict my sexual activity to my Master and to those to whom my Master gives his permission, and to those he desires to give me to.

3. As slave, I recognize that my Master is my Lord and Master and that my Master's cock, needs, wants, and all desires are the object of my obedience and worship.

4. As slave, it is my duty to obey any and all commands given me by my Master, and to do all of his biddings without question.

5. As slave, I shall address Master as "Master" or "Sir" or by whatever title he so chooses.

6. As slave, I shall do my best to never be an encumbrance upon my Master or to make him uncomfortable by my presence.

7. For the period of my slavery, the Master will control my (slave's) schedule and routine when I (slave) am with Master.

8. As slave, I shall accept, without complaint or protest, whatever punishments my Master may decree.

As slave, I accept these conditions and will strive to perform them without failure, without rebellion, and without hesitation.

As Master, I accept this slave into my loving care and protection.

We acknowledge that this agreement binds us as Master and slave dedicated to the accomplishment of our goals. This relationship will in no way prohibit the maintenance or development of relationships with others, except that for the duration of the slavery, the slave will make the attainment of the goals herein described her first priority and the conduct of her slavery, in light of these goals, will take precedence, when such precedence is required, over all other relationships, goals, and activities.

By our agreement to this document, the slave gives the Master the right to transfer the duties, rights, and obligations of this agreement to any person, at any time, for the duration of this agreement. Those persons to whom the Master transfers these rights by gift, rental, or sale shall be deemed holding the rights of this agreement in the Master's place and shall receive the same respect, service, and obedience as due the Master.

This voluntary servitude may be renewed at the Master's discretion.

By my signature and my sealing, I, *Steven Toushin* accept you as my slave *puppy sharon,* dated: *May 21, 2005*

I, *puppy sharon*, willingly submit myself to the above-described slavery, commit myself to the herein described goals, and accept *Steven Toushin* as my Master for the duration of this slavery. By my signature and sealing I accept you as my Master, dated: *May 21, 2005*

Steven Toushin _____

puppy Sharon _____

* * *

Steven writes:

It was a lovely, easy ceremony with just puppy and I. When I was ready for the ceremony to begin, I had puppy, who was naked, kneel in front of me and read her offering. When she finished, I accepted her offering as my slave and took her into my service. I put my collar around her neck and locked it. Puppy, who was still on her knees, took my cock into her mouth and I fed her. When I finished, I took puppy over to the table where we signed and dated the contract and her offering. She was now officially my property. I then played with her and when we were finished, we went out for dinner

Sun, 22 May 2005
sharon wrote:

Dear Master,

i thought i would feel different being collared, but i don't feel any different...just like i don't feel any different being divorced... seems odd. i wonder how long it will take for these things to seem real. i guess i was already in the mindset for quite a while (gradual process) and the formalities haven't changed that, though it seems like they should.

(chuckle) i just had a thought... what if this collar sets off the security alarm at the airport? That happened to a woman last time i flew, so she had to remove all of her jewelry to get through security. Can You be available at 7 a.m. to make an emergency trip to O'Hare? Or to Milwaukee on Tuesday in case the return trip becomes a problem?

Thank You for the wonderful weekend.

Love,
Your slave puppy

Wed, 25 May 2005

sharon wrote:

Dear Master,

Would it be okay if i stay home tomorrow night and try to get some stuff done? It is almost midnight and i just got home from the hospital. They didn't take my mother into surgery until after 6:00 this evening. She was still groggy and having a lot of pain when i left, but she will be fine and hopefully will be going home tomorrow. i feel like i haven't been home in a week. If i'm going to be gone four days over the weekend, i really need to get some stuff done. Then i will work twice as hard to please You on Friday 😊.

i love You.

Your slave puppy

Thu, 26 May 2005
Steven wrote:

Dear puppy,

Please tell me how you felt about the collaring and ceremony. I am disappointed and sad that you are not feeling the meaning and connection with the collar, that the symbolic meaning of its presence is somewhat lost. Does this have anything to do with what happened in Wisconsin? I am sorry about what happened in Wisconsin. I never thought about a situation like that. Please tell me what happened? What was your reaction and feelings?

Sir

Steven writes:

The collar was a short, silver chain necklace that I bought at Tiffany and Co. and it had a small silver key lock. It was part of their "Return to Tiffany" jewelry collection. This piece had to work with all of her clothing. It couldn't be recognized as anything other than an attractive piece of jewelry.

The Monday after the ceremony, puppy went to Wisconsin, to one of the company's branch offices, for two days. Within five minutes of her arrival, one of the administrative nurses said curtly, "What is that on your neck? How could you wear such a thing?" Puppy was stunned. After a few moments, she asked "What's wrong with it?" The nurse told her that she was wearing a piece of gang jewelry. A few of the others nurses chimed in with their disapproval.

Puppy was taken aback. Was this person serious or trying to put puppy in her place? Puppy was the new consultant from the Big City, and to get people's cooperation, she needed their respect. This was not the way to get it. To make matters worse at that moment, I had the key so the chain and lock were not coming off until she came home.

My opinion is that these people did not want an outsider coming into their territory and setting policy; and this was their way of bringing her down a few notches. They were pointing out that she couldn't relate to their patients or their area, so how could she set policy.

I won't do anything to hurt puppy in her work; and I felt bad that the collar had caused her a problem. I was also annoyed that nobody took a close look at the necklace. In my opinion, the woman who made that statement had an agenda. When puppy came back, I took the collar off. Now she only wears it when she's with me.

After the Wisconsin trip, I decided to speed up puppy's commitment to me. What I planned would be in two parts, starting at IML and completed two weeks later.

After six months of being my collared slave, I planned to have both sides of puppy's inner pussy lips pierced and have gold rings inserted to signify a deeper commitment. I now will have her pierced at IML. At the end of one year, when we renewed our contract, I originally planned to have her tattooed with a decorative design directly above her pussy. The tattoo would say, "Property of S.T." or "slave owned by Steven Toushin." Now the tattoo would be done two weeks after the piercings a few weeks from now. Puppy would then feel her commitment. She would feel my presence 24/7.

Thu, 26 May 2005
sharon wrote:

Dear Master,

Are You all rested up and ready for the big weekend? If i remember correctly, You said IML is at the Hyatt Regency, right? Will You be spending the day tomorrow setting up? Arthur's girlfriend is dying of curiosity about the event. She says she's going to stop by sometime over the weekend to see what it's all about...that ought to be interesting.

Love

Ysp

Thu, 26 May 2005
Steven wrote:
Dear puppy,

  We set up today. The vending starts tomorrow around 10:30 and ends at 5:00.
  I saw some lovely jewelry that I like for your pussy lips. Since the collar was a bust, in that it was not the symbol of commitment that worked for you, besides the problem you had with it at work – until I can think of something more appropriate for your work environment, I feel this will keep you with me at all times. I am determined that you will feel and see my presence, so I will start by having you wear my rings. This gives me the ability to lock your pussy lips together when we go out, so you will feel the lock dangling between your legs, how delicious. The tattooing and piercing will be within a week or so of each other.
  Where did Arthur's girlfriend ever hear about IML and why is she so curious?
  Yes, it is the Hyatt Regency on Wacker.

Sir

Thu, 26 May 2005
sharon wrote:
Dear Master,

  Question...won't pierced pussy lips interfere with fisting... or fucking for that matter? Have You known any women who had this done? And who does this? i can't picture myself sitting in the middle of a shopping mall for this procedure!! And who is going to tattoo someone's pussy? This all sounds very painful! You are going to make me a nervous wreck with all this talk.
  If the vending is done at 5:00 already, i guess i will just meet You at Your house tomorrow night.
  i don't remember how it all came up, but i told Arthur & Joyce about IML. She has been wanting to go to a club or event and has wanted us to take her sometime, which is not something i care to do. So i told her about IML, figuring she could go on her own if she wants to. Arthur said he's not going anywhere near there. If it's anything like last year, i doubt

she'll make it past the lobby if she shows up at all. Then again, i could be wrong....though i think she's just getting off on the idea of it all...the fantasy. Perhaps she has a bit of slave blood running through her veins?

Love,
Your slave puppy

Thu, 26 May 2005
Steven wrote:

Dear puppy,

     I will take care of the piercing and tattoo. You just think about it and let the anticipation make you a nervous wreck. Where on God's earth did you come up with the idea of a shopping mall? It must be the country girl in you. The piercing is being done by a Gay Leather Devil Worshiper from California, so you'll be in good hands with Satan.

Sir

Thu, 26 May 2005
sharon wrote:

Dear Master,

     Well, i will sure sleep better tonight knowing that 😈. i only have one pussy You know...and it has to last for the rest of my life... can't have it being damaged or non-functional or my Master might disown me... Satan better have good credentials.

     If Arthur and his girlfriend come to IML, it would be far too weird for me.

Love,
Your slave puppy

Tue, 31 May 2005
sharon wrote:

Dear Master,

     i'm not sure i know or understand what i felt about the collaring and ceremony. It didn't make me feel like i thought it would. i think if it had happened a year ago, it would have meant everything to me. But considering all that has taken place in the past year between You and i, as well as in my own life, it seemed sort of... after-the-fact...like i had given myself to You a long time ago and this was just an outward symbol for other people to see. i really like the collar; i like wearing it; and i like for other people to know i am Your slave. i felt very happy to be wearing Your collar, but it didn't seem to change how i felt about You or how i felt about our relationship. Whether You knew it or not, i would have said those same words shortly after i met You... it was not a new commitment. i think it validates things, makes it "official." i feel it is a gift You have given to me because i offered myself to You, and i am proud to wear it.

The thing is, i don't know what i expected to feel. The weeks just prior to the ceremony were kind of a whirlwind with rushing to finish *Destruction*, starting the new job, and finalizing the divorce. i guess i was rather frazzled, still running in circles, not having the time to sit down and absorb the experience. i intended to do that when i got to Wisconsin... kind of wallow in my slavery ☺...get my thoughts together, sort of evaluate where i was and where i was going. i was floating when i got there, feeling like the world was full of sunshine, blue skies, and beautiful people. i was totally unprepared for the reaction i got when i stepped through the door of the office.

There were probably ten people in the room and all eyes must have gone directly to the shiny lock & chain around my neck. Before i could even say hello, several people started making comments: "Interesting necklace," "Don't you think that's inappropriate to wear to work?" "Why are you wearing a lock?" "Where did you get that?" "We have a dress code around here." It reminded me of a bunch of ill-tempered librarians with glasses perched on the ends of their noses while they looked above them to reprimand the juvenile delinquents who dared to speak out loud amongst the sacred books. i was so surprised, all i could stammer was, "It was a gift." They were not impressed. i was asked to take it off and i pretended to ignore them because...i had no choice.

Fortunately, i was not in a position where i had to answer to any of them, or follow their dress code, or justify my choice of adornments. However, i had lost their respect. my job depends on my ability to gain cooperation from such people and it was obvious over the course of my stay that they had no intention of following my advice as long as i was wearing the lock and chain, which they associated with gangs. i highly doubt they thought i was in a gang, but it was a symbol they strongly disapproved of. As i looked around, the only jewelry i saw anyone else wearing were small, delicate crosses or angel pins.

After i left the office that first day, i went to the hotel where i spent the entire evening thinking about how i would ever be able to explain to You that i could not wear the collar at work. i even woke up several times during the night worrying about it. i almost called You about 3 a.m., but figured no sense in both of us losing sleep. i didn't want to take it off. i spent a lot of time trying to figure out how i could cover it up so as not to offend certain people, but with it being summer time, i figured they would really think i was nuts if i showed up wearing turtlenecks every day. i tried turning it around so the lock was in the back, so it could be covered up by a dress collar, but the chain was too short (or the lock too heavy) and it was strangling me. i even considered changing careers. By the time the plane landed back in Chicago, i had worn myself out trying to come up with a solution and had decided to just present You with the facts and let You come up with an answer.

i had a whole speech worked out, which immediately evaporated the minute i saw You. When You asked how the trip was, i started babbling and You immediately removed the collar before i had a chance to explain. i didn't want You to take it off. i wanted You to figure out how i could continue wearing it without offending anyone... irrational, but Masters are supposed to be all-knowing and all-powerful, right? 😊 i sat there holding the chain that was supposed to be around my neck and feeling like a failure. i only had it for a couple days and it was gone again. i was hugely disappointed.

You were very understanding and accepting of the situation, almost too understanding. i wanted You to put up a fight and say the chain was staying on no matter what. i would have done whatever You said, You know. However, You are the rational and practical one and You didn't want the collar to interfere with my job.

i was glad when You said You would come up with something else in place of the collar, like a bracelet or an ankle chain or something. i was hoping You would decide to just go with a smaller, less noticeable lock on the neck chain. Then when You starting talking about piercing, branding, tattooing, i thought, You can't be serious...that would be waaaaay too painful, not to mention permanent. In my ignorance, i thought You would spend weeks or months talking about it until i could get used to the idea. i really thought You were going to come up with something else.

325

So five days later, i found myself laying on a table in a hotel room, legs spread wide, while You and another man decided where to place Your rings. Owwwwwww!!!!!!!!!!!!! It seems You've solved the problem!

Love,
Your slave puppy

Puppy went to Wisconsin again in July. Here is what she had to say about that trip:

Thu, 21 Jul 2005
sharon wrote:

Dear Master

    Everything went very well in Wisconsin, but i'm happy to be back home. The group in that office was fine. The one who had started the whole thing about the necklace the last time was unusually subdued. i think someone must have put her in her place.

Love
Ysp

Wed, 1 Jun 2005
sharon wrote:

Subject: IML 2005

Dear Master,

    i felt very comfortable and had fun at IML this year. i really enjoyed the whole weekend. Last year i felt overwhelmed, lost, naive, like i didn't belong there...seems like a long time ago. i've always felt very comfortable around gay men, but last year i felt like i was intruding on a private party... my own perception, not theirs. This year, it didn't make any difference. Less of an egocentric view i guess...my presence or absence was meaningless to anyone else. Like i told Natasha, she and i could walk around the place totally naked and no one would even notice or pay attention. i find that quite amusing. We (women) tend to take ourselves far too seriously, thinking everyone is going to notice a hair out of place or a piece of lint on the sleeve when, in fact, no one else cares...in any environment. So conceited we all are. As i'm writing this, i'm thinking maybe the reason she was scared has something to do with trust.

Anyway, everyone i talked to there was polite, friendly, and helpful...the attendees, that is. The hotel staff seemed rather unhelpful and ignorant of where things were. i really enjoyed just watching all the people walk by. Definitely some beautiful bodies...not just handsome and attractive bodies...more like art appreciation or enjoying the beautiful things in nature... the art of body sculpting...like moving statues. i also enjoyed the fact that there were people of all different ages, shapes, and sizes and that everyone seemed so relaxed and comfortable in expressing affection. It must be a very romantic weekend for many people. It's funny to think how everything seemed so outlandish last year and warm, fuzzy, and friendly this year. Do You suppose i'm the only one to describe IML as warm & fuzzy? Probably not what they had in mind!

Every so often, people would stop in front of the table to watch the videos behind me. They would be cringing or wincing or turning away, so i would turn around to see what caught their attention and watch for a couple minutes. The thing i noticed was that the videos didn't create that kind of emotional reaction in me. Again, it was more like watching art, just like when we watched *Fisting Ballet* at Your house... fascinating and beautiful to watch, but that was all. i don't remember if You and i discussed it or if it was my own conclusion while working on Your book, but i think the emotional reaction is a value judgment...good (as in turn-on) or bad... and a self-centered perspective, like "I don't want that to happen to me." i think that's one way i've grown since i've known You. i never would have condemned anyone for their lifestyle or sexuality, but since i've known You, i've come to really appreciate the art and beauty of all lifestyles and sexualities. Does that make sense?

i was really surprised when Arthur and Joyce showed up. i don't know how she got him to go. All i could think about at the time was my newly pierced pussy and trying to get into a comfortable sitting position. Then they just appeared out of nowhere. i heard someone say my name and there they were. You had such a shocked expression on Your face when i introduced them to You. i think that's the first time i've seen You speechless!

i also enjoyed that evening when we went to Jack & Patrick's. They are wonderful and gracious hosts and just plain good people who i feel privileged to know. And Patrick is an excellent chef.

i'm still in a cloud about the piercing and i definitely feel you all the time. i don't know how i'll ever be able to concentrate at work. As for the tattoo....Your desire is my command Master.

Love,
Your slave puppy

Steven writes:

I was busy with people at my booth when puppy said, "Master, I want you to meet Arthur and Joyce." I sat there staring with my mouth open for a least a year and a half. It took me at least a moment to get my bearings anyway. I was stunned to say the least. Hopefully, it didn't look too obvious.

I had asked Natasha to join me at IML. I instructed her to wear black slacks, a sport jacket, no shirt, and no bra. When she arrived, she spent some time walking around before she came to the booth with a glass of wine in her hand. She was wearing a shirt and bra. When she came over to me, she did not formally greet me and she seemed uneasy. I quietly let her know that I was not pleased. She didn't do as she was told, and she didn't follow the correct procedure. We spoke a little and she laughed nervously. I asked her why she didn't obey my request. She replied that she had been nervous all day and didn't know what to expect. I asked what there was to expect and what she thought would happen. She said she didn't know. I asked her to go to the bathroom and take off her shirt and bra. She was hesitant, but then went and later returned without them on. Then she greeted me properly.

For the rest of the day, Natasha seemed uncomfortable, but she did not express why. We had always played either in my home or once in a private club, where she expressed bewilderment and excitement. I think the event and the public display of sexuality, gay sexuality, was too overwhelming for her.

Puppy, Natasha and I left IML and went over to Jack and Patrick's home for their yearly IML dinner party. Natasha remained quiet for the rest of the evening. When we left, we went back to my home, but Natasha did not join puppy and I.

A few days passed without any communication from Natasha, so I contacted her to see if she was all right. By that time, I knew that our relationship had ended.

Wed, 1 Jun 2005
Steven wrote:
Dear puppy,

Do you have Monday's receipt slips from IML?

Sir

Wed, 1 Jun 2005
sharon wrote:

Dear Master,

    The receipts are in the gray cash box which, i think, is on the table downstairs by the door.
    The swelling must be going down because Your rings definitely jingle when i walk. The one on the right side is more sore... will probably take longer to heal.

Love,
Your slave puppy

Wed, 1 Jun 2005
Steven wrote:

Dear puppy,

    Walk softly. I don't want you to wake up the whole neighborhood. In about four to five weeks the piercings won't bother you. It will take about 12 weeks for them to be fully healed. We will be playing again within a week.

Sir

Wed, 1 Jun 2005
sharon wrote:

Dear Master,

    i just want to say that i hope these things are giving You an extreme amount of pleasure.

Love,
Your slave puppy

Wed, 1 Jun 2005
Steven wrote:

Dear puppy,

I know you are thinking about me with the fondest of thoughts throughout your day.

Sir

Wed, 1 Jun 2005
sharon wrote:

Dear Master,

Yes, You are constantly on my mind...with the fondest of thoughts... ☺. i think all of this careful maneuvering is wearing me out though... you'd think i just had major surgery... such a lightweight!

Love,
Your slave puppy

Thu, 2 Jun 2005
sharon wrote:

Dear Master,

Your pussy was very sore by the time i got home last night and all day today. i think i must have had a reaction to the stuff i've been using to clean it. i am now slithering in Vaseline and feeling tremendous relief...thank God. If i could have found some ice cubes at work today, i wouldn't have hesitated to fill my panties with them.

Love,
Your slave puppy

Fri, 3 Jun 2005
Steven wrote:

Dear puppy,

What were your thoughts when I told you that I was going to have you pierced? When you knew for sure that you were going to be pierced? When it actually happened? How did you feel afterwards and now?

Sir

Fri, 3 Jun 2005
sharon wrote:

Dear Master,

    First of all, i want to say that i never in my life had any desire for piercings or tattoos or any other body modifications. As You well know, i am not a flashy person and i prefer not to draw attention to myself. And, believe it or not, i have a very low pain tolerance outside of a sexual scene...and i'm not even going to attempt to explain that one.

    When You first started talking about piercings and tattoos, i told myself it was just talk, it wasn't really going to happen, and if it did, it would be in the far distant future, so i could worry about it when the time came. i am a verrrrrry slow learner.

    i liked the idea of You having it done for Your pleasure, but these things are quite permanent and would be rather difficult to explain to anyone else in the future. i guess what it all boils down to is the difference between words and feelings. Regardless of what You said, i always felt that You would, at any time, get tired of me and it would be over...and i would be left with Your permanent marks while You moved on to someone else. In other words, i would give myself totally to You, but You would not necessarily take total ownership of me. i think that's why the collar didn't make me feel so much different...it could be removed in a moment.

    When the collar didn't turn out to be very practical and You started talking more about the piercings and tattoo, i still thought it would be at some distant point in the future. In fact, when You took me to look at the rings at IML and then bought them, i still thought it would be weeks or months before You would do anything with them. i was totally unprepared for it to happen the next day. my anxiety level skyrocketed to say the least. i could think of a thousand reasons to refuse and only one reason to go through with it... because You wanted it. So i never gave any consideration to refusing.

    The rings do make me feel very different. i feel connected to You all the time, especially because no one else can see them. i feel like somehow the collar represented me giving myself to You and the rings symbolize You accepting me. i feel like it's more of a commitment on Your part...that You wouldn't ask for this if You planned on discarding me tomorrow.

    Having my labia pierced is also a very humbling experience...pretty much eliminates any speck of privacy or modesty. Now there is no doubt that You are my Master and i am Your slave, Your property. Now i feel more owned, more safe and secure...and despite the fact that my pussy is still quite tender, i find myself smiling and thinking of You...with the fondest of thoughts.

Love,
Your slave puppy

Fri, 3 Jun 2005
Steven wrote:

Dear puppy,

You are going to be tattoed as my property. What are your thoughts and feelings about the tattoo at this time?

Sir

Fri, 3 Jun 2005
sharon wrote:

Dear Master,

As much as i would like to think that the tattoo is going to be months away, i suspect that it will be much sooner. See, i do eventually learn! A tattoo is more permanent than a piercing...not to mention, more prolonged pain during the process. i feel like it's a matter of degree. When You first talked about the tattoo, my thought was, "There's no way that's going to happen!" Even last week when You talked about it, i thought a tattoo was going too far...not something i wanted to do. But now i feel differently. i think the tattoo will make me feel more complete. i like the idea that whenever You look at me, You will see Your marks and You will be reminded that i am Your property, that i belong to You. i think the tattoo will be even more humbling than the rings and i will feel even more owned. Then the next thing You know, i'll be wanting to show off my (Your) pussy everywhere we go. In fact, i'm already having the urge to play show & tell with the rings. 😊

Love,
Your slave puppy

Sun, 5 Jun 2005
sharon wrote:

Dear Master,

    Everything You said today started to sink in on the way home tonight and i was feeling rather overwhelmed. Then when i got home and looked at the price tag on the jacket, i felt really overwhelmed and really unworthy of such a gift. It actually brought tears to my eyes. It is, by far, the nicest gift i've ever received. Thank You.

    i'm also feeling unworthy of everything You said about a permanent relationship, love, being Your primary slave, etc. You seem to know me, the real me, better than anyone else and the idea that You still find me acceptable to that degree is... well, it's hard to comprehend. i am not afraid of making a commitment, but i never expected that much commitment in return. i am only familiar with one-way relationships. It seems so strange that a Master-slave relationship would be more mutual than anything else i've known.

    i'm glad that we're going through this three-phase solidification of the slave contract. It is much more meaningful this way because apparently i'm only able to absorb small pieces at a time. All things seem to work out for the best. A long time ago i spent a lot of time praying for a person such as You to enter my life. Perhaps God does answer prayers after all... even if it takes many years for him to get around to it... something to think about. Thank You for coming into my life and for making the world a better place to be.

i love You.

Your slave puppy

Wed, 15 Jun 2005
sharon wrote:

Dear Master,

    It was so funny last night when i started my car and a woman's voice immediately came on the radio and said, "So if you're having pelvic pain, it could be serious. Call this number now." If i could have caught the phone number, i would have called to see just what she would do for me!

    The tattoo stings or burns on and off, not bad, just enough to know it's there. The lotion works well to soothe it. It looks smaller than i thought it would, especially since it felt like it was about five times that big while he was doing it. The writing doesn't look very clear when looking at it upside down or backwards in a mirror, but i will assume it's legible when looking straight at it.

Psychologically and emotionally...i feel happy. i do feel owned. Now there is no doubt that my well-adorned pussy definitely belongs to You! i hope You are pleased with how it looks. i'm having the urge to show it off to everyone. i'm also feeling like i'm spending a lot of time taking care of it. i may have to get a bigger purse just to carry around all the stuff to take care of my (Your) pussy.

It wasn't that i didn't feel connected to You before because i did. i think the rings and tattoo demonstrate how connected to You i do feel. They wouldn't be there if i didn't want them, if i didn't feel the connection, if i didn't want to be Your slave.

There is something unique about the process of getting them though...of having You at my side deciding what should be done and how it should be done. It makes me feel secure, cared for. It taps into something that has apparently been missing in my life. For as long as i can remember, i've been taking care of everyone else – both physically and emotionally – but any time anything has happened to me (good or bad), i've been all alone. i never thought much about it, never learned to expect anything more, never felt deprived or needy, but the idea that You were right there for both procedures...well, it is a new experience for me. Even inquiring about my physical, psychological, or emotional status is something no one else has ever done...or wants to hear about.

At the risk of sounding excessively drippy... You have touched my "inner child." Thank You. i feel proud to be wearing Your rings and Your brand, and i feel proud to be Your slave...and i am still thinking of You, with the fondest of thoughts...every time i move.

Love,
Your slave puppy

Wed, 15 Jun 2005
Steven wrote:

Dear puppy,

How is my pussy and tattoo doing? How was your day with such an adored front and bottom? Were you resting your leg on the sink with your dress up above your waist, throwing water on your cunt to cool yourself off?

When you have healed in the next couple weeks, I have devised a little piece of jewelry to hang from my rings, so you will always be aware of your Master.

Sir

Wed, 15 Jun 2005
sharon wrote:

Dear Master,

The thought did cross my mind... a spray bottle filled with ice cold water for my "front bottom area" as well as my "middle bottom area!" mmmmm... the lock hanging from Your rings did feel rather nice. Of course, i can't walk around with a smile on my face all the time...people might think i was up to something 😬.

Love,
Your slave puppy

Steven writes:

I asked puppy to tell me how she's getting along with her ex-husband since their divorce three months ago. They're still living in the same house and, as always, splitting the bills for the boys' schooling, household expenses, mortgage, etc.

Wed, 3 Aug 2005
sharon wrote:

Dear Master

Friendship with Arthur now:

We get along pretty well now because he no longer finds it necessary to nag me all the time. We help each other out with things if needed. Well, actually he helps me more than i help him since he's pretty self-sufficient and there are a number of things i am ignorant about. He pretty much runs the household and i'm the upstairs tenant who shows up a few nights a week. He hired someone to come in and clean the house, mostly because i never get around to cleaning up my half and it drives him crazy. We get along fine, each have our own separate lives and are rarely here at the same time. i see him a total of maybe 15 minutes a week. i would have to say we are good friends. i feel like i could count on him if i needed to and vice versa. i trusted him enough to get the brakes fixed on my car, so i think that says a lot!

Love,
Your slave puppy

Steven, 2006

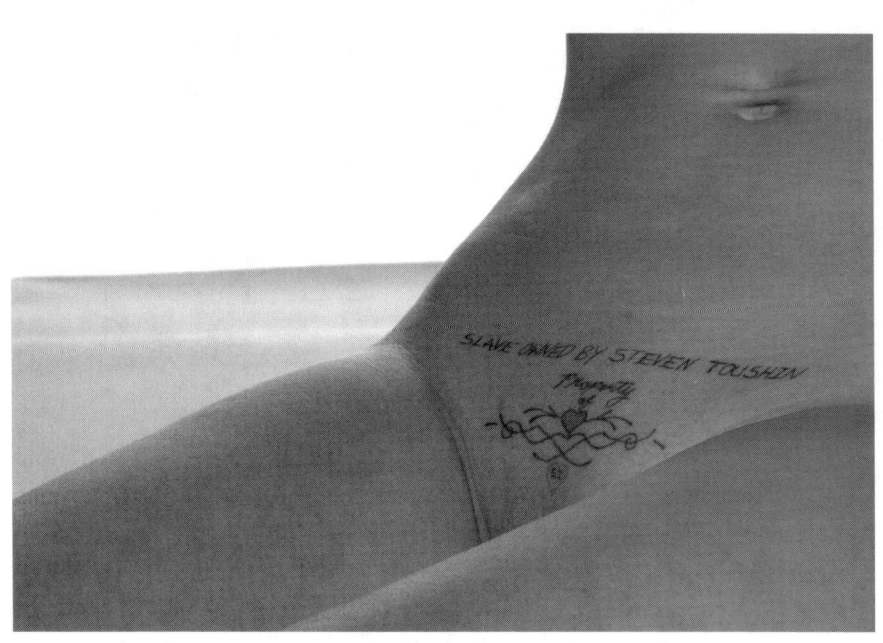

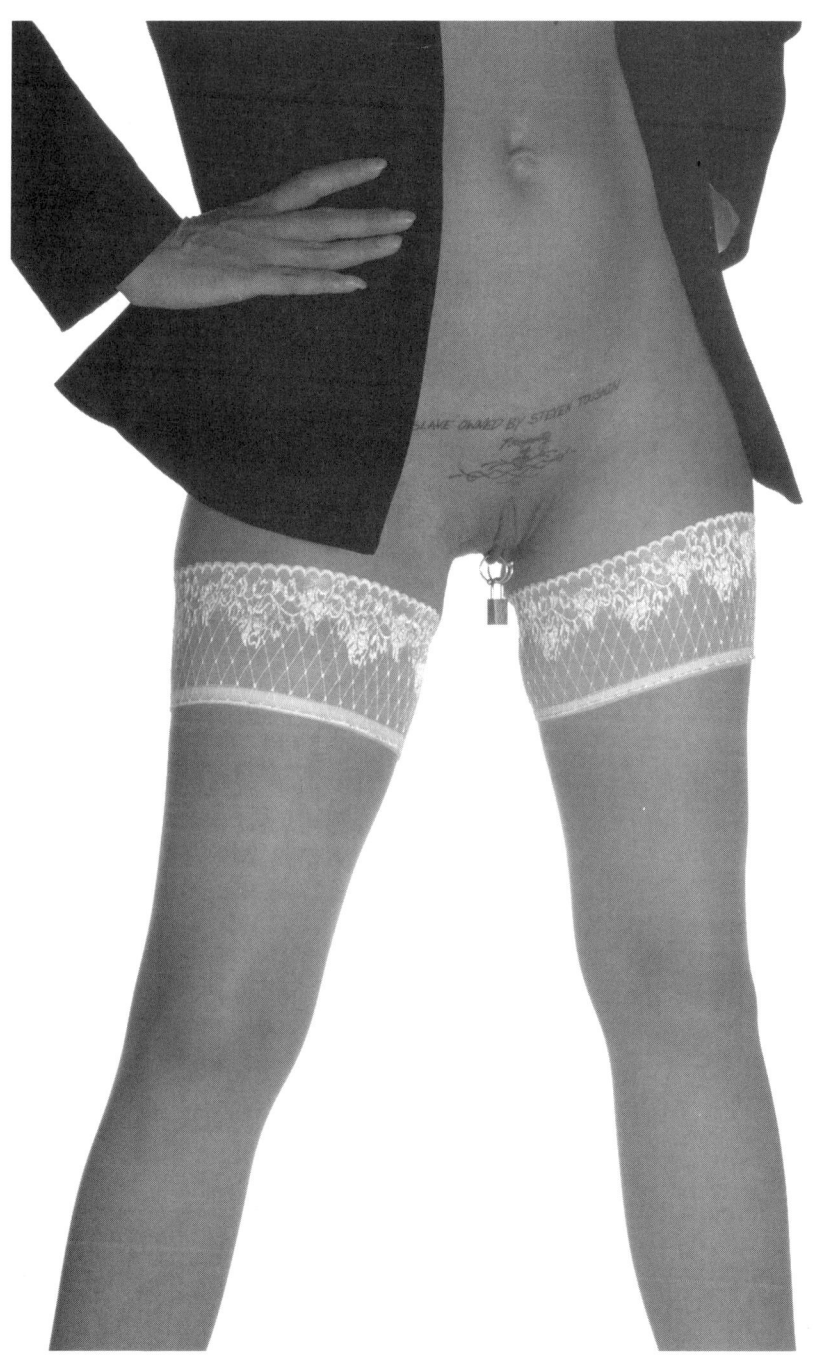

*GoldDust Pearl (foreground), BB Gun, Pirate,
Steven Toushin, Desperado (background, left to right)*

In Memory of BB Gun and Desperado

BB Gun
Born 1994 – Died 2006
Adopted 1999

    When I was growing up, we had a family dog. When I worked in Maine cutting trees, the Indians I lived with had a dog named Rex. Other than those times, I never really cared to have a dog.
    Thirty-five years later, I decided to get a dog after having lived with my daughter's dog, Ms. Charley. But it had to be a dog that was friendly to small pets because I have parrots and didn't want any of them harmed. I occasionally watch a show called *Animal Planet* on television,

and one day they were discussing Greyhounds. I was intrigued with what I heard, so I did some research and decided I wanted a Greyhound. Greys are a beautiful, elegant, easy, mellow, lazy breed of dogs.

My first Grey was BB Gun, a super thin, long Grey who retired from racing when he was five years old, after running 200 races. BB was all black with white shoes (feet), a white tuxedo front (chest), and a long strip of white at the end of his tail. His demeanor was quiet and laid back. He would bark once a year. He was elegant in stature, with long thin legs, and the longest tail you can imagine. But it was his gait that caught people's attention: he pranced like a horse with his head held erect.

BB Gun was a quiet Alpha dog, but he and I had some issues; and we had arguments and disagreements over these issues. I tried resolving the problem with obedience training. Consequently, he became super obedient, but it didn't resolve our issues. These issues only happened with me and only in our house, never with anyone else or anywhere else. The problem was that when BB needed to pee, he would come over to where I was and pee right in front of me. Now, please understand that when a Greyhound pees it becomes a lake, which meant I spent a lot of time cleaning up. I eventually smartened up and resolved the problem by putting diapers on Mr. BB Gun.

Desperado
Born 1993 – Died 2006
Adopted 2000

I had BB Gun for eight months when I adopted my second Grey, "Desperado." Desperado was six and half years old when I adopted him, and he had lived in the racing kennels all his life. He was light fawn in color with a black muzzle. He was a solid, muscular, thin dog who retired from racing at five and a half years old, after running 180 races. Desperado was the opposite of BB Gun. He was nervous and hyperactive, especially for a Greyhound. Desperado always had to be near me, or at least in a position to see me. He cared about nothing but me. In his racing days, Desperado was an ugly runner; he ran like a full back, willing to go through a brick wall to get to the finish line. He was all heart and was determined to win every race. That was my Desperado.

Pirate
Born 1995 – Died 2004
Adopted 1999

Four months after Desperado moved in, I adopted Pirate. Pirate was the biggest, most beautiful, but dumbest lug you can ever imagine. Pirate had lived with me for three years when he was diagnosed with bone cancer. He was eight and half years old at the time of the diagnosis. When it came time, I had to put him to sleep; I felt his last breath.

GoldDust Pearl
Born 1998
Adopted 2000

Six months after Pirate arrived, I adopted GoldDust Pearl. Goldie, who ragged on Pirate all the time, was depressed for two months after he died.

Mr. Blue
Born 1999
Adopted 2004

Six months after Pirate died, I adopted Mr. Blue.
In May, 2006, I boarded the Greys (BB Gun, Desperado, Goldie, and Mr. Blue) for four days. When they came back to me, they all had worms and diarrhea. I took the dogs to the vet and got medication to take care of the problem. But Desperado continued to have loose stools, and his weight dropped from 72 lbs to 50 lbs. No matter how much I fed him, he never gained any weight back; his body did not seem to absorb the food. As it turned out, Desperado was full of cancer.

Friday July 7, 2006: BB Gun passed away today of heart failure at the age of 12.

Over the last few days, BB seemed very tired. Thursday night, his legs gave out on him and it became very hard for him to stand up. I carried him down to the street so he could go to the bathroom, and then carried him back upstairs to the bedroom where I laid him down on his bed, so he could be in the room with us. My feeling was that if he couldn't walk the next day, I would consider putting him to sleep.

During the night, BB got up and moved to one of the other dog beds. The next morning, I let BB stay in the bedroom while I took the other dogs out, fed them, and took them to the office. Then I went back upstairs to attend to BB.

Up in the bedroom, BB got up and walked over to me. I smiled and carried him down to the kitchen so he could eat, then carried him down to the street so he could do his business. Then he walked up the stairs to the office on his own. He was doing fine, not wobbly at all. He slept and walked around the office for the next few hours.

At 3:00 that afternoon, I took the guys out to the bathroom; BB came downstairs on his own shortly after the others. When I gathered the dogs and put their leashes on, I called BB over to me and somehow BB and Blue knocked into each other, which was nothing out of the ordinary. However, BB's back legs went out on him and he fell; Goldie barked; and BB became terrified. When I picked BB up, he seemed to be disoriented, so I took him alone with me outside. On the stoop, I hugged him for a moment; his legs were a little shaky. We went around the corner of the building, about 10 feet from the stoop, and then BB seemed to loose his equilibrium. His back legs went out from under him again.

I picked BB up with my arms apart under his chest, which meant my hand was on his heart. His breathing was fast and then his heartbeat became faint. I carried him back over to the stoop in my arms, and then his heart stopped and he went limp. I sat down on the stoop, still holding him in my arms. His breathing came back again for a moment as I talked to him, told him goodbye, and told him it was a pleasure to know him and to live with him. I also called him a pain in the ass and told him how much I loved him and would miss him at the same time.

BB died of old age. He was very lucky because he had no pain and he died naturally and quickly. He was a good boy and I'm proud to have known, loved, and cared for him.

September, 2006: Desperado's Last Day

Desperado never complained. He always stayed near me, and he was the only one of my dogs who barked when he wanted something. I had been worried about Desperado for a while. He was getting weaker; I was carrying him up and down the stairs; and I had been preparing myself for his death for several months. I made an appointment for him to see the vet as well as to pick up his medication. On our way to see the vet, I was thinking about how this dog's love for me is never ending, how he wouldn't allow himself to leave me, to die. We walked very slowly down the block. Then he stopped to do his business, and blood just poured out of him. I bent down and hugged him. I became very sad, for now I was walking with Desperado to the vet to put him to sleep.

We walked at a very slow and leisurely pace since he was still curious about doorways and smells. We stopped a few times, and he'd rub his head on my leg. Desperado was tired. The vet is only three blocks from my office. When we got there, the attendants had Desperado's medication ready and told me the doctor would see us in a few minutes. I told them the medication was not necessary, and that I needed a room for Desperado. I needed to spend just a little more time with him. They were not expecting this and one of the techs, who had always taken care of my guys, started to cry.

I took a handful of chocolate kisses from the receptionist counter and led Desperado into one of the examining rooms. In the exam room, I fed him a chocolate kiss. I had never given him chocolate before; he was happy. He put his head in between my legs to be petted, and I bent down to hug and kiss him. I started to cry. Desperado, who was always a nervous dog, was now calm. He knew. I spent a half hour talking to him until it was time to say our final goodbye.

The doctor came into the room and prepared him for the injections. Desperado didn't panic like he usually did for the vet. Instead, he let me hold him; he let me take care of him. He trusted me to take away his pain. I said goodbye to Desperado as I had my hand on his heart. I felt his last breath. When I laid him down, his muscles relaxed and blood poured out of him.

I feel honored to have been with my guys when they've crossed over into the next life. With each one, I felt their last breath and had the opportunity to tell them that I loved them, to tell them how proud and honored I was to be part of their lives, and to tell them how I appreciated the love they had for me.

GoldDust Pearl: Left Behind

Goldie is quite a girl. She has always let the guys know she was the boss. When she was annoyed, she let the guys know it. When she wanted to make a statement, she had the guys trembling in the corners of the room. She had her ways of letting them know who was in charge. For example, she would move her bed so it blocked the pathway to other areas of the room. This way, when the guys wanted to go to those other areas, they had to go around her, which gave Goldie the opportunity to growl and bark at them. At this point, the boys would either whine or bark for someone to help them because she wouldn't let them pass.

Goldie doesn't move her bed in the pathways any more. She sleeps more than usual and has become very quiet. Goldie has always been in a dog pack, at the kennels where she grew up and raced, and at my/our home with her three "brothers." Now, all of the dogs in her original pack are gone.

Four or five weeks after Desperado passed on, Blue and I left the room, so Goldie was left alone. About five minutes had gone by when I heard her crying. I went to the bedroom to get her and when I opened the door, she ran out and went downstairs looking for Blue. When she found him, she couldn't stop kissing him. He is the only one she has left.

Reviews

The Puppy Papers
Reviewed by Kym Olsen on www.Amazon.com

November 1, 2004 4 stars

I couldn't decide whether to call this book a biography or an autobiography. It is through a series of emails, over a period of six months, in which Steven Toushin asks puppy sharon probing questions about her past and her understanding of sexuality (in particular hers) that sharon's story comes out but it is through her writings that we get to know her. It could be thought of as an interview as well. Perhaps structurally it is a hybrid. Personally, I like that I can't easily classify this book. It allows it to function as all of the above and creates the ability to enter the material in a variety of ways.

Conceptually it is interesting to find myself (as the reader) participating as voyeur in the budding relationship between Toushin and puppy. To observe as she slowly opens up revealing a fascinating sexual life from childhood to the present. Steven stays out of the way, revealing very little about himself, creating plenty of room for her to divulge her sexual awakenings. The correspondence between the two plays out much like life. There are the mundane emails, the "how are you. I'm fine" aspects, but tucked in between those are treasures of information. Some of which most women growing up in rural and suburban middle America will surely recognize and others that are truly unique to sharon; her openness to exploration reveals a woman self-possessed enough not to be bogged down in the guilt and shame of a slow but maturing understanding of her sexual desires and needs.

sharon's descriptions of her introduction to the BDSM world are absorbing, typically awkward, and sometimes funny as she talks about the pitfalls, as well as the satisfying encounters. Her point-of-view is adventurous and sometimes reveals a naiveté that is inevitable when entering a new world of experience. It is encouraging for those new to this sexual realm to read from a woman's point-of-view who remains intact despite unsuccessful experiences. A woman who handles the situations with calmness, self-possession and a sense of humor not allowing others to defeat or discourage her from continuing her quest to find sexual satisfaction. She seems to know this is all a part of her sexual education, which she is clearly in charge of. It's refreshing to read a woman's story that does not revolve around exploitation.

For those like me, if you begin to become suspicious of who this Steven Toushin guy is (especially after sharon reveals stories about some of the creeps she's encountered) never fear. Check out the appendix. There is plenty of information about him there. Though I do wish he would have included more about himself within the context of the email exchanges I understand the attempt to stay out of the way of sharon's story. It is sometimes successful, sometimes not. There are times when I begin wondering more about who he is which becomes a distraction from sharon.

This book is open-ended leaving the reader with many questions, particularly regarding sharon and Steven's growing relationship. It's some of the most titillating aspects of the book and if you want arousing material then you'll be clamoring for more details regarding their intense sexual interactions. I smell a sequel, which I'd buy. My curiosity has been piqued. The reader is given enough information to keep interested but there is still plenty that is to be explored. Again it is a strategy that points to one of life's conundrums, the inability for one person to fully know another person's mind and the desire to probe their lives all the more intensely. It also reminds us that one cannot judge a person by the way they look. There are plenty of professionals, suburban mothers, and other "normal" everyday people who have interesting and even amazing hidden lives. Makes you want to stop and find out what lurks behind the façade of normalcy that so many exude. It's good to know there are people from all walks of life waking up sexually and being brave enough to follow their inner desires.

The Puppy Papers
Reviewed by TammyJo Eckhart on www.amazon.com
September 11, 2004 5 stars
A Unique and Interesting Reading

In the beginning of many relationships a pattern of communication is established that seems to hold steady for most of its duration. In the realm of sex this varies from the "let's just try it" approach, to the "talk to anyone but each other" idea, to the "let's always talk about our feelings" therapeutic method. Steven Toushin likes to get to know his partners, and he does it in a different way than most people are used to: he asks questions and demands answers. *The Puppy Papers: A Woman's Life and Journey into BDSM* grew out of questions he asked his new partner, Puppy Sharon.

The sexual biography is becoming more common and generally is either autobiographical in nature or, if one is famous enough or rich enough, written by another person. In a way this book is a sexual biography of not just one woman, as the title suggests, but also of her relationship with Toushin and those who came before him. It is written as a series of emails and thus does not fit neatly into any normal classification for the purpose of review.

Not all the questions that Toushin asks show up in his emails, which are far outnumbered by Puppy Sharon's. From her wording we can see that he asks these questions when they meet, and from her answers we get the impression that what she has difficulty saying out loud in his presence she can type about later. It's common for a person to communicate in some ways better than others, and a good dominant knows how to use what works for the individual and their relationship.

Toushin believes in "four basic things" that he tells Sharon before they even meet; these are what I would call his ethics for BDSM as he practices it (p. 11). All of them focus on communication, because while he may be the master, it is a relationship with mutual needs and desires. This foundation makes Toushin radically different from the earlier partners Puppy Sharon describes in her emails.

By the end of the book I was feeling so sorry for Puppy Sharon's earlier adventures in kink. Her childhood may be relatively commonplace for females growing up in the 1960s and 1970s; you'd have to judge for yourself whether or not it was. This book grew out of her emails with a caring and experienced man, but her earlier experiences only showed me how very limited finding good partners over the Internet can be.

About a third of the way through the emails (p. 115) Toushin begins to explain that he will begin asking for more detailed information because he's thinking of a book project, this book. Normally this approach might result in a very artificial feeling for the remainder of the book, but he lets his Puppy's answers dictate the next set of questions, so she continues to explain in her normal way.

The book is separated into sections that describe the overall focus of that series of emails. The earliest are organic, developing out of the early relationship between dominant and submissive. The later emails get into more details about her past. Throughout, however, real life comes up. Imagine that! She and Toushin have lives outside of their kinky relationship. Too often this reality is glossed over in biographies and how-to books on kink, so it was nice to see it.

Overall the book is not straightforward, just as life and relationships aren't. It may be difficult for some folks to read, because it is rather organic in its storytelling and its layout. There's no focus on Top J then she moves to Top M; they mix together as she remembers and tells her new dominant about her experiences. That makes *The Puppy Papers* unique and interesting reading.

The Puppy Papers

A Woman's Life and Journey into BDSM
by Puppy Sharon and Steven Toushin

The Destruction of the Moral Fabric of America is a fascinating book made up of many parts, all centering around events in Steven Toushin's life, including his federal SM obscenity trial in 1989 in Nashville, Tennessee. This trial originated out of Attorney General Messe's Commission on Pornography (Operation PostPorn).

This book reprints the interviews of authors, activists and filmakers in the SM and leather community that were taken by Toushin's attorneys in the preparation of his defense against the government. The people and organizations interviewed are Guy Baldwin, Tony DeBlase, Gayle Rubin, GMSMA, John Rowberry, Jim Ward, Geoff Mains, David Rosen, and mental health experts Dr. Richard Green and Robert Stoller. Also included is the trial testimony of Park Dietz, member of the Meese Commission, and the sentencing of Rosen and Toushin.

Interwoven into this fascinating legal story are essays on BDSM and the Sexual future; Certifying Masters, Mistresses, slaves, and ProDommes; Sexual History, the Power of the word NO; letters between Guy Baldwin and Steven Toushin; a story about Jeffery Dahmer who killed an employee of Toushin's; Toushin's life in prison; the making of the Slave and Master films; an interview of Steven Toushin; America's Enemies; government documents exposing a morally corrupt government agency; the government raid on Toushin's companies (The Big Bust); and Thomas Jefferson and Toushin discussing *The Destruction of the Moral Fabric of America*.

This book will make you think. You will agree and disagree. It will have you talking to yourself; and it will have you discussing its issues, thoughts, and statements with your friends.

1989 Adult Video News Award Show (Las Vegas)
Reuben Sturman Memorial Award
(previously "Special Achievement Award")
Steve Toushin / Bijou Video
For Legal Battles on Behalf of the Adult Industry

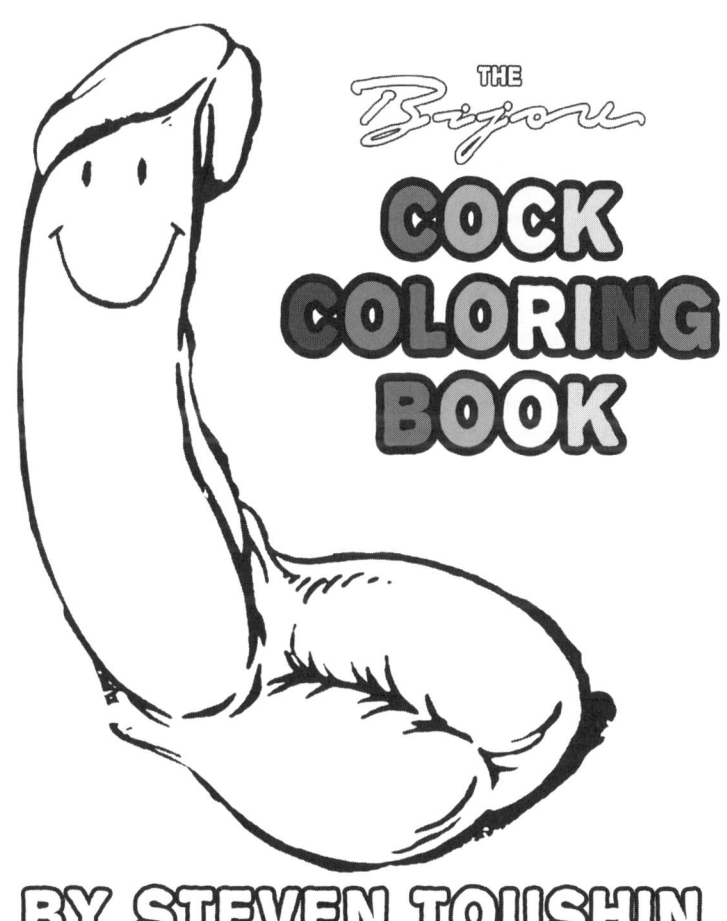

A Bijou Book by Steven Toushin

With best wishes, *Dick Cheney*

$12.87

To order, call 1-800-932-7111